Preface

Aim

The aim of this book is to provide an activity-based approach to the understanding of the quantitative techniques needed to help improve the quality of business decisions.

It assumes a knowledge of introductory business statistics as covered in a book such as *Understanding Business Statistics – An Active Learning Approach* (Saunders & Cooper) or *Business Mathematics and Statistics – A Complete Course Text* (Francis), both by the same publisher.

Typical courses on which it can be used include:

- ❏ HNC/D BTEC courses in Business Studies
- ❏ Undergraduate/professional courses (eg ACCA, CIMA, CII) on which there is a decision making, operational research, operations management or other quantitative analysis component.

Need

Changes in teaching methods and reduced resources in many institutions have resulted in a need for a new type of book – one that can allow the lecturer to delegate a proportion of the teaching process to students themselves, enabling the lecturer to concentrate on managing students' self-teaching.

This book is flexible enough, however, to be used in any one of the following teaching modes:

a) as a support text for fully taught lessons;

b) as a self-teaching package with minimum, if any, lecturer support, ie as part of a distance/open learning mode of study;

c) as a combination of (a) and (b), according to individual circumstances.

Approach

There are three main sections to the book:

> Section 1 – Discovering Quantitative approaches to Decision Making
> Section 2 – Information Bank
> Section 3 – Developing Knowledge and Skills

❏ **Section 1** is the main driving force of the book. It comprises 20 units following the experiences of a junior member of the central services department of a manufacturing and retailing company, who comes across problems that can be solved using quantitative techniques.

Scenarios set business quantitative techniques in a 'real life' context; Quick Answer Questions (with answers on the following left-hand page) prompt problem recognition; and tasks and problem-solving activities motivate the reader to seek solutions (help lines direct the reader to Section 2 – Information Bank). Guidance is given where the use of spreadsheets for certain tasks would be advantageous. Full model solutions to the tasks and problem-solving activities are given in an appendix.

Note: To help with course planning, Section 1 has been designed to have very few restrictions on the sequence in which units are tackled. The study planning chart on pages vi–vii and the introduction at the beginning of Section 1 highlight the link between this and other sections.

❏ **Section 2** provides a concise summary of the relevant quantitative techniques, written in a student-friendly manner. Whilst it is organised in the same sequence as Section 1, it is not meant to be read in the same way as a conventional text book, ie the reader should consult this section in order to carry out the tasks in Sections 1 and 3.

❏   **Section 3** consists of a mixture of tasks and professional examination questions with answers (to help the reader confirm his or her understanding) and tasks without answers. The latter, together with assignments, enables a lecturer to gauge the students' levels of competence.

Note for lecturers

A Lecturers' Supplement (in the form of a $3\frac{1}{2}''$ disk) is provided free of charge to lecturers adopting the book as a course text. This includes: outline answers to those tasks without answers; guidance notes for the assessment of the assignments; graphic files of key diagrams; files for the spreadsheet tasks; and guidance for group work.

How to use this book

The introduction to Section 1 includes an outline scenario of the PLC in which the 'hero' works in the central services department. Each unit in Section 1 uses the scenario as a 'peg' for the relevant quantitative techniques or principles.

The planning chart on pages vi–vii is intended to help lecturers map out their courses, and students plan their revision.

LA Oakshott
July 1993

Quantitative Approaches to Decision Making

L.A. Oakshott MSc

Senior Lecturer in the Department of Mathematical Sciences,
University of the West of England, Bristol

DP Publications Ltd
Aldine Place
London W12 8AW
1993

owledgements

ld like to thank the following bodies for giving me permission to include a selection of their ex-
ination questions in Section 3 of this book.

The Chartered Association of Certified Accountants (ACCA)

The Chartered Institute of Management Accountants (CIMA)

The Chartered Insurance Institute (CII)

The University of the West of England, Bristol

I am also grateful to colleagues and students at UWE, Bristol, for their suggestions and for help in
proofreading the text.

A CIP Catalogue Record for this book is available from the British Library

First Edition 1993

ISBN 1 85805 026 X
Copyright L.A. Oakshott © 1993

Printed by
The Guernsey Press Company Ltd
Braye Road, Vale
Guernsey, Channel Islands

Contents

Study planning chart

All the major topics in the Information Bank (Section 2) are covered by the 20 units in Section 1. Other topics are covered via tasks, with answers, in Section 3.

To help you with the planning of your course of study/revision, the chart below shows you where all topics in the Information Bank (Section 2) are covered by either Section 1 or Section 3.

Information Bank (Section 2) topics	Section 1 unit	Section 3 question with answer
Probability		
The probability of compound events	1	2
Conditional probability		2
Tree diagrams	1	2
Bayes' theorem		2
Expected value	1	
Probability distributions		
The binomial distribution	2	6
The use of the binomial distribution in quality control	2	
The Poisson distribution	3	
The normal distribution	4	11, 14
Decision analysis		
Payoff tables	5	15, 18
Value of perfect information		15
Decision trees	5	15
Sensitivity analysis	5	
Estimation		
Point estimates	6	
Confidence interval for a population mean using the normal distribution		21
Confidence interval for a population mean using the t-distribution	6	
Confidence interval of a proportion	6	21
Statistical process control	7	25
Hypothesis testing		
The z-test for a single sample mean		26
The t-test for a single sample mean	8	
Hypothesis test of two independent sample means	9	29, 31
Hypothesis test for samples that are not independent	10	32, 33
Hypothesis test of a proportion	8	
Hypothesis test of two proportions		32
The 'goodness of fit' test		34
The χ^2 test of association	11	36

Information Bank (Section 2) topics	Section 1 unit	Section 3 question with answer
Correlation and regression		
Scatter diagrams	12, 13	38
Pearson's product moment correlation coefficient (r)	12	38
Spearman's rank correlation coefficient (R)		39
Linear regression	13	40, 42
Analysis of errors		42
Prediction and estimation using linear regression	13	
Non-linearity	13	45
Time series analysis		
The decomposition model	14	
Analysis of errors	14	
Seasonally adjusted series	14	52
Forecasting using the decomposition model	14	49
Exponential smoothing	14	52
Network analysis		
Critical path analysis	15	55, 58
Resource scheduling	16	58
Cost scheduling	16	55
Pert analysis	15	
Inventory control		
Costs of holding stock	17	60
Economic order quantity (EOQ) model	17	60, 61
Discounts	17	60
Uncertainty in demand	17	61
The economic batch quantity model (EBQ)		62
Linear programming		
Linear programming formulation	18	
Graphical solution of linear programming problems	18	64, 65
Sensitivity analysis	18	64, 66
Minimisation problems		65
Multivariable linear programming		66
The transportation and assignment algorithms		
The transportation algorithm	19	67, 68, 69
Alternative solutions	19	69
Maximisation problems		68
The assignment algorithm		70
Simulation		
Validation of simulation models	20	
Random numbers	20	71, 74
Manual simulation	20	71
Analysis of simulation experiments	20	74
Variance reduction techniques	20	74

Intoduction to Riglen PLC

Riglen PLC was formed in 1984 by the merger of a food and confectionery manufacturer based in Bristol and the supermarket chain Rigmarts. Since 1984 substantial expansion has taken place with several new premises acquired for the manufacture, storage and sales of its product. The company now produces a range of household and toiletry products and it has also expanded its food range.

The head office and manufacturing plant of Riglen is at Bristol. Warehouses are located at Watford, Birmingham and Bristol.

Riglen employs 1200 staff at its factory and a further 850 staff at its 55 supermarkets. Turnover during the last five years has been as follows:

19x1	19x2	19x3	19x4	19x5
£50m	£76m	£84m	£102m	£100m

Although the growth in turnover has slowed, it is confidently expected that the further planned investment will help to continue the growth. In particular, much of the machinery is old and is in need of replacement. A rolling programme of replacement has been initiated and this has been linked with a staff training scheme to enable the latest technology to be employed.

Organisational structure

Riglen consists of a manufacturing division and a retail division. Within the manufacturing division there are three production departments and these are outlined below:

Department	Product range
Food	Fresh meat, bread, biscuits, cakes, confectionery, preserves, cereals, frozen fruit and vegetables
Cooked meat	Sausages, pies and cold meats
Household products	Washing powder, detergents, disinfectants and general cleaning products

Within each department, products are divided into profit centres. Each profit centre is the responsibility of a product manager. Under him is the production manager and the sales manager. The three managers hold regular meetings to agree production and sales targets and to set budgets for the coming period. Each product manager reports to the departmental manager who in turn reports to the Production Director at head office.

There is also a packaging department, which handles the packaging and despatch of all Riglen produce.

The organisation of the supermarkets is slightly different in that each store has a manager who reports to his regional manager. The regional manager together with his store managers will decide the products that are to be purchased and agree an inventory policy. Although some 'key' Riglen products must be purchased, the regional manager has the authority to purchase merchandise in whatever quantity he requires and from whoever he likes. The regional managers report to the Supermarket Director at head office.

The organisational tree of Riglen is shown below where it will be noticed that there are also non-line managers responsible for the departments of Finance, Personnel, Central Services and Distribution.

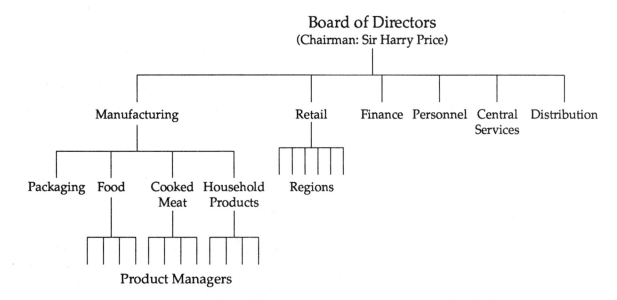

The Central Services Department provides a consultancy service to both the manufacturing and retail divisions. It consists of a number of analysts who apply statistical and mathematical techniques to problems that arise in the company. You, the reader, have joined this department as a junior analyst.

Section 1: Discovering Quantitative Approaches to Decision Making

Introduction

This section comprises 20 units describing the experiences of a junior member of the central services department of Riglen PLC, who needs to use business statistics in her work. Via these experiences you are encouraged to learn the quantitative techniques you will need to use in business decision making.

Each unit covers one topic and contains sufficient material for one or two weeks work (depending on your level of knowledge). The structure of each unit follows a common pattern:

1 **Prerequisites and objectives** – These state the knowledge required at the start of the unit and the knowledge and skills you will have on successful completion of the unit.

2 **The scenario** – In all scenarios you assume the role of the junior member of the central services department of Riglen. You are called upon to solve problems of a quantitative nature in a particular department or function.

3 **Quick answer questions** – These are intended to give you a feel for the problem, assuming no prior knowledge. Answers to these are always on the next left-hand page.

4 **Tasks** – These allow you to discover for yourself the appropriate quantitative skill, or the need for the skill. 'Help lines' direct you to the appropriate part of the Information Bank (Section 2) to assist you. Answers to all tasks are in Appendix 1.

5 **Problem solving activities** – These require you to use the skills learned from the tasks. Help lines to the Information Bank are provided, and answers are in Appendix 1.

6 **Spreadsheet tasks** – Certain tasks can best be solved using spreadsheets. In these cases the required spreadsheet applications are given.

7 **Developing Knowledge and Skills** – Particular questions in Section 3 which you can tackle on completion of any unit, are indicated for further practice/revision/evidence of competency.

You should read the overall introduction to Riglen PLC around which all unit scenarios are based on page viii–ix above.

Contents

Note: Certain units build on others. Therefore, if you are not working through the units *in sequence*, ensure that you have covered the prerequisite units as indicated in the contents below.

Unit 1: Probability

Prerequisites

There are no prerequisites for this unit. At the end of this unit you should be able to:

❏ Calculate simple probabilities.

❏ Calculate probabilities of compound events using the rules of addition and multiplication.

❏ Use probability trees to solve problems.

❏ Calculate expected values.

Scenario: *Machine breakdowns in the cooked meat department*

Riglen produces a very popular range of meat pies which is bought by many supermarket chains as 'own brand' produce. The three machines for cooking and packaging the pies are rather old and recently they have been suffering frequent breakdowns. These breakdowns are not normally serious but when they occur the machine is out of action for an hour. This is because the machine has to be allowed to cool before the breakdown (usually a blockage) can be attended to.

During the rolling programme of machinery replacement, a proforma has landed on the desk of the departmental manager, Kevin Giles, asking him for details of any machinery that he thinks needs replacing. As he has been through this process before (and been unsuccessful), Kevin decided to ask Central Services for their help. You attended a meeting with Kevin and senior analyst Bob Franks in which the problem of machine breakdowns was discussed. Bob advises that before a case can be made out it is necessary to collect more details on frequency of machine breakdowns and you are given the task of obtaining this data.

Following this exercise you report the following facts:

1. The three machines are identical and operate independently; that is, a breakdown of one machine does not effect the operation of the other machines.

2. A log is kept for each of the three machines. This log is updated hourly and includes details on throughput, any problems encountered and whether the machine is currently in working order.

You decide that an analysis of the number of times a machine is reported as not working may be useful, so you analyse the log of each machine over several months.

Machine	A	B	C
No. of times working	1400	1250	1480
No. times not working	200	350	120

Q | **Quick answer questions 1**

(i) Why was it necessary to analyse the log over a long time period.

(ii) What factors may effect breakdowns?

(iii) Under what conditions might the breakdown of a machine be dependent on the status (that is working or not working) of the other machines.

T | Tasks

You discuss these figures with Bob Franks and you both agree that, although useful, the figures on their own will not be sufficient as justification for the replacement of the machinery. The team in charge of the rolling programme like to see calculations involving probabilities, particularly where there are more than one machine involved. Bob gives you a list of questions, which you should provide answers for, in time for the next meeting with Kevin Giles.

(i) From your survey what is the maximum number of times that a machine could have been found working?

(ii) What is the probability that if you turned up in the cooked meat department at any time, machine A would

> Help? See Section 2: Probability: Introduction, page 55.

    (a) have broken down and

    (b) still be working

(iii) What is the probability that machines A **and** B would have broken down?

> Help? See Section 2: Probability: The probability of compound events, page 56.

(iv) What is the probability that machine A **or** B would have broken down?

(v) The 'tree' diagram below represents the status (that is, working or not working) of each of the three machines. Re-draw this diagram and alongside each 'branch' write the probability of this outcome occurring.

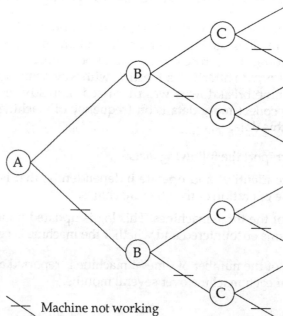

    ⤬ Machine not working

Using your diagram, calculate

(a) The compound probability of each 'route' of the tree.

(b) The probability that if you turned up in the cooked meat department at any time, all machines would be working?

> Help? See Section 2: Probability: Tree diagrams, page 57.

(c) The probability that at least one machine would have broken down?

(d) The probability that exactly two machines would have broken down?

P Problem solving activities

Your results were presented to the meeting and it was agreed that the figures suggest that new machines are justified. However the rental cost of these machines is high at £1500 per week per machine and some financial justification is required. You have been asked to provide figures to show the effect of replacing the three old machines with new models. You have been told that the probability that a new machine will break down is 0.05 and the maximum throughput for a machine (both old and new) is 2000 pies per hour for 80 hours a week. You can assume that the profit on each pie is approximately 10p and the scrap value of the old machines is zero.

(i)   What is the expected number of pies made each week with the old machines?

> Help? See Section 2: Probability – Expected value, page 60.

(ii)   Re-calculate the expected pie production using the new machines.

(iii) Can the replacement of the three machines be justified on financial grounds?

Spreadsheet tasks

(i)   A higher return on the investment may be achieved by only replacing some of the machines. Use a spreadsheet to investigate this idea.

(ii)   Try different values of the profit per pie. Plot a graph of net profit (or loss) against these values.

You should now be able to attempt questions 1 to 3 of Section 3, page 183.

Comments on quick answer questions 1

(i)   A shorter time period may not be representative of the long run behaviour of the machines

(ii) Utilisation (throughput), time since last service or time since last repair.

(ii) When the usage of a machine is dependent on the number of machines currently in working order.

Unit 2: The binomial distribution

Prerequisites

❏ Probability (Unit 1, page 3)

Objectives

At the end of this unit you should be able to:

❏ Draw a tree diagram for a binomial problem

❏ Calculate probabilities of getting any number of 'successes' in a sample

❏ Apply the binomial distribution to a quality control problem

---

Scenario: *Bar code inspection*

All packaged products at Riglen have a bar code label glued to the outside of the product. This labelling process can at times develop a fault, where a fault is a label with a defective bar code. Until recently the policy of the packaging department was to take a random sample of 5 items from the batch and if one or more items was found to have defective bar codes the entire batch was examined and any with defective bar codes were re-labelled. However during a cost cutting exercise it was decided that *two* or more items with defective bar codes should be the criterion for rejection.

Since this change in the inspection procedure, an unusually large number of complaints has been received from stores concerning the bar codes. Sue Jones, the manager of the packaging department, has investigated this and she has found that at the time of the policy change, problems were experienced with the labelling process. Sue would like to know why the new inspection procedure didn't spot this increase in defective bar codes and whether the old procedure would have done better. You have been asked to apply your statistical knowledge to the problem.

Q | **Quick answer questions 2**

(i) Is it possible to have zero defects? Why might it not be a good policy?

(ii) Why wouldn't it be a good idea to have 100% testing of the bar codes?

T | **Tasks**

You are told that the acceptable level of defective bar codes is 5%.

(i) Draw a tree diagram for all 5 items.

(ii) How many ways are there of getting 0,1,2,3,4,5 defective bar codes?

> Help? See Section 2: Probability – Tree diagrams, page 57.

(iii) What is the probability of getting no defective bar codes in a sample (assuming 'p' = 0.05)?

(iv) Take any 'route' in your tree that gives you one defective bar code and work out its probability. What is the probability of getting one defective bar code in a sample of size five? Repeat this for 2,3,4 and 5 defective bar codes.

> Help? See Section 2: Probability – The probability of compound events, page 56.

(v) What is the probability of

    (a) 1 *or more* defective bar codes?

    (b) 2 *or more* defective bar codes?

(vi) Discuss the advantages and disadvantages of both the old and new inspection procedures. Why would the previous scheme have more likely detected an increase in defective bar codes?

> Help? See Section 2: Probability Distributions – The binomial distribution, page 61.

P Problem solving activities

Following your analysis, Sue has negotiated a new agreement on quality with one of Riglen's major customers. In this agreement the acceptable level of defective bar codes stays at 5% but a maximum of 20% will be tolerated. If the defective rate exceeds 20% the store can claim compensation.

(i) Using this new information, analyse the old and current inspection procedures. In both cases what is the probability that a good batch will be rejected and the probability that a bad batch will be accepted?

> Help? See Section 2: Probability Distributions – The use of the binomial distribution in quality control, page 65.

(ii) Another inspection procedure has been suggested. In this procedure a batch would be accepted if no more than 2 defective bar codes were detected in a sample of size 20. Is this scheme better?

Spreadsheet tasks

The ideal inspection plan would be when the producer's and consumer's risk are both less than 5%. In practise this may be difficult to achieve and many inspection procedures need to be analysed before an acceptable one is found. This is very tedious to do manually but easy using a spreadsheet.

(i) If the acceptable and maximum level of defective bar codes is 5% and 20% respectively, use a spreadsheet to decide on an appropriate inspection scheme. That is how large a sample should be chosen and how many defective bar codes can be permitted in the sample?

(ii) Try increasing the maximum proportion of defects from 20% to 30% in steps of 1% and repeat (i) above.

You should now be able to attempt questions 4 to 6 of Section 3, page 183.

Comments on quick answer questions 2

(i) With better equipment and improved monitoring of its performance, the number of defects could possibly be reduced to zero. However, could the cost of doing this be justified, particularly with something that doesn't effect the quality of the product?

(ii) Again the answer is cost.

Unit 3: The Poisson distribution

> **Prerequisites**
> ❑ Probability (Unit 1, page 3)
> **Objectives**
> At the end of this unit you should be able to:
> ❑ Use the Poisson distribution to calculate probabilities of 'rare' events

Scenario: *Accident statistics*

Riglen is proud of its excellent safety record and over the past five years only 24 employees have had accidents while at work. This is less than half the rate of similar companies. However, during the first six months of the current year, 4 employees have already had accidents and the Health and Safety Officer, Cecil Philips has been asked to investigate.

Cecil's first reaction is that the number of accidents is still less than the average number of accidents in a year and it is quite possible that no more accidents will occur this year. However, after further pressure Cecil has reluctantly asked Central Services to investigate.

Q	**Quick answer questions 3**

(i) Do you think that just because an accident has not occurred for some time, there is more chance that one will happen in the near future?

(ii) Are accidents likely to be influenced by time of day or day of the week?

T	**Tasks**

Your remit is to decide if the apparent increase in accidents during the half year is due to chance effects or to some real deterioration in the accident rate.

(i) What has been the average annual number of accidents over the last 5 years? (Ignoring the accidents over the last 6 months)

(ii) Use this average figure to calculate the probability of getting 0,1,2,3,4,5,6,7 accidents in a year?

(iii) What is the probability of 8 or more accidents in a year?

(iv) What is the mean number of accidents in 6 months?

(v) What is the probability of 4 or more accidents in six months?

(vi) What conclusion have you come to regarding the accident rate?

> Help? See Section 2: Probability Distributions – The Poisson distribution, page 67.

You should now be able to attempt questions 7 and 8 of Section 3, page 184.

> *Comments on quick answer questions 3*
> (i) Unlikely, as it would be hoped that accidents happen independently. However, this may be so if people become complacent and less careful.
> (ii) Maybe. People get tired at the end of the day or week, which may make them more susceptible to accidents.

Unit 4: The normal distribution

> **Prerequisites**
> ❏ Probability (Unit 1, page 3)
> ❏ The binomial distribution (Unit 2, page 6)
>
> **Objectives**
> At the end of this unit you should be able to:
>
> ❏ Use the normal distribution to calculate the probability that a variable has a value between specified limits
>
> ❏ Use the normal distribution to calculate the values of a variable that correspond to a particular probability
>
> ❏ Calculate any one parameter of the normal distribution if the other parameters are known

Scenario: *'Weights and measures'*

Riglen has recently been prosecuted for selling an underweight jar of coffee and this has resulted in a good deal of bad publicity. The Chairman of the Riglen group, Sir Harry Price, has taken an interest in the case and the manager of the Food department, Shirley Watts has been summoned to a meeting with the Board. During this meeting Shirley explained that it was impossible to ensure that under weight products were not sold, although the risk could be reduced – at a cost. Several member's of the Board were rather surprised at this statement and openly questioned Shirley's fitness for her position as manager. However, before any move was made in this direction it was decided to ask Central Services to carry out an investigation.

The head of Central Services, Bob Franks, has been asked to give this investigation top priority and he has sent you to collect information on the filling process. Since it was a 100g jar of coffee that caused the problem, you decide to concentrate on this product. You discover that the jars are filled automatically and the filling machine can be pre-set to any desired weight. For the 100g jars of coffee a weight of 101g is set. There is no subsequent checking of the weight of individual jars although samples are occasional taken to check for quality. Bob suggests that you now attempt to obtain more information on the accuracy of the filling process. You telephone the supplier of the filling machine and following a conversation with the Technical Manager you discover that the weight of product that is discharged into the jar is normally distributed with a mean as set by the operator. The standard deviation will depend to a certain extent on the mean weight but for weights between 90g to 110g it is virtually constant at 1.5g

Q | Quick answer questions 4

(i) Do you think it would be possible to design a filling machine that would give you exactly 100g every time?

(ii) Is weight a continuous or discrete measure?

T | Tasks

You have been asked to apply your knowledge of probability distributions to the problem. In particular you have been told that prosecution only occurs when the product is underweight by more than 2%, so you need to find the probability that such a weight could happen by chance.

(i)   Assuming that the mean weight is 101g, what proportion of jars are:
    (a)   under 100g in weight
    (b)   under 98g in weight
    (c)   under 97g in weight
    (d)   over 100g
    (e)   within 2g of the marked weight.

> Help? See Section 2: Probability Distributions – The normal distribution , page 69.

(ii) If 50,000 jars of coffee are sold per week, how many jars are less than 98g in weight?

> Help? See Section 2: Probability – Expected value , page 60.

(iii) Weights and measures inspectors carry out spot checks of products either in the factory or at retail outlets. Assuming that they sample ten 100g jars a week, what is the probability that a jar weighing less than 98g will be discovered?

> Help? See Section 2: Probability Distributions – The binomial distribution , page 61.

(iv) What should the mean weight be set to in order that the probability of a jar weighing less than 98g is less than 0.1%?

> Help? See Section 2: Probability Distributions – The normal distribution , page 69.

P   Problem solving activities

Following your work on this problem it was decided to re-set the machine so that the mean weight of coffee was 102.5g. You are told to randomly sample the production of 100g jars of coffee over the next few days in order to decide if the change has had the desired effect. To your dismay you discover that 0.5% of jars are below 98g in weight.

(i)   What is the expected proportion of jars below 98g? Why might the actual proportion of jars be different to this figure?

(ii) Assuming that the mean weight is correct and weights are normally distributed, calculate the standard deviation of the weights of 100g jars of coffee.

(iii) Using this value of the standard deviation, decide what the correct value of the mean should be so that the proportion of jars below 98g is as given in (i) above.

> Help? See Section 2: Probability Distributions – The normal distribution , page 69.

(iv) The cost to Riglen of the coffee is £2 per kg. How much would the adjustment to the mean weight cost Riglen in a week?

You should now be able to attempt questions 9 to 14 of Section 3, page 185.

Comments on quick answer questions 4

(i)   In theory the answer is no since there will always be some variation even if it was only of the order of one mg.

(ii) A continuous measure since weight is not restricted to any particular value.

Unit 5: Decision analysis

Prerequisites

To complete this unit successfully you should have a good knowledge of the following:

❏ Probability (Unit 1, page 3)

❏ Expected value (Unit 1, page 3)

❏ Tree diagrams (Unit 1, page 3)

Objectives

At the end of this unit you should be able to:

❏ Construct decision trees for decision problems

❏ Use the 'roll-back' technique on a decision tree

❏ Apply sensitivity analysis to decision problems

Scenario: *'What, no meat?'*

Riglen's laboratory's have recently come up with a method of producing joints of 'chicken' from non-animal products. The process is quite revolutionary and the taste and texture of the 'meat' is believed to be indistinguishable from the real thing. The product should also have an advantage in terms of price and shelf life (the product need not be stored in a refrigerator and will stay in good condition for up to two weeks).

However, the cost of setting up production is very high at £1m and it is not at all certain that consumers will accept the product. The marketing department have assessed the risk and believe that there is only a 30% chance that consumers will approve of the product. If consumers do approve then sales are estimated to be around £2.5m p.a, but if the reaction is negative then sales will amount to no more than £0.7m p.a (the catering market is virtually guaranteed to want the product).

The risk could be reduced by carrying out a survey to gauge public reaction to the product. From past experience this kind of survey produces accurate results 85% of the time. (That is, if the survey indicates a favourable response, the probability that a favourable response occurs is 0.85 and similarly, if the survey suggests a negative response, the probability that a negative response occurs is 0.85). The cost of this survey will be £100,000.

Q **Quick answer questions 5**

(i) The marketing department estimate that there is only a 30% chance that consumers will react favourably to the product. How accurate do you think this figure is?

(ii) What kind of marketing survey will need to be carried out?

T **Tasks**

The product manager assigned to this new product line is Graham Green and he has requested your help in deciding whether to commission a survey or to proceed immediately with full production. You explain that the decision is perhaps more complicated than he thinks and the following options are available to him:

1. Proceed with full production

2. Commission a survey. Whatever the results of the survey there are two further options, that is proceed with full production or abandon the project.

3. Abandon the project.

Following discussions with the marketing department, you decide that carrying out the marketing survey before going into full production will not effect the expected sales revenue. You have also assumed that the probability that the survey will indicate a favourable response is 0.3.

(i)   What would be the net expected monetary value (EMV) under option 1 (proceed with full production)?

> Help? See Section 2: Decision Analysis – Pay-off tables, page 78.

(ii) Draw a tree diagram to represent the different courses of action. Use squares to represent decision nodes and circles to represent probabilistic (chance) nodes. Along each branch from a decision node add the cost of making this decision (for example, the cost of the full production decision is £1m). Along each probabilistic branch add the probability of this outcome and at the end of each route of your tree add the expected sales revenue.

(iii) Working backwards along your tree (that is, from right to left) calculate the EMV at each chance node. When you get to a decision box, take that decision which gives you the highest net EMV (after any costs have been deducted). Cross out all decision branches which are *not* taken.

(iv) What is the final net EMV and what should your decision(s) be?

> Help? See Section 2: Decision Analysis – Decision trees, page 80.

P Problem solving activity

Although Graham agrees with your analysis, he is concerned that much of the data supplied by the marketing department are little more than guesses. In particular he believes that the probability that consumers will react favourably to the product is likely to be higher than 0.3.

> Help? See Section 2: Decision Analysis – Sensitivity analysis, page 83.

Investigate the sensitivity of your answer to task (iv) to changes to this probability.

Spreadsheet tasks

Use a spreadsheet to investigate the sensitivity of your recommended decision to changes in the probability of an accurate survey result and *simultaneously* to changes in the probability of a good response.

You should now be able to attempt questions 15 to 19 of Section 3, page 187.

Comments on quick answer questions 5

(i)   Probably only an educated guess based on past experience.

(ii) The public will need to given samples to try and this will be best done by a 'face to face' survey.

Unit 6: Confidence intervals

Prerequisites

To complete this unit successfully you should have a good knowledge of the following:

❏ Probability (Unit 1, page 3)

❏ The normal distribution (Unit 4, page 9)

Objectives

At the end of this unit you should be able to:

❏ Calculate the confidence interval for a population percentage

❏ Calculate the confidence interval for a population mean

❏ Calculate the size of sample required to give a specified margin of error

---

Scenario: *'Trips to France'*

The latest internal accounts for the supermarket business show that the annual sales of wines and spirits has fallen by more than 30%. This fall has been blamed on the relaxation of the limits of duty free goods that can be brought into Britain from EEC countries from 1993. If this is the case then very little can be done to improve the situation and Riglen may be forced to discontinue this line in some of its smaller supermarkets. However before this decision is made Susan Kelly, the manager responsible for the London and South East region, decided to ask a random sample of shoppers if they intend to travel to France this year. Of the 75 shoppers questioned, 27 were certain to go to France at least once. She also sent one of her assistants to Dover to ask a random sample of 60 returning holiday makers how much they had spent on duty free alcohol. Of these 60, eight refused to answer and for the remaining 52 people the average spend was found to be £37.26 with a standard deviation of £35.97.

Q **Quick answer questions 6**

(i) Could there be any other reason for the fall in sales of wines and spirits?

(ii) If another sample of 75 shoppers were chosen and asked the same question would you expect to get the same result?

(iii) Is the size of the sample important? why?

(iv) Does it matter that eight people refused to answer the question on amount spent?

T **Tasks**

Susan was quite pleased with the survey results as it showed that only a minority of customers intend to take advantage of the higher duty free limits. She was also relieved that the average amount spent on duty free alcohol was less than the average national expenditure on alcohol for the home of £45.45 per adult per annum. She deduced from this that all shoppers will continue to purchase some alcohol in Britain.

However, during a subsequent seminar on statistics that Susan attended, much discussion took place on the problems on analysing survey results. She came away from the seminar wondering if she had interpreted the survey results correctly and has come to you for help.

(i) What is the percentage of shoppers who said they were definitely making at least one trip to France this year?

Help? See Section 2: Estimation – Point estimates, page 86.

(ii) What is the standard error (STEP) for this percentage?

(iii) Calculate the 95% confidence interval for the true percentage of shoppers who intend to travel to France this year? Interpret this interval.

Help? See Section 2: Estimation – Confidence interval of a proportion, page 93.

(iv) What is the standard error of the mean (STEM) of the amount spent on duty free alcohol?

Help? See Section 2: Estimation – Sampling distribution of the means, page 87.

(v) Calculate the 95% confidence interval for the true mean of the amount spent on duty free alcohol for all holiday makers returning from France via Dover.

(vi) Does your analysis suggest that the average amount spent on duty free alcohol is really less than the national average amount spent on all alcohol purchases for the home?

Help? See Section 2: Estimation – Confidence interval for a population mean using the t-distribution, page 90.

P Problem solving activities

Following the presentation of your results Susan decides that the survey results were not sufficiently accurate to be of any use. She would like to repeat the survey and has asked you to advise her on the sample sizes required.

(i) Calculate the number of shoppers to be questioned so that the 'half width' of the confidence interval is no more than 3%.

(ii) The half width of the confidence interval for the average spend on duty free alcohol wants to be reduced to £5. How many holiday makers need to be sampled?

(iii) What reservations (if any) do you have about this kind of survey?

Help? See Section 2: Estimation – Calculation of sample size, page 92.

Spreadsheet tasks

(i) Use a spreadsheet to calculate the half width of the confidence interval for sample sizes from 10 to 300. Plot a graph of half width against sample size and comment on the graph.

(ii) If an interviewer is paid £0.50 for each person sampled, use your spreadsheet to calculate the total cost for the range of sample sizes used in (i). Plot a graph of cost against half width. What do you consider would be a sensible half width to accept, given the cost of the exercise? What sample size does this represent?

You should now be able to attempt questions 20 to 23 of Section 3, page 190.

Comments on quick answer questions 6

(i) There could be many reasons. The general demand could have fallen due to price rises or shoppers may be able to purchase drink cheaper elsewhere.

(ii) You would expect to get slightly different results from different groups of people.

(iii) The larger the sample the more reliable the results should become. This is because you are including more of the 'population'

(iv) If the reason for not answering the question was that the people concerned had bought an excessive amount of alcohol, then the average has been underestimated.

Unit 7: Statistical process control

> **Prerequisites**
>
> To complete this unit successfully you should have a good knowledge of the following:
>
> ❏ Probability (Unit 1, page 3).
>
> ❏ The normal distribution (Unit 4, page 9).
>
> ❏ Confidence intervals (Unit 6, page 13).
>
> **Objectives**
>
> At the end of this unit you should be able to:
>
> ❏ Calculate the limits for the mean control chart.
>
> ❏ Plot sample means onto this chart.
>
> ❏ Determine when a process is 'going out of control'.

Scenario: *Tin cans*

Riglen purchases large quantities of tin cans from the 'Tin Can' company. The cans are made of steel with a thin coating of tin on the inside to prevent rusting. Recently a whole batch of cans had to be returned to 'Tin Can' because it was noticed that the tin had started to 'lift' from the can. Tin Can were most apologetic and had sent Philip Matt, their Production Director to discuss the problem with Riglen. You have been asked to attend the meeting as you had recently attended a course on quality control.

Philip explained that the problem has only arisen since a new tinning process has been installed. The original process gave a relatively high coating of tin, which was unnecessary and expensive. The new process is designed to reduce the thickness of tin by a factor of 10 but it needs constant attention to prevent it malfunctioning. When the process malfunctions the thickness of tin falls below acceptable levels and this can cause 'lifting' of the tin. The speed at which this malfunction is identified depends on the skill of the operator and on occasions large numbers of defective cans have been produced. These are usually discovered during the inspection stage but as with any inspection scheme, poor batches can sometimes be accepted. Philip assured the meeting that everything is being done to prevent this problem recurring and the inspection of cans is to be increased to prevent defective cans from being sent out of the factory.

You are then introduced as Riglen's quality control 'expert' and it is agreed that you will spend a few days at Tin Can's factory checking their improved quality procedures.

On arrival at the factory you are surprised to discover that no checks are made on the process itself. The only quality control in evidence is on a sample of the finished product and this is done simply by inspection – if no faults are evident the batch of cans are passed as satisfactory. Further questioning reveals that a machine is available in the company's laboratory for measuring the thickness of tin on a can. You suggest that it may be possible to identify problems *before* they occur by measuring the thickness of tin on samples of steel sheet as they are coated. Philip agrees that it is worth proceeding with this idea and is willing to provide you with whatever assistance you require.

From observation of the process you discover that the steel sheet arrives in rolls, each roll producing about 1000 cans. The sheet is passed through the process in one continuous operation and it is not possible to stop the process before the end of the roll. The coated sheet is then cut up and rolled into cans by another process. The coating process is designed to produce coatings with a mean thickness of 20 microns and a standard deviation of 1.5 microns. If the coating thickness falls below 15 microns lifting can occur.

Q Quick answer questions 7

(i)   Would it be possible to check the mean and standard deviation of the process?

(ii) Why might it not be possible to take a large sample of measurements?

T Tasks

Following discussions with Philip you decide that a sample of 4 thickness readings is the best that could be achieved and this will be done for each roll. Based on this information you are ready to produce a control chart for the mean thickness of coating.

(i)   What is the value of 'Z' for a probability of

    (a)   0.025 and

    (b)   0.001

> Help? See appendix 3: The normal table, page 250.

(ii) Calculate the standard deviation of the sampling distribution of the means (STEM) for a sample size of 4.

> Help? See Section 2: Estimation- Sampling distribution of the means, page 87.

(iii) Calculate the 95% and 99.8% confidence intervals using your answers from Tasks (i) and (ii).

(iv) Copy the diagram below onto graph paper and draw in the two confidence intervals that you calculated in Task (iii).

> Help? See Section 2: Estimation – Confidence intervals for a population mean using the normal distribution, page 88.

> Help? See Section 2: Estimation – Statistical process control, page 94.

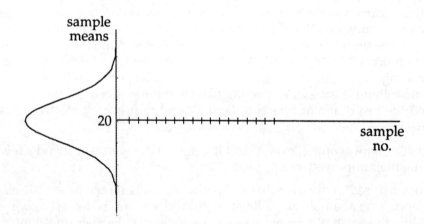

P Problem solving activities

Before handing the control chart over to Philip, you ask the machine operators to take a sample of 4 measurements of coating thickness for each roll. This is carried out each day for 5 days and the mean of each sample is given as follows on the opposite page:

Day	Sample no.	Mean		Day	Sample no.	Mean
1	1	20.5		2	1	19.7
	2	21.6			2	19.7
	3	19.8			3	18.8
	4	20.1			4	19.3
	5	19.7			5	19.4
					6	19.0

Day	Sample no.	Mean		Day	Sample no.	Mean
3	1	19.2		4	1	20.0
	2	20.9			2	19.2
	3	20.4			3	17.2
	4	18.3			4	19.9
	5	18.4			5	20.2

Day	Sample no.	Mean
5	1	20.8
	2	20.5
	3	19.7
	4	19.9
	5	19.6
	6	19.4

(i)   Plot the means for each day onto the chart that you produced in Task (iv). (You can assume that the machine is re-set before the start of each day.) For each day decide if the process is in or out of control. Give reasons for your answer.

> Help? See Section 2: Estimation – Statistical process control, page 94.

(ii) Is it likely that the coating thickness has fallen below 15 microns on any day?

You should now be able to attempt questions 24 and 25 of Section 3, page 191.

Comments on quick answer questions 7

(i)   Yes, a large sample of measurements could be taken when the process is known to be working correctly, and the mean and standard deviation calculated from this sample.

(ii) It may take a long time to make one measurement and as this task is 'unproductive' work the sample size will need to be kept small.

Unit 8: Hypothesis testing of a sample mean and proportion

Prerequisites

To complete this unit successfully you should have a good knowledge of the following:

❐ Standard errors (Unit 6, page 13)

❐ Use of the Z and t tables (Unit 6, page 13)

❐ Degrees of freedom (Unit 6, page 13)

Objectives

At the end of this unit you should be able to:

❐ Set up the null and alternative hypotheses for a given problem

❐ Determine the critical values from tables

❐ Use the t-test on a sample mean

❐ Use the Z-test on a sample proportion

❐ Decide if there is sufficient evidence to reject a null hypothesis

---

Scenario: 'Peaches and cream'

The food department buys in various fruit and vegetables for processing and canning. One of the items are peaches and these are purchased from a supplier (Tinsler) in tins with a supposed net weight of 20kg. Riglen have never thought it necessary to weigh the incoming produce as the relationship with the company has always been good. However, since the founder, Bob Tinsler, retired, a number of problems have arisen. In particular it has been noted that the number of tins of peaches that Riglen cans from a consignment of Tinsler peaches has been declining during the last few months. Before accusing Tinsler of supplying underweight tins, Shirley Watts, the manager of the Food department has asked for your assistance.

You decide to take a sample of 30 tins from the next consignment of peaches and weigh the contents carefully. The contents of 4 of the tins were 'blown', that is the fruit had started to ferment. These tins were discarded and 4 further tins selected and weighed.

From the sample of the 30 tins you found that the mean weight of the contents was 19.234kg with a standard deviation of 2.622kg.

Q | **Quick answer questions 8**

(i) Why was it necessary to sample such a large number of tins? Wouldn't a smaller number have been satisfactory?

(ii) Why was it necessary to discard the 'blown' tins.

T | **Tasks (1)**

You decide to use an hypothesis test, at the 5% significance level, to discover if Tinsler are supplying underweight tins?

(i)   Set up the null and alternative hypothesis for this problem.

(ii) What is the critical value at the 5% significance level?

(iii) Calculate the standard error of the sampling distribution of the means (STEM).

> Help? See Section 2: Hypothesis testing – Introduction, page 99 and Hypothesis test involving a single sample mean, page 100.

(iv) Calculate the test statistic for this problem.

(v)   Do your results suggest that the null hypothesis should be rejected?

> Help? See Section 2: Hypothesis testing – The t-test for a single sample mean, page 103.

T   Tasks (2)

You now turn your attention to the 4 tins that were discarded. It is accepted that a few tins will be defective in some way but it is very unusual for more than 5% of tins to have to be discarded. You wish to find out if the proportion of defective tins in your sample was significantly greater than 5%.

(i)   What is the proportion of defective tins in your original sample?

(ii) What are your 'null' and 'alternative' hypotheses for this problem?

(iii) What is the critical value at the 5% significance level?

> Help? See Section 2: Hypothesis testing – Introduction, page 000 and Hypothesis test of a proportion, page 109.

(iv) Calculate the standard error of the sampling distribution of the sample proportion (STEP).

(v)   Calculate the 'test statistic' for this problem.

(vi) Do your results suggest that the null hypothesis should be rejected?

(vii) Do you have any reservations with your analysis? What could you do to overcome these reservations?

> Help? See Section 2: Hypothesis testing – Hypothesis test of a proportion, page 102.

P   Problem solving activity

After you have completed these calculations and written your report, you realise that as the entire consignment is only 200 tins you should have adjusted STEM using the finite population correction factor.

Would this adjustment cause you to change your conclusion concerning the mean weight of the entire 200 tins?

> Help? See Section 2: Estimation – Finite populations, page 94.

You should now be able to attempt questions 26 and 27 of Section 3, page 179.

You should now be able to attempt questions 26 and 27 of Section 3, page 179.

Comments on quick answer questions 8

(i)   A large sample gives improved accuracy and avoids having to make normality assumptions for the entire consignment.

(ii) The weight may have been affected in some way- perhaps the tins were leaking.

Unit 9: Hypothesis testing of two independent sample means

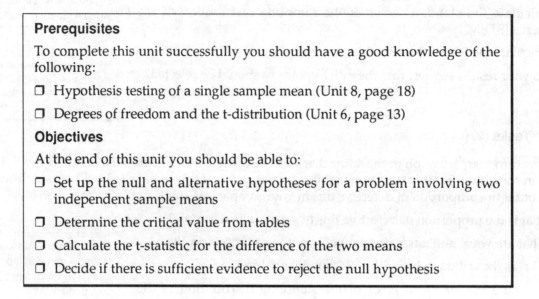

Prerequisites

To complete this unit successfully you should have a good knowledge of the following:

❑ Hypothesis testing of a single sample mean (Unit 8, page 18)

❑ Degrees of freedom and the t-distribution (Unit 6, page 13)

Objectives

At the end of this unit you should be able to:

❑ Set up the null and alternative hypotheses for a problem involving two independent sample means

❑ Determine the critical value from tables

❑ Calculate the t-statistic for the difference of the two means

❑ Decide if there is sufficient evidence to reject the null hypothesis

Scenario: *Dust filters in the Cooked Meat department*

An inspection by the Environmental Health Department has recently taken place at Riglen and concern was expressed at the amount of dust that was detected in the air within the Cooked Meat department. Although the quantity of dust does not exceed the legal limit, the inspectors recommended that the dust filters be replaced as soon as possible.

Following a meeting between Kevin Giles, the departmental manager and Cecil Philips, the Health and Safety Officer at Riglen, it was decided to investigate the relative merits of the various filters on the market at the current time. Following this investigation, Cecil has reduced the choice to just two, the 'Ameba' and the 'Bewax'. In order to decide which one to purchase, the manufacturers have loaned Riglen one unit of each type in order that a comparison can be made.

Cecil first installed the Ameba and each week for the next six weeks the filters were weighed, cleaned and replaced. The Ameba unit was then removed and the Bewax unit placed in the same position and the experiment repeated. The amount of dust (in grams) collected by the two units was as follows:

Ameba: 5.7,   6.4,   6.1,   4.8,   7.2,   2.9

Bewax: 2.9,   4.7   6.3   3.0   7.0   3.5

(Note: During the third week of the Bewax experiment, the technician responsible for the filter cleaning was off sick and the filters were not weighed prior to cleaning. To compensate for not having any results for week 3, the experiment was continued for another week.)

Q **Quick answer questions 9**

(i) Why was it necessary to install the two units in the same position?

(ii) Was it necessary to extend the Bewax experiment for another week? Could the Bewax analysis be carried out on 5 weeks instead of 6?

T | Tasks

Cecil was hoping that it would be obvious which filter unit was better but he feels the results are inconclusive. You have heard about the experiment and offered to carry out a statistical analysis on the results.

(i)   What are the null and alternative hypotheses for this problem?

(ii)   How many 'degrees of freedom' does this problem have?

(iii) What is the critical value at 5% on these degrees of freedom?

(iv)   Calculate the mean and standard deviation of each sample.

> Help? See Section 2: Hypothesis Testing – Comparison of two sample means page 105 and Hypothesis test of two independent sample means, 105.

(v)   Use the two standard deviations found in task (iii) to calculate the 'pooled' estimate of the population standard deviation.

(vi)   Calculate the standard error of the difference of the two means.

(vii)   Calculate the test statistic for this problem.

(viii)   Do your results suggest that the null hypothesis should be rejected? What are your conclusion regarding the relative merits of the two filter units?

> Help? See Section 2: Hypothesis Testing – Hypothesis test of two independent sample means, page 105.

You should now be able to attempt questions 28 to 31 of Section 3, page 193.

Comments on quick answer questions 9

(i)   The dust density may be different in other parts of the department, so a more reliable comparison would be made if the two units were in approximately the same position.

(ii) It wasn't essential to extend the experiment since it is only the means that are being compared.

Unit 10: Hypothesis test on paired data

Prerequisites

To complete this unit successfully you should have a good knowledge of the following:

❐ Hypothesis testing of a single sample mean (Unit 8, page 18)

❐ Degrees of freedom and the t-distribution (Unit 6, page 13)

Objectives

At the end of this unit you should be able to:

❐ Set up the null and alternative hypotheses for a problem involving paired data

❐ Determine the critical value from tables

❐ Calculate the t-statistic for the mean of the difference between the two samples

❐ Decide if there is sufficient evidence to reject the null hypothesis

---

Scenario: *Sales campaign*

You have been asked to help in the design and analysis of a sales campaign involving a selected number of supermarkets. Janet Graves, the Marketing Manager, believes that it is the 'caring image' of the business that attracts customers rather than price cuts alone.

To test this idea Janet obtained approval to invest in staff training and other expenditure to generate a friendly atmosphere within a supermarket. Advertising on television and local radio was also to be increased during the campaign. You randomly selected 8 supermarkets throughout the country representing different areas and spending patterns.

Following staff training, the campaign is started and continued for a month.

The sales turnover (in £000's) for each supermarket for the month before and after the campaign was noted and is as follows:

Supermarket:	A	B	C	D	E	F	G	H
Sales: Before	150	75	110	300	120	560	350	185
After	178	60	150	400	180	540	350	235

Q **Quick answer questions 10**

(i) What other factors may effect turnover at a supermarket during the month in question?

(ii) Why was it important to obtain a cross section of supermarkets from different areas?

T | Tasks

Janet's view before the campaign started was that sales would increase. However, she knows that she won't get further support from Head Office unless she can prove conclusively that the campaign has worked.

(i)   What is the null and alternative hypotheses for this problem?

(ii) What are the critical values at 5% and at 1%?

(iii) Calculate the increase (or decrease) in sales turnover for each supermarket. (A decrease should be represented by a minus sign)

(iv) Calculate the mean and standard deviation of the difference in turnover.

(v)   Calculate the standard error of the differences (don't forget to adjust the standard error that you calculated in task (iv)).

(vi) Calculate the test statistic for this problem. What conclusions can you draw regarding the success of the marketing campaign.

> Help? See Section 2: Hypothesis Testing – Hypothesis test for samples that are not independent, page 107.

You should now be able to attempt questions 32 and 33 of Section 3, page 195.

Comments on quick answer questions 10

(i)   The time of year may effect turnover or a campaign by a rival chain of supermarkets.

(ii) The campaign is likely to have different effects in different areas.

Unit 11: The χ^2 hypothesis test

Prerequisites

To complete this unit successfully you should have a good knowledge of the following:

❐ The concept of hypothesis testing (Unit 8, page 18)

❐ The multiplication rule of probability (Unit 1, page 3)

❐ Degrees of freedom (Unit 6, page 13)

❐ Confidence intervals for a proportion (Unit 6, page 13)

Objectives

At the end of this unit you should be able to:

❐ Set up the null and alternative hypotheses for a test of association between two categories

❐ Determine the degrees of freedom of a contingency table and use this to find, from tables, the appropriate critical value

❐ Calculate the test statistic and decide if there is sufficient evidence to reject the null hypothesis

---

Scenario: *'You can't teach old dogs new tricks'*

In conjunction with machinery replacement, Riglen has instigated a major programme of re-training for all its production employees. In order to assess the effectiveness of this training programme, a sample of 110 employees were appraised before and after the training. Based on the comparisons of the two appraisals each employee was classified according to how well they had benefited from the training. This classification ranged from 'worse', which means they now perform worse than they did before, to 'high', which means they perform much better than they did before the training. The results of this appraisal can be seen in the table below where you will notice that employees have been further classified by age.

Age of employee	Level of improvement				Total
	Worse	None	Some	High	
Below 40	1	5	24	30	60
40+	4	5	31	10	50
Total	5	10	55	40	110

Q **Quick answer questions 11**

(i) What other classifications could there be apart from age?

(ii) What form might the appraisal have taken?

(iii) What are the problems associated with appraisal of the production function?

T **Tasks**

The Head of Training at Riglen is Alan Bright and he is interested to discover if level of improvement at their job and age are related. He has asked you to analyse the table above and to report your findings.

(i) What are the null and alternative hypotheses for this problem?

Help? See Section 2: Hypothesis Testing – The χ^2 hypothesis test, page 103 and The χ^2 test of association, page 113.

(ii) If you selected a production employee at random, what is the probability that:

    (a) He would be under 40 years old?

    (b) His level of performance has got worse?

    (c) He would be under 40 *and* his level of performance has got worse?

Help? See Section 2: Probability – The probability of compound events, page 56.

(iii) What is the *expected* number of employees who should be both under 40 years old and worse at their job?

Help? See Section 2: Probability – Expected value, page 60.

(iv) Calculate the expected numbers of employees in each cell of the above table. (You should be able to find a quicker method of calculating these expected numbers)

(v) You should find that some of these expected numbers are less than 5. Combine suitable categories until the expected number in each cell is greater than 5.

(vi) Calculate the *difference* between the observed number (O) and the expected number (E) for each cell.

(vii) Square this difference to remove any negative signs and then divide by the expected number to 'normalise' the resulting figure.

(viii) Place the figures you obtained from task (v) to (vii) into a table similar to the one below.

O	E	(O – E)	(O – E)^2	$\dfrac{(O-E)^2}{E}$

(ix) Add up the values in the last column- this is your test statistic.

(x) How many ways are there of choosing the numbers that go into the original table, given that the row and column totals are fixed? This is the number of degrees of freedom for the table.

(xi) Use the χ^2 table in the appendix (page 000) to obtain the critical value at the 1% significance level and compare this figure with your test statistic. Would you accept or reject the null hypothesis?

(xii) What conclusions can you come to regarding the association (if any) between level of improvement at the job and age?

Help? See Section 2: Hypothesis Testing – The χ^2test of association, page 113.

P   Problem solving activity

Following from your results above, Alan has asked you to analyse in more detail, the results for the employees who showed a high level of improvement at their job.

Help? See Section 2: Estimation – Confidence interval of a proportion, page 93.

What is the 95% confidence interval for the proportion of all employees who showed a high level of improvement at their job.

You should now be able to attempt questions 34 to 37 of Section 3, page 196.

Comments on quick answer questions 11

(i) Sex of employee, number of years with company or paper qualifications

(ii) The quality or quantity of the product produced

(iii) Many difficulties. There may not be any obvious output that can be measured or perhaps employees work in teams. Appraisal may have to be on a subjective basis.

Unit 12: Correlation

Prerequisites

There are no prerequisitesfor this Unit, although a knowledge of simple X–Y graphs is assumed.

(In order to answer Problem solving activity (iii), some knowledge of hypothosis testing is assumed – see Unit 8 page 18.)

Objectives

At the end of this unit you should be able to:

❑ Draw and interpret scatter diagrams

❑ Calculate the product moment correlation coefficient.

❑ Apply a test of significance to the correlation coefficient

Scenario: *Supermarket sales*

You have received a request from Jane Holt, the supermarket manager for the Midlands region, to analyse some data that she has obtained on sales turnover.

Jane believes that the annual turnover of a supermarket can be explained by a number of external factors. She is hoping that it will be possible to quantify these factors and use them for monitoring existing stores and for the siting of new ones.

She considered many factors but decided that the following were worth looking at and the data would be easy to obtain.

(a) Distance of the supermarket from the centre of the nearest town.

(b) The number of car park spaces at the store.

(c) The population of the catchment area of the store.

(d) The percentage of unemployment in the nearest town.

The table below relates to the eight supermarkets in the Midland region.

Supermarket	A	B	C	D	E	F	G	H
Turnover (£000's)	85	60	105	98	40	130	76	75
Miles from town	0.2	0.0	2.5	3.0	4.0	0.0	2.0	6.5
Car park spaces (000's)	1.0	1.2	3.2	3.5	0.75	5.0	4.5	1.0
Population (000's)	3.6	1.0	55.0	20.0	0.5	60.0	3.5	5.0
Unemployment(%)	20.0	17.5	10.0	33.0	22.5	20.0	11.25	31.0

Q Quick answer questions 12

(i) What other factors might affect turnover?

(ii) How might an analysis of this data help when planning new stores?

T Tasks

Jane wants you to analyse the data in a way that she can understand. She likes 'graphs and things' so you decide to try plotting five *scatter diagrams*- one for each factor.

(i) Draw a scatter diagram of 'miles from town' against turnover. The X axis should represent the distance factor and the Y axis should represent turnover. Don't join up the points. Draw a smooth closed loop round all the points making the area within the loop as small as possible. Is this loop an ellipse shape or more like a circle? Is the loop pointing upwards or downwards?

(ii) Repeat (i) for the other three factors, always making turnover the 'Y' variable.

(iii) Using the distribution of the points on the diagram and the shape and direction of the loops, categorise the four scatter diagrams into: positive, negative or no association; strong or weak association; linear or non-linear association.

(iv) Do you think that this graphical analysis has enabled you to identify which factor or factors is associated with turnover?

> Help? See Section 2: Correlation and regression – Introduction, page 116 and Scatter diagrams page 116.

P Problem solving activities

Following this graphical analysis, Jane has asked you to quantify the importance of each factor.

(i) Obtain a suitable correlation coefficient for each factor against turnover.

(ii) Using the values obtained from (i), categorise the factors into: positive, negative or no association; strong or weak association. Does this agree with your earlier answers? Try and explain any discrepancies.

> Help? See section 2: Correlation and regression – Correlation, page 118 and Pearson's Product moment correlation coefficient (r), page 118.

(iii) For each correlation coefficient you obtained in (i), decide if the value is significantly different from zero.

> Help? See Section 2: Correlation and regression – Significance of **r**, page 119.

(iv) Make recommendations regarding the factors that appear to influence turnover. Comment on any reservations you might have with either the data or the analysis. Could your results be extrapolated to other regions?

Spreadsheet task

Use a spreadsheet to investigate the sensitivity of the correlation coefficients you calculated above to small changes in the data. In particular what happens if supermarket 'F' is omitted?

You should now be able to attempt questions 38 and 39 of Section 3, page 199

> Help? See Section 2: Correlation and regression – Computational aids in correlation and regression analysis, page 124.

Comments on quick answer questions 12

(i) Price of goods is probably the most important factor. Other factors could include the number of other supermarkets within the catchment area, opening hours and the size of the store.

(ii) An analysis of the data may indicate which factors are important and this could be taken into account in the planning stage. For example car parking space may be more important than distance from the town centre.

Unit 13: Linear regression

Prerequisites

To complete this unit successfully you should have a good knowledge of the following:

❏ Scatter diagrams (Unit 12, page 26)

Objectives

At the end of this unit you should be able to:

❏ Understand the meaning of the least squares criterion

❏ Calculate and interpret the regression line

❏ Calculate the coefficient of determination and understand its relationship to regression

❏ Obtain point and interval estimates of the dependent variable

❏ Appreciate the limitations of simple bivariate linear regression analysis.

Scenario: *Sales of 'White-Glo' detergent*

The Household Products Department produce a range of detergents called White-Glow. The sales of these detergents have fallen during the last year and an investigation is under way to find the cause.

John Marla, the sales manager of the White-Glow range, believes that the advertising policy of the Department is partly to blame for the decline in sales. This policy states that the advertising expenditure for the current month cannot exceed 10% of the sales revenue of the preceding month. John thinks that a fixed budget should be allocated and he has decided to initiate a project to investigate this idea.

The first stage in this project was to collect data on sales revenue and advertising expenditure. These data are shown in the table below. (All figures are in £000's).

Month	Jan	Feb	Mar	Apr	May	June	Jul	Aug	Sept	Oct	Nov	Dec
Sales	60	60	58	45	41	33	31	25	24	23	23	23
Adv.	6.0	6.0	6.0	5.8	4.5	4.1	3.3	3.1	2.5	2.4	2.3	2.3

Q **Quick answer questions 13**

(i) What do you think is wrong with the current policy?

(ii) What factors, apart from advertising, might affect sales?

(iii) Do you think it would be useful to have a statistical relationship (an equation) between sales and advertising expenditure? Why?

(iv) Do you think that this relationship would be linear?

T **Tasks**

In order to help John Marla with his project you have been asked to do some preliminary analysis of the data. In particular he wants you to investigate the possible linear relationship between advertising expenditure and sales.

(i)   Plot a scatter diagram of the data given in the table above. Comment on the strength of the association between the two variables.

(ii)   Draw a straight line through the scatter diagram. This line should pass close to as many points as possible. Is there any evidence that the relationship between advertising expenditure and sales is non-linear?

> Help? See Section 2: Correlation and regression – Scatter diagrams, page 116.

(iii)   Use your line to estimate the sales for an advertising expenditure of £6,000. Repeat for the remaining advertising expenditure figures given in the table.

(iv)   The difference between the actual sales figures and those you estimated in (iii) represents the error in your estimates. Calculate the 12 errors and identify any outliers (extreme values). Do you think your line is a 'good fit' to the data?

(v)   To decide if one line is better than another the sum of the individual errors could be found. Why wouldn't this be particularly useful? What other measures of the total error might be appropriate?

> Help? See Section 2: Correlation and regression – Linear regression, page 120.

P   Problem solving activities

Your preliminary analysis suggests that there is an association between sales and advertising expenditure and that the relationship, over the range of the data provided, is approximately linear. John Marla has now asked you to continue the analysis and to obtain the following:

(i)   The 'line of best fit' between sales and advertising expenditure.

> Help? See Section 2: Correlation and regression – Method of least squares, page 121.

(ii)   An idea of how well the equation obtained in (i) fits the data.

(iii)   The expected sales given an advertising expenditure of £5000.

> Help? See Section 2: Correlation and regression – Coefficient of determination, page 122 and Analysis of errors, page 122.

(iv)   Whether your analysis proves that increased advertising implies increased sales.

(v)   Your recommendations regarding the advertising budget.

> Help? See Section 2: Correlation and regression – Prediction and estimation using linear regression, page 123.

Spreadsheet tasks

(i)   Use a spreadsheet to plot the 95% confidence intervals for sales revenue given values of the advertising budget from £2000 to £6000.

(ii)   Use a spreadsheet to investigate whether the 'log' transformation will help 'straighten' the data; that is, will the fit be improved by this transformation.

You should now be able to attempt questions 40 to 46 of Section 3, page 200.

> Help? See Section 2: Correlation and regression – Computational aids in correlation and regression analysis, page 124. Also Prediction and estimating using linear regression, page 123 and Non-linearity, page 125.

Comments on quick answer questions 13

(i) The main problem with the current policy is that advertising expenditure is made to be dependent on sales. Therefore if sales are really dependent on advertising expenditure and sales fall then a downward spiral could result.

(ii) There are many possible factors that could affect sales such as price, competitors advertising policy, the life cycle of the product etc.

(iii) Yes. This would allow the effects of changes in advertising expenditure on sales to be estimated.

(iv) Unlikely for the whole range of advertising expenditure. An increase in advertising when advertising is low is likely to increase sales more than when advertising is high. This is because as advertising expenditure is increased beyond a certain level saturation may occur, so that any further increase will have little or no effect.

Unit 14: Time series analysis

> **Prerequisites**
>
> There are no prerequisites for this Unit, although a knowledge of simple X-Y graphs is assumed.
>
> **Objectives**
>
> At the end of this unit you should be able to:
>
> ❏ Use the technique of moving averages to isolate the trend in a time series.
>
> ❏ Understand the circumstances where the additive and multiplicative models should be used.
>
> ❏ Calculate the seasonal component for both the additive and multiplicative models.
>
> ❏ Obtain the seasonally adjusted series.
>
> ❏ Apply the technique of exponential smoothing in appropriate circum-stances.
>
> ❏ Use time series analysis to make forecasts.

Scenario: *The 'long weekend'*

Scenario: The 'long weekend'

All companies suffer from absenteeism and Riglen is no different in this respect. Riglen employees lose pay for each day sick but their absence can still increase costs because of production problems that can occur when certain key staff are absent.

There has been several instances recently where production has been held up because of absenteeism and the matter has been raised at the weekly product manager's meeting. The following is an extract of the conversation between Alan Smith, the Production manager, Peter Fish, the Personnel manager and Sarah More, a product manager:

A. Smith	"During the last week our output has fallen by 10%. Why is this?"
S. More	"My section has suffered high absenteeism recently, which has caused severe problems. I blame the new productivity scheme that too easily allows employees to make up lost pay."
P. Fish	"I do not agree with this. The graph I have prepared shows that absenteeism has hardly changed over the last five weeks."
A. Smith	"I don't want to start an argument, I just want someone to analyse those absenteeism figures and tell me how many employees are likely to be absent next week. We can then plan accordingly."

The time series graph referred to above is reproduced in Figure 1 and the figures for the absenteeism over the last five weeks are given below:

		Number of employees absent				
		Mon	Tues	Wed	Thurs	Fri
Week	1	101	52	23	47	84
	2	115	45	16	37	96
	3	98	53	26	41	75
	4	148	101	53	75	100
	5	104	43	15	30	70

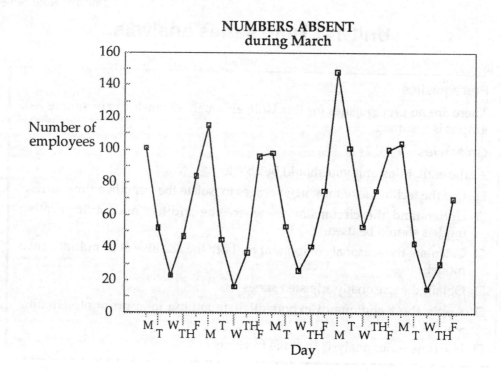

NUMBERS ABSENT during March

Number of employees (y-axis: 0 to 160)

Day (x-axis: M T W TH F repeated across weeks)

Q Quick answer questions 14

(i)   Absenteeism for week four is higher than for the other weeks, what could the reason be for this?

(ii) Do you think that the absenteeism is higher for any particular day? Why might this be?

(iii) Do you think Alan Smith is handling the problem correctly? What would you have done?

T Tasks

Peter Fish has agreed to analyse the figures and realises that before any forecasts are made he really needs to smooth the data, that is, to remove the 'seasonal' fluctuations. His first attempt was to find the average number absent for each of the five weeks and plot this on the graph. However he is not sure if this is correct and has come to you for help.

(i)   Explain why the method suggested by Peter Fish to smooth the data is not very satisfactory.

(ii) A better method is the method of *moving averages*. To use this method first re-write the data into one long column. Then sum the data for the first 5 days and write this value in the next column alongside Wednesday. Now subtract 101 from this total, which is the value for Monday of the first week and add 115, which is the value for the Monday of the second week. Write this value alongside Thursday. Repeat this process for the remainder of the data. For each total, divide by 5 to obtain the average and place these values in the next column.

(iii) Plot the original series and your moving average series on the same graph. Has the moving average series smoothed the data? What does this series represent?

> Help? See Section 2: Time Series Analysis – The decomposition model, page 127 and Isolating the trend, page 127.

(iv) Extrapolate your moving average series into week six. What are your forecast trend values for week six?

P | Problem solving activities

To enable forecasts for each day to be obtained, Peter has asked you to let him have information on the daily variation of absence rates (that is the 'seasonal' component). He also would like to know how reliable such forecasts will be and whether it would be possible to obtain future forecasts without having to repeat the analysis.

(i) Use an appropriate decomposition model to calculate the average seasonal component for Monday to Friday.

> Help? See Section 2: Time Series Analysis – Isolating the seasonal component, page 130.

(ii) Use the average seasonal component and the moving avaerage series to calculate the predicted number of employees absent for each day.

(iii) Analyse the errors between the actual and expected figures for numbers absent. What can you deduce from this analysis?

> Help? See Section 2: Time Series Analysis – Analysis of errors, page 132.

(iv) Using the seasonal constants found in (i) and the forecast trend figures, obtain the expected numbers of employees absent during week six.

> Help? See Section 2: Time Series Analysis – Forecasting using the decomposition model, page 134.

(v) De-seasonalize the time series using the seasonal constants found in (i).

> Help? See Section 2: Time Series Analysis – Seasonally adjusted series, Page 134.

(vi) Use exponential smoothing on the last four values of the seasonally adjusted series in order to forecast the numbers absent for Monday of week six. You should use a smoothing constant of 0.3 and a forecast of 56.6 as your first forecast.

> Help? See Section 2: Time Series Analysis – Exponential smoothing, Page 135.

> Help? See Section 2: Time Series Analysis – Analysis of errors, page 132.

Spreadsheet tasks

Use a spreadsheet to investigate the sensitivity of the forecast obtained in the problem solving activity (vi) to changes in the smoothing constant. Which value of α gives the smallest value of the MSE statistic?

You should now be able to attempt questions 47 to 52 of Section 3, page 203

Comments on quick answer questions 14

(i) Probably a flu epidemic or something similar.

(ii) Absenteeism for Mondays and Fridays is higher than the other days. Perhaps some employees are taking days off in order to extend the weekend?

(iii) Alan Smith doesn't seem concerned about the underlying cause of absenteeism, that is, is it genuine or the result of poor morale? The first thing to do would be to check whether absenteeism rates have increased over the long term.

Unit 15: Network analysis

Prerequisites

There are no prerequisites for this Unit, although to successfully attempt Problem solving activity (ii) a knowledge of the normal distribution is required – Unit 4, page 9.

Objectives

At the end of this unit you should be able to:

❑ Construct an 'activity-on-node' network to represent a project.

❑ Calculate the earliest and latest start and finish times for each activity.

❑ Calculate the float for each activity and identify the critical path.

❑ Apply the PERT technique in order to take uncertainty into consideration.

Scenario: *Launch of a marketing campaign for the new 'Green Household Products'*

Critical path analysis

The Household Products Department has decided to market a new 'greener' range of household products. The first product to be produced is a washing powder and if this proves successful other environmental friendly products will be produced. Before the product is to be available nationwide, a marketing campaign is to be launched in a selected region.

Sue King, the marketing manager for the Household Products Department has been asked to handle the campaign and her first task is to estimate the likely time this project will take. She has heard that critical path analysis would give her this information and she has approached you for help and advice. Together you have identified the important activities connected with the campaign and Sue has obtained estimates of the durations for each activity. The details are given below.

Activity	Description	Duration (weeks)	Immediate Predecessors
A	Arrange meetings to formulate campaign	2	-
B	Design publicity material	3	A
C	Design TV advertising	4	A
D	Design newspaper advertising	3	A
E	Specifications sent to advertising agency	1	C and D
F	Preparation of TV and newspaper advertisements	10	E
G	Distribution of washing powder within the Midlands TV region	3	-
H	Run campaign in the Midlands TV region	6	B,F and G
I	Assess results	2	H
J	Arrange national campaign	4	I

Q | Quick answer questions 15

(i) The sum of the durations of all the activities is 38 weeks. Why is this an over-estimate of the time required?

(ii) Why do think it is necessary to test market the product in a selected region?

(iii) What are the disadvantages of test marketing the product in one region?

(iv) Why has a TV region been chosen?

T Tasks

Sue has asked you to use the above data to estimate how many weeks it will be before the national campaign can start. She would also like to know which activities are 'critical' to the project, that is which activities need careful monitoring.

(i) Use boxes (nodes) to represent activities and lines between the boxes to represent the dependencies. For example E cannot start until both C and D have been completed so a line from both C and D should be connected to E. You will need a START and END node so that all activities have at least one line entering and one line leaving.

> Help? See Section 2: Network Analysis – Activity-on-node, page 139.

(ii) Make a *forward* pass through the network calculating the earliest start time (EST) and the earliest finish time (EFT) for each node. The EST should be written at the top left hand corner of the node and the EFT at the top right hand corner. Assume that the start of the project is at time zero.

(iii) Starting at the END node, make a *backward* pass through the network calculating the latest finish time (LFT) and the latest start time (LST) for each node. Write this information at the bottom of the node.

(iv) How long will it be before the national campaign could start?

(v) Determine how much slack or *float* there is in each activity. Which activities are *critical*, that is do not have any float?

> Help? See Section 2: Network Analysis – Critical path analysis, page 138 and Calculation of the floats, page 141.

P Problem solving activities

Some of the activity durations that you were given by Sue have been disputed by Alan Smiles, the Product Manager. He believes that some of the figures are incorrect while for others he believes that there is some degree of uncertainty and this should be taken into account.

(i) Alan believes that activity B could be completed in 1 week and activity F in 8 weeks. What effect would this have on the project duration?

(ii) Activities C, D and J are considered by Alan to be uncertain and he has provided an optimistic, a pessimistic and a most likely time estimate for each of these three activities. They are as follows.

> Help? See Section 2: Network Analysis – PERT analysis, page 145.

Activity	Optimistic	Pessimistic	Most likely
C	2	7	3
D	2	6	3
J	3	6	5

Using these figures and the durations given for B and F in (i), prepare a new estimate of the total project time.

(iii) What is the probability that the project will be completed in less than 29 weeks?

> Help? See Section 2: Probability Distributions – The normal distribution, page 69.

You should now be able to attempt questions 53 and 54 of Section 3, page 206

Answers to quick answer questions 15

(i) The duration of 38 weeks assumes that the activities take place sequentially. However some activities can run in parallel, for example activities B,C and D can take place at the same time.

(ii) Results of the test market may indicate the likely demand that will be generated nationally. It may also indicate problems that need to be addressed either in the technical specification of the product or in the marketing campaign.

(iii) The region chosen may not be typical of the country as a whole. Another reason is that it gives notice of your intent to competitors.

(iv) Since TV advertising is to be used it makes sense to use a TV area.

Unit 16: Resource and cost scheduling

Prerequisites

To complete this unit successfully you should have a good knowledge of the following:

❏ Critical path analysis (Unit 15, page 34)

Objectives

At the end of this unit you should be able to:

❏ Use a Gantt chart and resource histogram to smooth the use of resources required by a project.

❏ Apply the technique of cost scheduling.

Scenario: *Modernisation of the canning plant*

There have been recurring problems with the food canning process and a decision has been taken at Board level to replace the machinery with more modern computer controlled equipment. Holder and Holder Consulting Engineers have been commissioned to advise on the system to purchase and their report is expected in 5 weeks time. Although the fine details of the recommended system will not be known until this report has been received, the essential characteristics of all the alternatives are the same. Planning for the installation can therefore start immediately and this is important because during the installation all food canning has to be contracted out and this will be expensive.

In order to ensure that the project is completed as quickly as possible and at minimum cost you have been asked to use the relevant network analysis techniques on the data given below. You should also note that fitters are to be employed on a fixed term contract and it is important that only the minimum number necessary are recruited.

Activity	Description	Duration (weeks)	Immediate Predecessors	Fitters required	Cost (£000's)
A	Obtain consulting engineer's report	5	-	0	5
B	Remove existing machinery	4	-	8	3
C	Purchase new machinery	5	A	0	50
D	Purchase electrics	7	A	0	15
E	Purchase computers	6	A	0	25
F	Install machinery	4	B and C	5	5
G	Install computers	3	E	6	5
H	Connect electrics	3	F and D	2	4
I	Recruit and train staff	6	-	0	3
J	Pilot production run	1	G and H	6	6
K	Prepare for full production	4	I and J	5	2

Q **Quick answer questions 16**

(i) Are there any alternatives to contracting out the canning work?

(ii) Do you think that there is any uncertainty with the activity durations? What might happen if some of these activities took longer than expected?

T   Tasks (1) Resource smoothing

In order to ensure that only the minimum number of fitters are recruited, you decide to 'smooth' the fitter requirements over the timespan of the project.

(i) Draw the network and calculate the start and finish times for each activity. How long will the project take and what are the critical activities?

> Help? See Section 2: Network Analysis – Critical path analysis, page 138.

(ii) Making the horizontal axis of a graph represent time, start at the top of the graph paper and draw a horizontal bar of length 5 to represent activity A. Continue this for all activities, starting at the earliest start time and finish at the earliest finish time.

(iii) To each activity on the chart you prepared in (ii) add the number of fitters required. Then for each week sum the total number of fitters required and write this at the bottom of your chart. What is the maximum number of fitters required and during what weeks does this occur.

(iv) Indicate with a dotted line on your chart the floats of the non-critical activities. By delaying the start of one or more of these activities try and reduce the maximum number of fitters required. What is the minimum number of fitters required that will still allow the project to be completed in the time found in (i) above?

> Help? See Section 2: Network Analysis – Resource scheduling, page 142.

T   Tasks (2) Cost scheduling

An attempt is to be made to reduce the total project time since for every weeks reduction a saving of £10,000 can be achieved through not having to contract out the weeks canning. This will be possible because some activities such as B can be completed in less time than scheduled. Of course this reduction in time will be at an increased cost. The activities that can be reduced (*crashed*) in time are given below.

Activity	Normal time (weeks)	Crashed time (weeks)	Normal cost (£000's)	Crashed cost (£000's)
B	4	2	10	16
D	7	6	15	21
F	6	3	5	20
G	3	2	5	12
K	4	3	2	10

(i) What is the total normal cost of the project including the £10,000 per week canning charge?

(ii) Using the figures above, calculate for each activity the cost of reducing the time by one week.

(iii) Starting with the critical path, make a list of all paths through the network. Alongside each path write down the duration in weeks of the path.

(iv) Try and reduce the critical path to the same duration as the next largest in the cheapest way possible. Now reduce both paths until the duration is equal to the next highest path and so on. Repeat this until no more reduction is possible. What is the new total cost of the project?

(v) What is the project duration that will minimise the total cost of the project?

Help? See Section 2: Network Analysis – Cost scheduling, page 144.

You should now be able to attempt questions 55 to 58 of Section 3, page 207

Answers to quick answer questions 16

(i) The company could build up large stocks or perhaps the new machinery could be installed in another part of the factory.

(ii) There could be some uncertainty with the durations, particularly with activities involving installations. If any activity was delayed, the project could be delayed if the delay exceeded the activities float.(Don't forget critical activities have zero float).

Unit 17: Inventory control

Prerequisites

There are no prerequisites for this Unit, although to successfully attempt Problem solving activity (iv) a knowledge of the normal distribution is required – Unit 4, page 9.

Objectives

At the end of this unit you should be able to:

❒ Calculate the costs associated with holding stocks.

❒ Calculate the order quantity that minimises these costs.

❒ Decide whether buying in bulk to obtain a price discount is worthwhile.

❒ Calculate a buffer stock to avoid stock-outs.

❒ Appreciate the limitations of the EOQ model.

Scenario: *Food canning*

Riglen cooks and cans food products for sale in its supermarkets. It uses 500,000 medium size cans per annum at a fairly uniform rate, which it purchases from the Tin Can company. Tin Can charge £100 per 5000 cans plus a delivery charge of £50 regardless of the size of the order. Riglen's current order policy is to order 10,000 cans every week but during a cost auditing exercise the canning department has been criticised for such frequent ordering. As a consequence of this criticism, Jeff Lea, the Canning Production Manager has been told to review the department's ordering policy.

Jeff has asked Central Services for their advice and you have just emerged from a meeting with Jeff and the stock controller, Alan Dawes. You found Alan quite hostile to the idea of inventory control because the last time it was attempted a stock-out occurred and production had to stop for two days while emergency supplies were obtained. However because of the insistence of head office, Jeff has given you the authority to proceed with the exercise.

Q **Quick answer questions 17**

(i) Why do you think that the current policy is to order weekly?

(ii) Can you think of any reasons why ordering less frequently may cause problems?

(iii) What kind of costs are associated with holding stock?

T **Tasks**

You decide to cost the current policy and then to determine whether an alternative policy would be cheaper. To help you in your study you obtained the auditor's report which had worked out it was costing the company 1.5p p.a to hold one can in stock. (This 1.5p is made up of interests charges and cost of storage facilities). The company works for 50 weeks a year.

(i) What is the average quantity of stock currently held? and how much does this cost the company each year in holding costs?

(ii) How many orders are made each year and what does this cost the company?

(iii) What is the sum of these two costs?

(iv) Try repeating tasks (i) to (iii) with different order quantities, from say 20,000 to 150,000 cans in intervals of 10,000 cans. Plot the order cost, holding cost and total cost on the same graph, using the X axis for the order quantity. From your graph estimate the order quantity that minimises the total costs.

> Help? See Section 2: Inventory control – Costs of holding stocks, page 148.

(v) Use the EOQ formula to check your answer in (iv). What is the saving in cost if this order quantity was used rather than the current order of 10,000. What is the time between orders with your calculated order quantity?

> Help? See Section 2: Inventory control – Economic order quantity (EOQ) model, page 148.

P   Problem solving activities

Following your recommendations, Alan has made the following observations.

(a) The cans are normally delivered in boxes of 5000 and an additional charge of £50 per order is made for delivery of part boxes.

(b) The Delivery time (that is, the time from making an order to the time it is received) is 4 weeks.

(c) If such large quantities are to be ordered, it will be better to increase the order quantity to 100,000, as at this quantity the price is reduced to £99 per 5000 cans.

(d) The weekly demand for cans is not constant but is normally distributed with an average of 10,000 cans and a standard deviation of 5,000 cans.

Investigate these observations; in particular

(i) Does the cost of part boxes change your recommendation?

(ii) What should the re-order level be if delivery time is 4 weeks?

(iii) Is it worthwhile taking advantage of the bulk order discount?

> Help? See Section 2: Inventory control – Economic order quantity (EOQ) model, page 148.

(iv) What re-order level would be required to ensure that the probability of a stock-out is less than 1%?

> Help? See Section 2: Inventory control – Discounts , page 152.

> Help? See Section 2: Inventory control – Uncertainty in demand, page 152.

Spreadsheet tasks

The cost (h) of holding one unit of stock is usually only an estimate. Use a spreadsheet to investigate the sensitivity of the EOQ figure you calculated in Task (v) to changes in h (currently 1.5p). Plot a graph of EOQ against h.

You should now be able to attempt questions 59 to 62 of Section 3, page 210

Comments on quick answer questions 17

(i) Probably for administrative ease.

(ii) Less frequent ordering will increase the quantity in stock and there may not be the space available to store it.

(iii) The two main costs are the cost of ordering and the cost of storage. The cost of storage reflects money that is tied up in the stock and the cost of providing the storage facilities. If goods deteriorate while in stock or are likely to get damaged this should also be reflected in the cost of storage.

Unit 18: Linear programming

Prerequisites

There are no prerequisites for this Unit, although a basic understanding of algebra is assumed.

Objectives

At the end of this unit you should be able to:

❏ Formulate linear programming problems

❏ Use a graphical method to solve two variable problems

❏ Understand the concept of shadow prices and be able calculate their value

❏ Carry out a sensitivity analysis on the problem

Scenario: *Hi-Fibre breakfast cereal*

The Food department has brought out a new breakfast cereal called Hi-Fibre, which uses a concentrated form of fibre developed by Riglen's research laboratory. This product has been test marketed in a few selected areas and the consumer reaction has been favourable. However several people questioned said that they would prefer a higher fibre content, so Dave Smith, the Product manager has decided to meet this demand with an additional product called Hi-Fibre Plus. This product will have double the fibre content of Hi-Fibre and will require additional cooking time. The selling price of Hi-Fibre Plus will be greater than for Hi-Fibre and the contribution to profits also will be higher. For Hi-Fibre, the contribution will be 12p per 500g packet, and for H-Fibre Plus it will be 15p per 500g packet.

During the period of test marketing, 500 packets of the product were produced each day. However from a commercial point of view at least 2500 packets of each product must be produced daily and it is expected that demand will soon exceed this figure. Dave's problem is that he is unsure of the quantities of each product to produce. Even if he assumes that he can sell all that he makes, the resources at his disposal are limited. The storage area can take a maximum of 12,000 packets so total daily production of the cereal cannot exceed this figure. He has one oven and one packaging plant that operates for twelve hours a day and the supply of concentrated fibre is, for the moment, restricted to 120kg per day. There is no practical limit to the other ingredients.

Q **Quick answer questions 18**

(i) If there were no limit on the amount of resources available and the company could sell all it could make, what production plan would you recommend?

(ii) Should Dave produce just Hi-Fibre Plus since this has the highest profit contribution? Why not?

(iii) Would Dave Smith have had the same problem if he had kept to one product? Why not?

T **Tasks**

Dave Smith has asked you to use the technique of linear programming to solve his production problem and he has given you the following additional information:

	Hi-Fibre	Hi-Fibre Plus
Cooking/packaging	3 seconds	5 seconds
Fibre content	5g	10g

All figures are based on 500g of cereal.

(i)   If he makes **F** packets of Hi-Fibre and **P** packets of Hi-Fibre Plus, write down the equation for the total profit contribution.

(ii) Production is limited to 12,000 packets because of storage space. Write down the inequation for this constraint.

(iii) If one packet of Hi-Fibre takes 3 seconds to produce and package, how long will **F** packets take? Similarly how long will **P** packets of Hi-Fibre Plus take? Since production can take place for up to twelve hours, write down the second constraint.

(iv) The third constraint concerns the quantity of fibre in each product. Write down this constraint using the fact that no more than 120kg is available.

(v)   The fourth and fifth constraints concern the minimum production that must be made. Write down both these constraints.

> Help? See Section 2: Linear programming – Introduction, page 157 and Linear programming formulation, page 157.

(vi) Using the X axis to represent Hi-Fibre (F) and the Y axis to represent Hi-Fibre Plus (P), draw the lines of the *equations* of the five constraints. The regions representing each inequation can now be shown by marking the side of the line *not* satisfying the inequation. Identify the region of your graph that satisfies all five constraints.

(vii) Investigate the various combinations of F and P within the 'feasible' region identified in (vi). Which combination gives you the largest profit?

> Help? See Section 2: Linear programming – Graphical solution of Linear programming problems, page 158. Also Finding the optimal solution – the isoprofit/cost method, page 159 and an alternative method, page 161.

P	**Problem solving activities**

Your recommendations concerning the quantities of each product to produce daily have been accepted but Dave would now like answers to the following questions.

(i)   How much of each resource (that is fibre, storage space and the working day) is left after the optimal quantities of cereal are produced? Which resources are 'scarce'? (that is, all used up).

> Help? See Section 2: Linear programming – Tight and slack constraints, page 161.

(ii) Is it worthwhile increasing any of the scarce resources? and by how much? The additional cost of increasing fibre production is £20 per kg, storage space would work out at 20p per packet and extending the working day would incur costs of £30 per hour.

> Help? See Section 2: Linear programming – Sensitivity analysis, page 161 and Changes to the right hand side of a constraint, page 162.

(iii) Would the optimal solution change if the profit contribution of either product changed?

> Help? See Section 2: Linear programming – Sensitivity analysis, page 161 and Changes to the objective function coefficients, page 162.

(iv) The Sales department believes that the demand for Hi-fibre Plus will be greater than for Hi-Fibre. If this is correct production of Hi-Fibre Plus needs to be higher than Hi-Fibre. What increase in profit contribution of Hi-Fibre Plus will be necessary if the total profit is to remain the same?

You should now be able to attempt questions 63 to 66 of Section 3, page 212

Comments on quick answer questions 18

(i) The best strategy would be to produce as much Hi-Fibre Plus as possible since this gives the largest profit.

(ii) Hi-Fibre Plus uses more resources and it is possible that a smaller quantity of cereal would be produced and consequently the profit would be smaller.

(iii) As there would be no competition for the limited resources, production could continue until one or more of these resources have been exhausted.

Unit 19: The transportation algorithm

Prerequisites

There are no prerequisites for this Unit, although an understanding of the general principles of linear programming would be helpful.

Objectives

At the end of this unit you should be able to:

❑ Set up an initial feasible solution for a transportation problem that has unmatched supply and demand

❑ Solve a transportation problem using the Transportation algorithm

❑ Obtain alternative optimal solutions

❑ Apply sensitivity analysis to the solution

Scenario: *'Coals to Newcastle'*

A report into transportation costs at Riglen has just landed on the desk of Kim Richards, the Chief Accountant. From this report Kim discovers that the cost of transporting goods around the country has doubled in the last 5 years and is now in the region of £8m p.a. Kim has arranged an urgent meeting with Andrew Giles, the Transport Manager, to discuss a possible cost cutting exercise. However, the meeting ended in disagreement as Andrew refused to consider any further economies on top of the ones he has recently made.

The disagreement eventually reached Board level and a decision was made to carry out a full independent study of the transport operation at Riglen. A team of consultants were hired, together with a team from Central Services. You are a junior member of the Central Services team and you have been asked to take a fresh look at the supermarket delivery policy.

Riglen owns 3 warehouses. These are at Watford, serving London and the Home Counties; at Birmingham, serving the Midlands and the North of England; and at Bristol, serving Wales and the South West. As a pilot study you decide to consider deliveries to 5 major regions. These are London, The South West, Wales, The North West, and The North East.

Goods from the warehouses are delivered in standard size boxes. The requirements for one particular day last week was:

London:	530 boxes
Wales:	350 boxes
North West:	450 boxes
North East:	500 boxes
South West:	400 boxes

It is not always possible to fully meet demand and any shortfall is made up on the next delivery. This was the case for the day being considered and the following numbers of boxes were allocated for delivery to the 5 regions by the 3 warehouses:

Watford: 500 boxes   Birmingham: 900 boxes   Bristol: 500 boxes

The deliveries were made from each warehouse to supermarkets within their own region on the basis of cheapest overall delivery cost. The delivery cost is estimated by multiplying the number of boxes delivered to a particular area by a 'cost per box'. This cost per box depends on such factors as distance, time taken and the type and capacity of the vehicle used. The average cost from each warehouse to each area is as follows:

Warehouse:		Destination				
		London	Wales	NW	NE	SW
	Wat	1.80	5.00	5.00	7.10	2.90
	Birm	4.50	4.10	3.40	10.00	4.70
	Bri	3.30	2.20	4.70	7.90	2.10

Costs are in £ per box

The reason for the high delivery cost from the Birmingham warehouse to the North East is that less economic vehicles are used on this route.

Q Quick answer questions 19

(i) Why do you think the warehouses are located at Watford, Birmingham and Bristol?

(ii) What assumptions have to be made in calculating delivery costs according to the cost per box formula. How reasonable is this?

T Tasks

You attend a meeting between the consultants and Riglen personnel at which the supermarket delivery policy is discussed. It was decided to use your pilot data to compare Riglen's present distribution policy with the policy of allowing delivery from a warehouse to any area.

(i) Using your pilot data and the current distribution policy, suggest what the transportation plan would have been for that day, and calculate the cost of this plan.

(ii) Now allow any warehouse to supply any area. Set up an initial feasible solution using the table below. That is, allocate as much as you can to the cheapest 'route', then the next cheapest and so on. Make sure that you balance rows and columns. (You will need to enlarge the table to accommodate the fact the supply does not equal demand). What is the cost of this allocation?

> Help? See Section 2: The transportation and assignment algorithms – Step 1, page 166.

Warehouse:		Destination					Available
		London	Wales	NW	NE	SW	
	Wat	☐	☐	☐	☐	☐	
	Birm	☐	☐	☐	☐	☐	
	Bri	☐	☐	☐	☐	☐	
Required							

Costs go in the boxes

(iii) Calculate the 'shadow costs' of all the unused routes in your initial solution. Are any of the shadow costs negative?

> Help? See Section 2: The transportation and assignment algorithms – Step 2, page 167.

(iv) Improve your solution by transferring as many boxes as possible to the route with the greatest negative shadow cost. Repeat step 2. Is your new solution optimal?

Help? See Section 2: The transportation and assignment algorithms – Step 3, page 168.

(v) What is the cost of your optimal solution? and what is the difference in cost between this plan and the one you devised in task (i).

(vi) If these savings could be repeated for all deliveries, how much could Riglen save in a year?

P Problem solving activities

The results of your investigation have been well received but before a full scale analysis is carried out you have been asked to use your pilot data to answer the following questions.

(i) Is there an alternative solution to the one you recommended in task (ii)?

Help? See Section 2: The transportation and assignment algorithms – Alternative solutions, page 170.

(ii) What would be the additional cost per box of using the Bristol to London route?

(ii) If more efficient vehicles were used on the Birmingham to the North East route the cost per box would be reduced. By how much does this cost have to fall before it becomes economic to use this route?

Help? See Section 2: The transportation and assignment algorithms – Sensitivity analysis, page 170.

You should now be able to attempt questions 67 to 69 of Section 3, page 215

Comments on quick answer questions 19

(i) Probably because they are on the motorway network.

(ii) This assumes that lorries would always be fully laden, which is probably reasonable.

Unit 20: Simulation

Prerequisites

There are no prerequisites for this Unit, although Problem solving activities (iii) and (v) assume a knowledge of hypothesis testing – Unit 8 (page 18) and Unit 10 (page 22).

Objectives

At the end of this unit you should be able to:

❑ Demonstrate the technique of simulation by manually simulating a simple system

❑ Understand the difference between terminating and non terminating systems

❑ Be able to analyse simulation results

Scenario: *Building of a new unloading bay at the Bristol factory*

Andrew Giles the Transport manager at the Bristol factory has just returned from a meeting with the Managing Director. He is clearly in a bad mood and has asked you to attend a hastily arranged departmental meeting. After a great deal of moaning about everything and anything he finally gets down to explain the problem. Apparently the police have received complaints from local residents about the parking of heavy lorries in the side streets near the factory. This is occurring because there is insufficient room in the depot for lorries to wait to be loaded/unloaded.

Andrew is particularly furious because his plans for a new larger depot were turned down by the Board only last year and without more space he doesn't see what can be done. The existing depot will only accommodate up to five lorries in total, yet there are frequently more than ten waiting. If lorries were turned away there would be complaints from the companies concerned and also from other departments within Riglen.

Once Andrew has calmed down you suggest that perhaps the solution is to speed up the loading/unloading process so that lorries spend less time at the depot. However Andrew dismisses this suggestion as a recent study has shown that the single loading/unloading bay is working efficiently. You then suggest that if you cannot speed up the process then a second bay should be built. Andrew is sceptical about this idea as the additional bay would reduce space within the depot and there is no guarantee this would solve the queueing problem. You then explain that you could develop a simulation model of the current operation and see the effects of having a second bay without any risk involved.

You finally convince Andrew that a simulation model is worth trying and you obtain his permission to study the current system and collect any data that you feel is necessary.

Following this data collection exercise you obtained the following information.

(i)   The depot is open from 0800 to 1800 Mondays to Fridays.

(ii)   Vehicles either require loading or unloading (not both)

(iii) 70% of lorries require loading and 30% unloading.

(iv) The frequency distributions of the loading/unloading operations found by timing a large number of lorries were as follows.

Time (minutes)	Loading % frequency	Unloading % frequency
0 to under 30	20	30
30 to under 40	35	40
40 to under 50	22	25
50 to under 60	15	4
60 to under 70	8	1

(iv) The frequency distribution of the *inter-arrival* time, that is the time between successive arrivals was as follows.

Time (minutes)	% frequency
0 to under 10	15
10 to under 20	40
20 to under 30	30
30 to under 40	5
40 to under 50	5
50 to under 60	3
60 to under 70	2

You have also made the following assumptions:

(i) The pattern of arrivals is constant throughout the day.

(ii) A second bay would be used like the first, that is for loading and unloading.

(iii) A single queue of lorries would form and a lorry could use either bay on a 'first come, first served basis'.

(iv) Any lorries in the queue at the end of the day would be loaded or unloaded.

Q **Quick answer questions 20**

(i) You have assumed that both bays could be used for loading and unloading. What other arrangement would be possible?

(ii) Is the 'first come, first served' basis a reasonable assumption?

T **Tasks**

To help explain the principle of simulation to Andrew you decide to carry out a manual simulation.

(i) Allocate two digit random numbers to the different loading time intervals so that the number of random numbers corresponds to the percentage within each interval. For instance the random numbers 00 to 19 represents 20% within the range 0 to under 30 minutes. (You will find it easier to do this if you work out the cumulative percentage frequency first).

> Help? See Section 2: Simulation – Random numbers, page 175.

(ii) Repeat (i) for the unloading time distribution, the inter-arrival time distribution and the proportion of loading and unloading lorries.

(iii) Use the random numbers 42, 17, 38 and 61 to generate loading times. (You will find this easier if you have worked out the mid point loading times first).

(iv) Using the layout below and the given random numbers, simulate three hours (180 minutes) of depot operation. How many lorries are in the queue at the end of the simulation and what is the average waiting time?

ARRIVALS						SERVICE				
RNo	Inter arr. time	Clock time	Queue size	RNo	Loading Unloading (L or U)	RNo	Time	Starts	Ends	Waiting time

Random numbers: 20, 17, 42, 96, 23, 17, 28, 66, 38, 59, 38, 61, 73, 76, 80, 00, 20, 56, 10, 05, 87, 88, 78, 15

Help? See Section 2: Simulation – The rail ticket office problem, page 174 and Manual simulation, page 176.

P Problem solving activities

Following the successful demonstration of the simulation technique, you have been given the go ahead to carry out the simulation of the depot operation using a simulation software package.

You made ten separate runs of your model, each of one days operation (10 hours). Five runs were for the current operation (one bay) and five runs for the proposed operation (two bays).

The results are as follows:

	One Bay			Two Bays		
Day	Av. time in system (minutes)	Av. no. in queue	Max queue size	Av. time in system (minutes)	Av. no. in queue	Max queue size
1	120.3	4.2	9	40.5	0.15	2
2	126.2	3.3	8	36.3	0.02	1
3	126.7	4.1	8	51.9	0.41	2
4	148.7	6.4	14	57.7	0.91	3
5	134.5	5.2	13	62.8	1.17	3

(i) Explain why one run of the simulation package would have been insufficient to decide if the simulation model is producing correct results.

(ii) Explain why a 'steady state' analysis wasn't necessary.

Help? See Section 2: Simulation – Analysis of simulation experiments, page 179.

(iii) A large survey of the current operation has shown that the average time in the system is 144.5 minutes. Does this figure agree with your simulation results?

(iv) The same random number stream was used for both the current and proposed operations. Why was this important?

Help? See Section 2: Simulation – Validation of simulation models, page 174 and Accuracy of simulation results, page 177.

(v) Do the results prove that two bays would give a significantly improved performance?

Help? See Section 2: Simulation – Variance reduction techniques, page 179.

(vi) There is a cost associated with lorries waiting to be loaded or unloaded. A conservative estimate is that the cost is £20 per hour per lorry. If the cost of the second bay is £100,000 and running costs of a bay is £15 per hour, would you recommend that the second bay be built? (Assume that the mean inter-arrival time is 21.4 minutes.

Help? See Section 2: Simulation – Analysis of simulation experiments, page 179.

You should now be able to attempt questions 71 to 75 of Section 3, page 218

Comments on quick answer questions 20

(i) One loading bay could be used for loading and one for unloading.

(ii) Probably, although it would be necessary to check as loading may have priority over unloading, for example.

Section 2: Information Bank

Contents

Probability

Introduction

You make decisions based on probability every day of your life. For example you have to decide what to wear – is it going to be cold, is it going to rain? The weather forecast says there is a 60% chance of rain so you decide to take your coat, or perhaps it rained yesterday so you decide it is likely to rain today.

This is a very common approach to probability but because it does not involve any numerical analysis it is called *subjective* probability.

Another method is the *empirical* approach. This method uses measurement to estimate probabilities. For example you may wish to decide the probability of a defective electrical component being produced by a particular process. If you test 100 components and find 5 defective then you would say that the probability of a defective component being produced is $\frac{5}{100}$ or 0.05. That is probability =

$$\frac{\text{Number of times a particular event occurred}}{\text{Total number of trials or 'experiments'}}$$

The particular event here is finding a defective component and the 'experiment' is picking, testing and classifying a component as either good or defective. To get an accurate estimate of the probability, a very large number of experiments would need to be performed. You can prove this for yourself by tossing a coin several times. If you tossed it 10 times you might get 7 heads and 3 tails, giving you a probability of 0.7 ($\frac{7}{10}$) of getting a head. However, if you tossed it 100 times you would get closer to the expected probability of $\frac{1}{2}$ or 0.5.

The third method is the *a priori* approach. This is similar to the empirical approach except that you can work out *in advance* how many times a particular event should occur. In the coin tossing experiment you know that there is only one head so that the **probability of a head is** $\frac{1}{2}$. If you picked a card from a pack, the probability of an ace is $\frac{4}{52}$ or $\frac{1}{13}$ since there **are 4 aces** in a pack. The definition can be written as:

$$\frac{\text{Number of ways in which a particular event can occur}}{\text{Total number of possible outcomes}}$$

This definition assumes that all outcomes are equally likely.

The value of a probability can be given either as a fraction, a decimal or as a percentage. An event with a probability of zero is termed impossible while an event with a probability of 1 or 100% is termed certain. Figure 1, below may help you picture the idea of the probability measure.

Probability scale

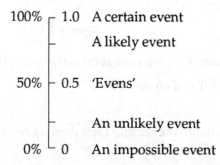

Figure 1

The probability of compound events

It is frequently required to find the probability of two or more events happening at the same time. For example an aircraft has many of its controls duplicated so that if one fails the other one would still function. But what is the probability that both systems will fail? The way that probabilities are combined depend on whether the events are *independent* or whether they are *mutually exclusive*. Two (or more) events are said to be independent if the occurrence of one does not effect the occurrence of the other. The two aircraft systems will be independent if the failure of one system does not change the probability of failure of the other system. Two (or more) events are mutually exclusive if either event can occur but not both. One card drawn from a pack cannot be both a Jack and an ace. However a Jack and a diamond are not mutually exclusive since the selected card could be both. When the set of all possible outcomes are known they are said to be *mutually exhaustive* and the sum of the probabilities of a set of outcomes that are mutually exclusive *and* mutually exhaustive must equal 1. For example, there are four suits in a pack of cards and the probability of selecting a card from either suit is $\frac{13}{52}$ or $\frac{1}{4}$. The sum of these probabilities is 1 since a card must come from one (and only one) of the suits. This idea will allow you to calculate a probability if the other or others are known. If say, the probability of a defective component is 5% then the probability that it is not defective is 95%.

Compound events can be more easily solved if a diagram is drawn. One useful diagram is the *Venn* diagram. A Venn diagram is made up of a square, the inside of which encloses all possible outcomes. The events of interest are represented by circles. The Venn diagram in Figure 2 represents two events A and B. Event A is being dealt a Jack, which has a probability of $\frac{4}{52}$ and event B is being dealt an ace, which also has a probability of $\frac{4}{52}$. The probability of being dealt either a Jack *or* an ace is

$$\frac{4}{52} + \frac{4}{52} = \frac{8}{52}$$

However if event B is being dealt a Diamond then the two events overlap as shown in Figure 3. If the two probabilities are now added the intersection of the two events (shown shaded) will have been added twice. This intersection, which represents the case of being dealt a Jack of Diamonds, must be subtracted from the sum of the two probabilities. That is

$$\frac{4}{52} + \frac{13}{52} - \frac{1}{52} = \frac{16}{52}$$

A = a Jack   B = an Ace   A = a Jack   B = a Diamond

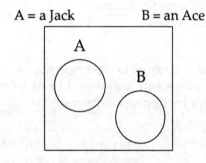

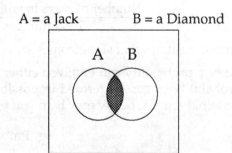

Figure 2   **Figure 3**

In general if P(A) means the probability of event A and P(B) the probability of event B then

$$P(A \text{ or } B) = P(A) + P(B) - P(A \text{ and } B)$$

This is known as the *addition rule*.

Note: If the two events are mutually exclusive as in the first example then there is no intersection and P(A and B) is zero.

Conditional probability

If the probability of event B occurring is dependent on whether event A has occurred you would say that event B is conditional on event A and is written P(B|A) which means probability of B given A has occurred.

When events A and B are independent P(B|A) = P(B). Sampling without replacement is a good example of conditional probability. If two students are to be chosen randomly from a group of 5 girls and 4 boys then the probability of the second person being a girl depends on the outcome of the first choice.

First choice	Probability of second choice being a girl
boy	$\dfrac{5}{8}$
girl	$\dfrac{4}{8}$

In the first case the number of girls remains at 5 but in the second case there are only 4 girls to choose from. Note that in both cases the total number of students left is 8 since one has already been chosen.

If you want to know the probability of the first student being a girl *and* the second student being a girl you will need to use the *multiplication rule*. If the events are dependent as in this example, the rule is:

$$P(A \text{ and } B) = P(A) \times P(B|A)$$

So P(girl and a girl) $= \dfrac{5}{9} \times \dfrac{4}{8} = \dfrac{20}{72} = \dfrac{5}{18}$

If two (or more) events are independent the rule simplifies to:

$$P(A \text{ and } B) = P(A) \times P(B)$$

For example if an aircraft has a main and a back-up computer and the probability of failure of either computer is 1% then the probability of both failing is .01 × .01 = .0001 or .01%.

Tree diagrams

A very useful diagram to use when solving compound events, particularly when conditional probability is involved, is the tree diagram. This diagram represents different outcomes of an experiment by means of branches. For example, in the student example the two 'experiments' of choosing an individual can be represented by the tree diagram in Figure 4. The first experiment is represented by a small circle or node and the two possible events are represented by branches radiating out from the node. The event and probability are written alongside the branch. The second experiment is again represented by a node and you will notice that this node appears twice, once for each outcome of the first experiment. Branches again radiate out from each node but notice that the probability is different depending on what happened in the first experiment.

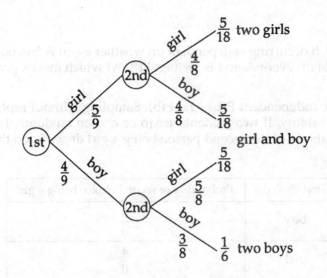

Figure 4

You will see that the compound events have been written at the end of each route in Figure 4. (The probabilities have been given as fractions to avoid rounding errors). If you add up these probabilities you will see that they sum to 1. This is because the routes are mutually exclusive and *mutually exhaustive*. They are mutually exclusive because one and only one of the routes can be followed and they are mutually exhaustive because all possible routes have been shown. From this diagram various probabilities could be evaluated using the law of addition. For example the probability of getting two students of the same sex is $\frac{5}{18} + \frac{1}{6} = \frac{4}{9}$.

It is unlikely that you would use a tree diagram to solve a simple problem like this, but consider the following problem.

The demand for gas is dependent on the weather and much research has been undertaken to accurately forecast the demand. This is important since it is quite difficult (and expensive) to increase the supply at short notice. If, on any particular day, the air temperature is below normal, the probability that the demand will be high is 0.6. However, at normal temperatures the probability of a high demand occurring is only 0.2 and if the temperature is above normal the probability of a high demand drops to 0.05. What is the probability of a high demand occurring if over a period of time the temperature is below normal 20% of occasions and above normal 30% of occasions?

The tree diagram is shown in Figure 5, on the next page. Since the demand *depends* on temperature the first node refers to temperature and there are three branches; below, normal and above normal. The probability of the temperature being normal is 1 − (0.2 + 0.3) = 0.5.

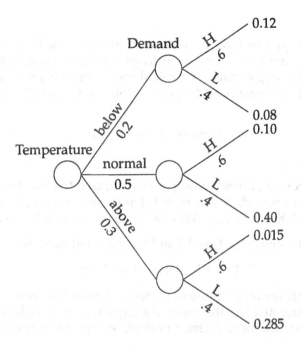

Figure 5

The compound probability for each route has been placed at the end of the route, so that the probability of there being a high demand given that the temperature is below normal is 0.2 × 0.6 = 0.12. Since there are three routes where the demand could be high, the law of addition is used and the probability is

$$0.12 + 0.10 + 0.015 = 0.235$$

Bayes' theorem

The multiplication rule for dependent events is

$$P(A \text{ and } B) = P(A) \times P(B \mid A)$$

But it can also be written as

$$P(A \text{ and } B) = P(B) \times P(A \mid B)$$

And this can be re-arranged as

$$P(A \mid B) = \frac{P(A \text{ and } B)}{P(B)}$$

This is known as Bayes' theorem. Essentially, Bayes' theorem allows a probability to be modified if further information is obtained. The result is called a *posterior* probability. For example, if on a particular day the gas demand was found to be high what is the revised estimate of the probability of the temperature being below normal on any day?

Re-writing Bayes' theorem for this example you would get

$$P(\text{below given high demand}) = \frac{P(\text{below and high demand})}{P(\text{high demand})}$$

The probability of high demand is 0.235 (see above) and from Figure 5, the probability of the temperature being below normal *and* the demand being high is 0.12, so the revised probability of the temperature being below normal is

$$\frac{0.120}{0.235} = 0.511$$

Expected value

If you toss a coin 100 times, you would *expect* 50 heads and 50 tails. That is, the expected number of heads is $.5 \times 100 = 50$. In general it is a long-run average, which means it is the value you would get if you repeated the experiment long enough. It is calculated by multiplying a value of a particular variable by the probability of its occurrence and repeating this for all possible values. In symbols this can be represented as

$$\text{Expected value} = \Sigma px$$

Where Σ means the 'sum of'.

For example, over a long period of time a salesperson recorded the number of sales she achieves per day. From an analysis of her records it was found that she made no sales 20% of the time, one sale 50% of the time and 2 sales 30% of the time. What is her expected number of sales?

The 'x' in this case takes on values of 0, 1, and 2 and the expected value is

$$.2 \times 0 + .5 \times 1 + .3 \times 2 = 1.1 \text{ sales}$$

This is just like working out the mean value of a group of numbers, where the probabilities are the frequencies or 'weights'. And just like the mean, the expected value will not necessarily be a whole number. Expected values are frequently used to calculate expected monetary values, or EMV (page 80).

Further reading

A First Course in Statistics, Booth, (DP PUBLICATIONS)

Introductory Statistics for Business and Economics, Wonnacott, (WILEY)

Statistics without Tears, Rowntree, (PELICAN)

Essential Statistics, Rees, (CHAPMAN & HALL)

Quantitative Approaches in Business Studies, Morris, (PITMAN)

Business Mathematics and Statistics, Francis, (DP PUBLICATIONS)

Probability distributions

Introduction

Although you may not be familiar with probability distributions, you would almost certainly have come across frequency tables (or distributions). For example, you decide to record the time it takes you to get to work or college and over a period of 50 days you get the following frequency table:

Time (minutes)			Frequency
15	to less than	20	5
20		25	10
25		30	15
30		35	10
35		40	8
40	or more		2

This table shows you how the journey time is *distributed* between 15 to 40+ minutes. You can see that journey times are not evenly spread between these limits so certain journey times are more likely than others. For example, a journey time over 40 minutes is quite unlikely. To see this more clearly the frequency could be divided by 50, the total frequency. This will give you the probability that a certain range of times will occur. (See page 55). The resulting *probability distribution* is shown below.

Time (minutes)			Probability
15	to less than	20	0.1
20		25	0.2
25		30	0.3
30		35	0.2
35		40	0.16
40	or more		0.04
		sum	1.00

So you can see that the probability that the journey time will take more than 40 minutes is only 0.04 or 4%. You will also see that the sum of the probabilities is 1.00, which is another way of saying that all possibilities have been taken care of.

It has been assumed here that journey times occur at random, that is, it is not possible to predict the time of tomorrow's journey. This is similar to tossing a coin, even if you had 9 heads one after another, the probability that the tenth toss will give you a head is still only 0.5.

Since time is a *continuous* measure, the probability distribution obtained above is a continuous probability distribution. If the variable could only take on whole (or *discrete*) values, such as the number of people on a bus, the distribution would be called discrete. Also, since the distribution was obtained by measurement it is referred to as an empirical probability distribution. More interesting distributions are those that can be derived mathematically.

The binomial distribution

This is a discrete probability distribution and arises when a variable can only take on one of two values. (That is, the outcomes must be mutually exclusive). The probability of the two outcomes must be constant from trial to trial and successive events must be independent. (See page 56). The obvious example to use here is a coin since it can be in one of two states, either a head (H) or a tail (T). However you will see that the binomial distribution is a very important distribution in the area of quality control.

If a coin is tossed once, there are only two outcomes with equal probability, but if you toss it twice (or toss two coins once) the outcome could take on one of the following:

> 2 heads
>
> or 2 tails
>
> or a head and a tail

There are two ways of getting a head and a tail since either coin could be head or a tail. The best way of illustrating the outcomes is by mean of a tree diagram (see page 57). Figure 1 shows that there are 4 'routes' to the tree. At the end of each route the *number of heads* has been indicated, together with the probability of that route. The number of ways of getting 2, 1, and 0 heads is 1, 2, and 1 respectively and the probability of any route is:

$$0.5 \times 0.5 = 0.25 \text{ (or } (0.5)^2).$$

Therefore the probability of getting 1 head is $2 \times 0.25 = 0.5$.

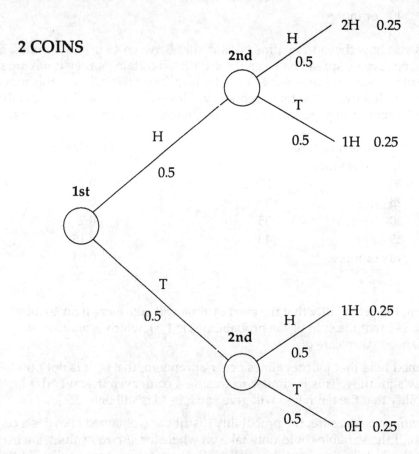

2 COINS

Figure 1

If three coins are now tossed, the tree has become a little more complicated and is shown in Figure 2. The number of ways of getting 3, 2, 1, or 0 heads is 1, 3, 3, and 1 respectively and the probability of following any route is now:

$$(0.5)^3 = 0.125$$

The probability of getting 1 head is therefore $3 \times 0.125 = 0.375$ and the probability of getting 2 heads is also 0.375.

If you repeat this for 4 heads you should find that the number of ways of getting 4, 3, 2, 1, 0 heads is 1, 4, 6, 4, and 1 respectively and the probability of following any route is $(0.5)^4 = 0.0625$. If you now write the number of ways of getting various combinations of heads in a table similar to the one below, you should see how easy it is to carry on the sequence.

1 toss				1		1		
2 tosses			1		2		1	
3 tosses		1		3		3		1	
4 tosses	1		4		6		4		1

Thus for 5 tosses the sequence will be 1, 5, 10, 10, 5, 1.

3 COINS

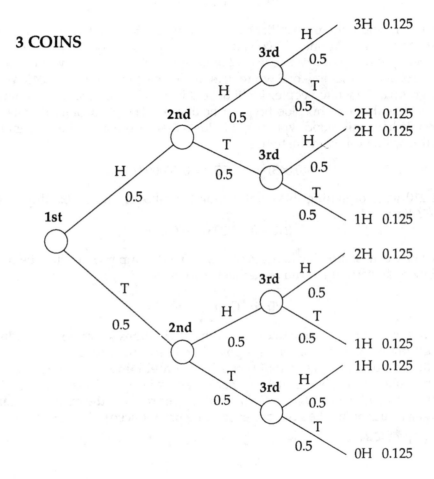

Figure 2

This known as Pascal's triangle and it gives you the number of ways an event will occur. Although it is quite feasible to do this for small number of tosses of the coin, what would happen if you tossed the coin 10, 20 or even 50 times? Fortunately this series is the same as finding the number of ways of choosing **r** items from **n** and is given by:

$$\frac{n!}{r!(n-r)!}$$

This formula is usually referred to as ^nC_r. (n! is read as *'factorial n'* and means $n \times (n-1) \times (n-2) \times (n-3) \times ....$)

For example, if you wanted to know the number of ways getting 4 heads from 10 tosses, then n = 10 and r = 4 and

$$^nC_r = {}^{10}C_4 = \frac{10!}{4! \times (10-4)!}$$

$$= \frac{10 \times 9 \times 8 \times 7 \times 6!}{4 \times 3 \times 2 \times 1 \times 6!}$$

$$= 210$$

(note: the 6! cancels)

(It is advisable to use a scientific calculator for these calculations as ^nC_r can then be obtained directly. A scientific calculator will also enable you to do all the calculations in this chapter and to store the result in the calculator's memory. This reduces the chance of 'rounding' errors)

The probability of any route must be $(0.5)^{10} = 0.0009765$ so the probability of getting 4 heads in 10 tosses is:

$$210 \times 0.0009765 = 0.2051$$

This is fine for a coin where the probability of each event is 0.5 but what about more general problems? Where an item can be in one of two states and the probability of both states is known (and sums to 1), the ideas just discussed can be used. For example, about 4.5% of white people are in blood type AB, so the probability that any one white person has this blood type is 0.045. What is the probability that in a group of 10 white people, 4 will have this blood type? This is a binomial problem because a white person either has this blood type or he doesn't. The probability that he doesn't is 0.955 (1-0.045). If 4 people have this blood type then it follows that 6 do not, so the probability of a route of the probability tree giving this combination is:

$$(0.045)^4 \times (0.955)^6 = 0.0000031.$$

Since there are 210 ways of getting this combination (see above), the probability of 4 white people with blood type AB is:

$$210 \times 0.0000031 = 0.00065$$

If **p** is the probability of a 'success', where success is defined as a person or item being in a particular state, then the binomial distribution can be defined as follows:

$$P(r) = {}^nC_r \cdot p^r \cdot (1-p)^{n-r}$$

This looks horrendous but if you have understood the calculations so far you shouldn't find this formula too difficult to follow. For example, suppose that you wanted to find the probability that 2 or *more* people in the group of 10 had blood of type AB. You could find the probability of 2, 3, 4, etc and then add the probabilities together. However there is an easier way. This is, to use the fact that the probabilities must sum to 1, so $P(\geq 2) = 1 - (P(0) + P(1))$. This reduces the number of calculations from 9 to 2. (With larger values of 'n', the saving is even more pronounced).

The calculation of P(0) is easy since there is only one route in this case and $^{10}C_0 = 1$. So

$$P(0) \quad = (0.045)^0 (0.955)^{10}$$

$$= 0.63101$$

(note: anything raised to the power of 0 is 1)

For the calculation of P(1), $^{10}C_1 = 10$, so:

$$P(1) \quad = 10 \times (0.045)^1 (0.955)^9$$

$$= 0.29733$$

and

$$P(r \geq 2) \quad = 1 - (0.63101 + 0.29733)$$

$$= 0.07166 \text{ or about } 7\%$$

The mean and standard deviation of the binomial distribution

The mean of a binomial distribution is np. (This is the *expected value* of the distribution – see page 60). So for the blood type problem, where n = 10 and p = 0.045, the mean number of white people with blood type AB in a group of 10 white people is:

$$10 \times 0.045 = 0.45$$

The standard deviation is given by the formula:

$$\sigma = \sqrt{np(1-p)}$$

So in the blood type example:

$$\sigma = \sqrt{10 \times 0.045 \times 0.955}$$
$$= 0.6556$$

The use of the binomial distribution in quality control

The most important application of the binomial distribution is in the design of inspection schemes for quality control. All processes produce defective items from time to time but the important thing is to identify when the number of defective items is greater than normal. If an item can be classified as either being defective or satisfactory then the binomial distribution can be used to help in this decision.

(**Attribute**) inspection schemes usually involve taking a sample of items from a batch and testing to see if any are defective. The inspection scheme will specify the action to be taken should the number of defective items exceed a preset limit. For example a random sample of 20 could be specified and if more than 2 items are found to be defective, the entire batch is rejected. Another inspection scheme could involve a second stage, such as, 'if more than 2 items are found defective, another sample is taken and then, if any items are found defective, the batch is rejected'.

These schemes are usually referred to as *acceptance sampling schemes* and are defined by **n**, the sample size and **c**, the maximum number of defective items allowed. It assumes that there is an acceptable quality level (**AQL**) for a batch which should not be exceeded. An ideal inspection scheme is shown in Figure 3 and in this scheme any batches that exceed this AQL level are rejected.

An Ideal Inspection Scheme

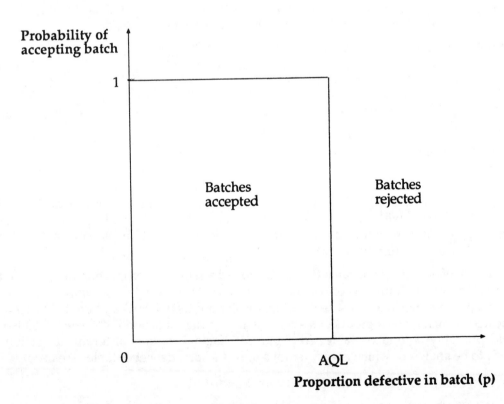

Figure 3

Unfortunately this scheme is impossible to achieve in practise unless 100% testing was carried out. When samples are tested, it is possible that the results from the sample are satisfactory even though the batch contains more than the acceptable level of defective items. Conversely, a good batch could be rejected because the sample had an unusually high number of defective items. To demonstrate this problem imagine that an inspection scheme specified that a sample of size 10 be taken, and the batch accepted if there are no more than 1 defective items. The probability of accepting the batch is the sum of the probability of none and one defective items and these probabilities will depend upon the proportion of defective items in the batch. For example, if the proportion was 5% then:

$$P(0) = (0.95)^{10} = 0.5987$$

$$P(1) = 10 \times 0.05 \times (0.95)^9 = 0.3151$$

and:

$$P(0) + P(1) = 0.9138$$

That is, there is a 91.4% chance that a batch containing 5% defective items is accepted. Put another way, if the AQL was 5% then there is a 8.6% chance (100 – 91.4) that the (good) batch is rejected. This is known as the *producer's risk* and clearly this wants to be as low as possible. However, if the proportion defective is higher than 5% the risk that a batch is accepted can be quite substantial. To demonstrate this, the above calculations have been repeated for different values of the proportion defective (p) and are shown in the table below.

p	P(0)	P(1)	P(<2)
0.01	0.9044	0.0914	0.9957
0.05	0.5987	0.3151	0.9139
0.10	0.3487	0.3874	0.7361
0.15	0.1969	0.3474	0.5443
0.25	0.0563	0.1877	0.2440
0.30	0.0282	0.1211	0.1493

So, if the proportion defective was 0.15 (15%), there is still a probability of 0.5443 that the batch would be accepted. Even with a proportion defective of 25% the probability is 0.244.

This probability of accepting a bad batch could be reduced by making the inspection scheme more demanding. For example, the size of the sample could be increased or the number of defective items allowed in a sample could be reduced. If a batch was accepted only if *no* defective items were found, the table above tells you that the probability of accepting a batch with 25% defective items is reduced to .0563 (This is the value of P(0) at p = 0.25). Unfortunately there is now a probability of 0.4013 that a batch with 5% defective items is rejected (1 – 0.5987).

To attempt to overcome these problems, another measure is specified. This is the *lot tolerance proportion defective* or **LTPD**. This measure specifies the maximum proportion that can be allowed in a batch. This means that some batches with a defective proportion between the AQL and LTPD will be tolerated but none above the LTPD. Unfortunately even this scheme is not practical and there is a chance that some batches with a defective proportion above the LTPD will be produced. This is called the *consumer's risk*. An inspection scheme is therefore required that keeps both the producer's and consumer's risk to a minimum (usually below 5%).

If the probability of accepting the batch (P($\leq$ 2)) is plotted against the proportion defective in the batch (p), the curve shown in Figure 4 is obtained. This curve is known as the *operating characteristic curve* and will depend on the inspection scheme adopted. The AQL (p = 0.04) and the LTPD (p = 0.39) has been indicated, which gives a producer's and consumer's risk of around 5%. The LTPD is very high and would probably be unacceptable. To obtain satisfactory values, different inspection schemes would need to be analysed, which is very tedious unless a spreadsheet or tables are used.

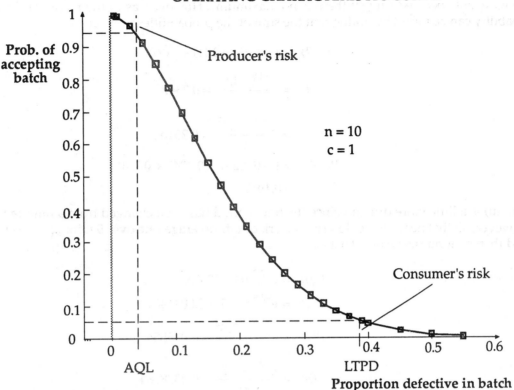

OPERATING CHARACTERISTIC CURVE

Figure 4

The Poisson distribution

The Poisson distribution is another example of a discrete probability distribution. It is particularly good at modelling events that occur in a random fashion. For example, the arrivals at a post office, breakdowns in a computer system, or accidents in a factory.

The formula for the Poisson is less complicated than the binomial and the probability of **r** events is as follows:

$$P(r) = \frac{e^{-m}m^r}{r!}$$

Where **m** is the mean number of events in a given time period and **e** is the constant 2.7182818... and can be found on many scientific calculators (usually in the form e^x).

A typical example of the Poisson distribution is as follows: The number of calls to a switchboard is random, with a mean of 1.5 per minute. What is the probability that

(i)   There are no calls in any one minute?

(ii) There are more than 2 calls in any one minute?

(iii) There are less than 6 calls in a 5 minute period?

For question (i) it is simply a matter of substituting m = 1.5 and r = 0 into the Poisson equation. That is:

$$P(0) = \frac{e^{-1.5} \times 1.5^0}{0!}$$

$$= 0.2231$$

(Since $e^{-1.5} = 0.2231$, $1.5^0 = 1$ and $0! = 1$)

It is not possible to calculate the answer to (ii) directly since the maximum number of calls that could be received is not specified (in fact there is no maximum). However, as in the binomial distribution the probability can be found by noting that the sum of the probabilities must be 1.

So,

$$P(r>2) = 1 - (P(0) + P(1) + P(2))$$

$$P(1) = \frac{e^{-1.5} \times 1.5^1}{1!} = 0.3347$$

$$P(2) = \frac{e^{-1.5} \times 1.5^2}{2!} = 0.25102$$

That is:

$$P(r>2) = 1 - (0.2231 + 0.3347 + 0.2510)$$

$$= 0.1912$$

Question (iii) is a little more difficult since the time period has been changed from a minute to 5 minutes. However, all that needs to be done is to work out the average rate over 5 minutes, which is 7.5 (5 × 1.5) and then continue as before. That is:

$$P(0) = e^{-7.5} = 0.000553$$

$$P(1) = e^{-7.5} \times 7.5 = 0.0041481$$

$$P(2) = \frac{e^{-7.5} \times 7.5^2}{2!} = 0.015554$$

$$P(3) = \frac{e^{-7.5} \times 7.5^3}{3!} = 0.0388884$$

$$P(4) = \frac{e^{-7.5} \times 7.5^4}{4!} = 0.0729163$$

$$P(5) = \frac{e^{-7.5} \times 7.5^5}{5!} = 0.1093745$$

To calculate the probability that there are less than 6 calls, the probabilities must be added.

So:

$$P(r < 6) = 0.2414$$

Note that the Poisson distribution is an example of a *recursive* formula. That is, the next value can be worked out from the last, since:

$$P(0) = e^{-m}$$

$$P(1) = e^{-m}m = P(0) \times m$$

$$P(2) = e^{-m}\frac{m^2}{2!} = P(1) \times \frac{m}{2}$$

$$P(3) = e^{-m}\frac{m^3}{3!} = P(2) \times \frac{m}{3} \qquad \text{etc ...}$$

The use of the Poisson distribution as an approximation to the binomial distribution

The Poisson distribution can also be used as an approximation to the binomial distribution. In order to use the Poisson distribution in this way, the following conditions should be met:

(a)   The number of trials, n, is large (greater than 30).

(b)   The probability of a success, p, is small (less than 0.1).

(c)   The mean number of successes, n × p, is less than 5.

For example, suppose a batch contained 1% defective items and a sample of size 40 was chosen. What is the probability that there are 2 defective items. This is a binomial problem and the answer using the binomial distribution is:

$$P(0) = 40C_2 \times (0.01)^2 \times (1 - 0.01)^{38}$$

$$= 780 \times 0.0000682$$

$$= 0.0532$$

If you used the Poisson distribution you would first note that the mean number of defects in a sample of size 40 is

$$40 \times 0.01 = 0.4$$

So:
$$P(2) = \frac{e^{-0.4} \times 0.4^2}{2!} = 0.0536$$

which is an error of less than 1%

As you can see, the Poisson distribution is easier to use, and this is particularly true if many probabilities have to be calculated.

The mean and standard deviation of the Poisson distribution

The variance of the Poisson distribution is equal to the mean. So the standard deviation, which is the square root of the variance is equal to the square root of the mean. In symbols this becomes:

$$\sigma = \sqrt{m}$$

The normal distribution

The normal distribution is an example of a *continuous* probability distribution and is the most useful and important distribution you will come across. Many observations that are derived from measurements follow this distribution. For example the heights of people and the weights of loafs of bread follow the normal distribution.

If you were to draw a histogram of either the binomial or Poisson distributions the chances are that the histogram would be skewed. However, the normal distribution is completely symmetrical or bell shaped. The mean, mode, and median of this distribution all lie at the centre of the bell as you can see in Figure 5, opposite.

The normal curve has the following properties:

(a) The curve is symmetrical about the mean.

(b) The total area under the curve is equal to 1 or 100%. This means that probability can be equated to area.

(c) The horizontal axis represents a continuous variable such as weight.

(d) The area under the curve between two points on the horizontal axis represents the probability that the value of the variable lies between these two points.

(e) As the distance between two points gets less, the area between the two points must get less. Taking this to its logical conclusion, the probability of a specific value is zero. It is therefore only meaningful to talk about ranges, such as 800g to 810g.

(f) The position and shape of the curve depends on the mean and standard deviation of the distribution. As the standard deviation gets larger, the curve will get flatter and extend further on either side of the mean.

The normal distribution

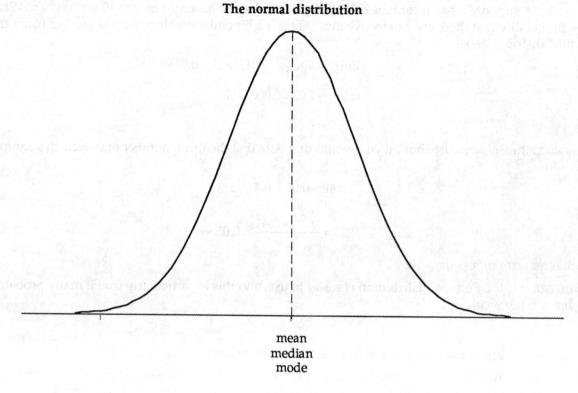

mean
median
mode

Figure 5

To illustrate how the normal distribution is used, imagine a baker making bread. The average weight of a 'standard' sliced loaf should weigh at least 800g. The actual weight of each loaf will depend on how accurately the dough is measured and the spread of weights around the mean will depend on the value of the standard deviation. Assuming that the mean weight has been set at exactly 800g and the standard deviation for one particular batch of loaves is 10g, what is the probability, that if a loaf is chosen at random, it will weigh more than 815g? This problem is illustrated diagrammatically in Figure 6, where the area representing all loaves with a weight exceeding 815g has been shaded.

Distribution of the weights of loaves of bread

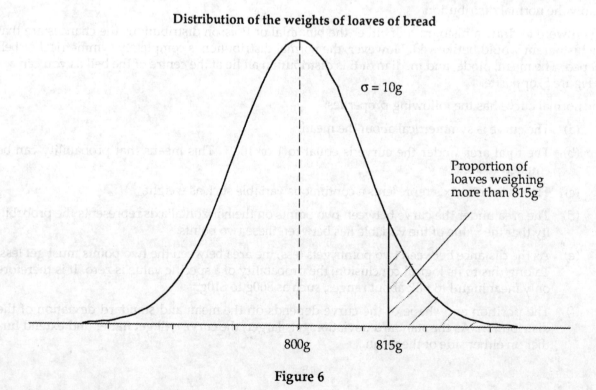

$\sigma = 10g$

Proportion of
loaves weighing
more than 815g

800g   815g

Figure 6

How do you find the shaded area? The formula for the normal probability function is far too complicated to enable probabilities to be found this way, so a table is used. Because the shape and hence the area depends on the mean and standard deviation, the table relates to one specific normal curve. This is the *standard normal* curve. The standard normal curve, which has been drawn in Figure 7, has a mean of zero and a standard deviation of 1. The figures along the horizontal axis are number of standard deviations and are called the **Z** values. You will see that the majority of the distribution is covered within ±3 standard deviations. To prove this and also to demonstrate the use of the normal table you should now refer to the extract of the table, given below. The full table is provided in appendix 3, page 250. The table provided in this book gives you the area (or probability) in the *right hand tail* of the distribution but other tables may give the area in a different way. (Once you have used one table you should find it a simple matter to use a different type).

Z	0.00	0.01	0.02	0.03	0.04	0.05	0.06	0.07	0.08	0.09
0.0	0.5000	0.4960	0.4920	0.4880	0.4840	0.4801	0.4761	0.4721	0.4681	0.4641
0.1	0.4602	0.4562	0.4522	0.4483	0.4443	0.4404	0.4364	0.4325	0.4286	0.4247
0.2	0.4207	0.4168	0.4129	0.4090	0.4052	0.4013	0.3974	0.3936	0.3897	0.3859
0.3	0.3821	0.3783	0.3745	0.3707	0.3669	0.3632	0.3594	0.3557	0.3520	0.3483
0.4	0.3446	0.3409	0.3372	0.3336	0.3300	0.3264	0.3228	0.3192	0.3156	0.3121
0.5	0.3085	0.3050	0.3015	0.2981	0.2946	**0.2912**	0.2877	0.2843	0.2810	0.2776
0.6	0.2743	0.2709	0.2676	0.2643	0.2611	0.2578	0.2546	0.2514	0.2483	0.2451
0.7	0.2420	0.2389	0.2358	0.2327	0.2296	0.2266	0.2236	0.2206	0.2177	0.2148
0.8	0.2119	0.2090	0.2061	0.2033	0.2005	0.1977	0.1949	0.1922	0.1894	0.1867
0.9	0.1841	0.1814	0.1788	0.1762	0.1736	0.1711	0.1685	0.1660	0.1635	0.1611

The first column gives the Z value to one decimal place and the first row gives the second place of decimals. For example, for a Z value of 0.55, you would look down the first column until you found 0.5 and then across until you were directly under .05. The probability (highlighted in the extract above) is 0.2912, or 29.12%. This is the probability of Z being greater than 0.55, that is,

$$P(Z > 0.55) = 0.2912.$$

To find the probability from the mean to a specific Z value you need to use the fact that half the distribution has an area of 0.5. So to find the area from the mean to Z = 1 you would use the normal tables to obtain P(Z > 1) = 0.1587 and subtract this from 0.5. That is 0.5 − 0.1587 = 0.3413. since the distribution is symmetrical, the probability from 0.0 to −1.0 is also 0.3413. The probability from −1 to +1 is therefore 0.6826. In other words, 68.26% of the normal curve is covered by ±1 standard deviations.

If you repeat this for Z = 2 and Z = 3 you should get the following result:

$$P(-2 < Z < 2) = 2 \times (0.5 - 0.0228) = 0.9544, \text{ or } 95.44\%.$$

$$P(-3 < Z < 3) = 2 \times (0.5 - 0.00135) = 0.9973, \text{ or } 99.73\%.$$

That is, 99.73% of the normal distribution is covered by ±3 standard deviations.

How does this help with our bread problem? The mean of a loaf of bread is not zero and the standard deviation is not 1 but the problem *can be* transformed into one that does have these values. If the mean value (μ) is *subtracted* from every value, that is, $X - \mu$, the distribution will still have the same shape; it will just have changed its position. If these transformed values are now *divided* by the standard deviation (σ), the final transformed distribution will have the required properties. This transformation is called the **Z** transformation and is given by:

$$Z = \frac{X - \mu}{\sigma}$$

In the bread example, μ = 800g, σ = 10g and X = 815g, so:

$$z = \frac{815 - 800}{10} = 1.5$$

The standard normal distribution

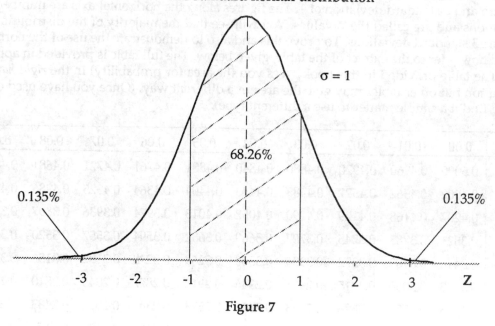

Figure 7

Since $P(X > 815) = P(Z > 1.5)$, it is simply a matter of looking up $Z = 1.5$ in the normal table. If you do this you should get a probability of 0.0668 or 6.68%.

That is:
$$P(X > 815g) = 0.0668.$$

The normal distribution can be used to solve various types of problems. To demonstrate this, several different problems using the bread example have been solved below. In each case it is assumed that a loaf is chosen at random. Notice that a diagram has been drawn for each problem – it is strongly recommended that you always draw a diagram when you solve normal distribution problems.

1. *What is the probability that the weight of the loaf is below 785g*

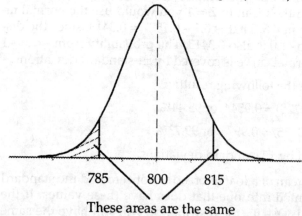

These areas are the same

Since the normal curve is symmetrical,
$$P(X < 785) = P(X > 815).$$

This problem has already been solved (see above), so the probability is 0.0668.

2. *What is the probability that the weight is between 790g and 805.5g*

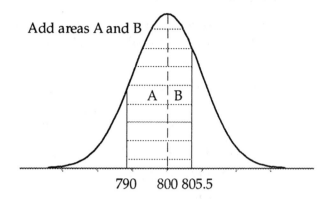

Add areas A and B

790   800 805.5

To solve this problem you should note that the required probability is the sum of two probabilities. That is:

P(800 <X< 805.5) + P(800 >X> 790).

Or area A + area B (see diagram)

Area A

$$P(800 <X< 805.5) = 0.5 - P(X > 805.5)$$

$$Z = \frac{805.5 - 800}{10} = 0.55$$

$$P(800 <X< 805.5) = 0.5 - P(Z > 0.55)$$

$$= 0.5 - 0.2912$$

$$= 0.2088$$

Area B

$$P(800 >X> 790) = 0.5 - P(X < 790)$$

$$Z = \frac{790 - 800}{10} = -1.0$$

$$P(800 >X> 790) = 0.5 - P(Z < -1)$$

$$= 0.5 - P(Z > 1)$$

$$= 0.5 - 0.1587$$

$$= 0.3413$$

So the required probability is 0.2088 + 0.3413 = 0.5501 or 55.01%

(The required probability could also be obtained by noting that

$$P(790 <X< 805.5) = 1 - (P(X < 790) + P(X > 805.5).$$

$$= 1 - (0.2912 + 0.1587)$$

$$= 0.5501)$$

3. *What is the probability that the weight is between 810g and 812g?*

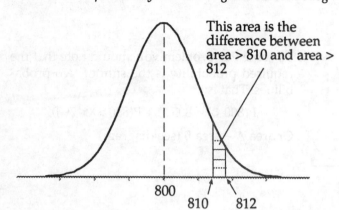

This area is the difference between area > 810 and area > 812

In this case the required probability is the *difference* of two probabilities. That is,

$$P(X > 810) - P(X > 812)$$

The two Z values are:

$$\frac{810 - 800}{10} = 1.0 \ and \ \frac{812 - 800}{10} = 1.2$$

So $P(Z > 1.0) - P(Z > 1.2)$

$$= 0.1587 - 0.1151$$

$$= 0.0436$$

4. *What is the probability that the weight is less than 805g*

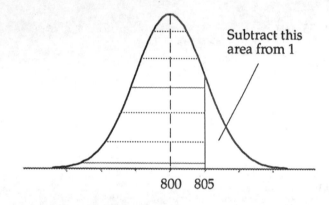

Subtract this area from 1

The easiest method here is to find the probability that a loaf weighs more than 805g and subtract it from 1. That is:

$$P(X < 805) = 1 - P(X > 805)$$

$$Z = \frac{805 - 800}{10} = 0.5$$

$$P(Z > 0.5) = 0.3085$$

So the required probability is:

$$1 - 0.3085 = 0.6915$$

5. *The baker wishes to ensure that no more than 5% of loaves are less than a certain weight. What is this weight?*

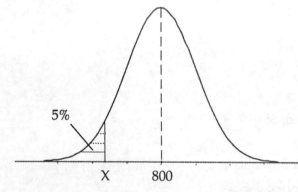

5%

In this example the normal table is used in reverse. That is, the Z value corresponding to a probability of 0.05 is first found. The nearest probabilities are 0.0505, corresponding to a Z value of 1.64 and 0.0495, corresponding to a Z value of 1.65. The most accurate answer would be the mean of the two Z values, that is 1.645.

This value corresponds to 5% in the upper tail of the distribution. For the lower tail, which is required here, the Z value must be –1.645.

So, if 'X' is the unknown weight:

$$-1.645 = \frac{X - 800}{10}$$

and:

$$X = 800 - 16.45$$

$$= 783.6g$$

6. *A large number of loaves were weighed and it was found that 8% weighed less than the figure found in (5.). Assuming that the standard deviation hasn't changed, what is the actual value of the mean?*

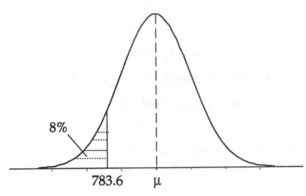

8%

783.6   μ

Again it is necessary to work backwards.

The Z value corresponding to a probability of 8% is 1.405.

$$-1.405 = \frac{783.6 - \mu}{10}$$

$$\mu = 783.6 + 14.05$$

$$= 797.7g$$

Although these 6 questions cover most normal distribution problems, there is one further problem you may be faced with. This is, the calculation of the *expected* number of items in a batch with some particular property(see page 60). For example, suppose the total number of loaves in a batch is 200, what is the expected number weighing less than 785g?

From question 1, the probability of a loaf weighing less than 785g is 0.0668. Therefore the expected number of loaves weighing less than 785g is:

$$200 \times 0.0668 = 13.36$$

The normal distribution as an approximation to the binomial distribution

Under certain conditions binomial problems can be solved by using the normal distribution. The conditions are that both n × p and n × (1-p) are greater than 5. This means that p needs to be near to 0.5 and n should be large.

For example, suppose the probability of a defective item is 0.3. If a sample of 30 were taken, what is the probability that at least 5 were defective?

To solve by the binomial distribution, the probability of 0,1,2,3,and 4 needs to be found and the sum of these probabilities subtracted from 1.

$$P(0) = (.7)^{30} = 0.0000225$$
$$P(1) = 30 \times (.3) \times (.7)^{29} = 0.0002897$$
$$P(2) = 435 \times (.3)^2 \times (.7)^{28} = 0.0018008$$
$$P(3) = 4060 \times (.3)^3 \times (.7)^{27} = 0.0072033$$
$$P(4) = 27405 \times (.3)^4 \times (.7)^{26} = 0.020838$$

So:
$$P(r > 4) = 1 - 0.03015$$
$$= 0.9698$$

To solve this problem by the normal distribution it is first necessary to calculate the mean and standard deviation. The mean is n × p = 30 × 0.3 = 9.0 and the standard deviation is:

$$\sqrt{np(1-p)} = \sqrt{30 \times 0.3 \times 0.7}$$
$$= 2.51$$

It is then necessary to make a *continuity correction*. This is because the binomial distribution is a discrete probability distribution whereas the normal distribution is a continuous distribution. To get around this problem it is assumed that the discrete value 5 is a continuous variable in the range 4.5 to 5.5. To find the probability greater than 4, the value 4.5 is used as you can see in the diagram following.

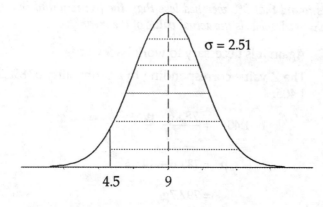

This problem now becomes one of finding $P(X > 4.5)$, which is $1 - P(X < 4.5)$ and:

$$Z = \frac{4.5 - 9.0}{2.51} = -1.79$$

$$P(Z < -1.79) = P(Z > 1.79)$$

and from the normal table the probability is 0.0367.

So the required probability is:

$$1 - 0.0367 = 0.9633$$

which compares well with the correct value of 0.9698.

The normal distribution as an approximation to the Poisson distribution

The normal distribution can also be used to solve Poisson problems. This is valid provided the mean is greater than about 10.

To illustrate the use of the normal distribution for this application, the switchboard problem solved on page 67 will be re-solved using the normal distribution. The mean is 7.5, which is less than the recommended level, so it will be interesting to see how good the approximation will be in this case.

The Poisson distribution gave a probability of 0.2414 that there would be less than 6 calls in a 5 minute period. To use the normal distribution, the continuity correction again needs to be applied. In this case the probability of less than 5.5 calls needs to be found. The standard deviation is the square root of the mean (7.5) which equals 2.739.

The calculation is straightforward using the normal distribution:

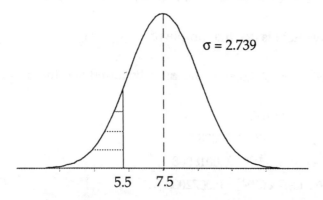

This gives a probability of 0.2327 which is not too far away from the correct value of 0.2414. (An error of about 3%).

Adding normal distributions

A statistically minded newsagents notes that the sales of the 'Sun' newspaper at his shop is normally distributed with a mean of 250 copies per day and a standard deviation of 45. The sales of the 'mirror' is also normally distributed with a mean of 142 copies a day and a standard deviation of 36. What is the mean and standard deviation of both newspapers combined?

This is a case where it is necessary to *add* normal distributions. If you add normal distributions, the resulting distribution is also normal, as you have probably guessed. You will also probably guess that the mean of the new distribution is the sum of the means of ones that you are adding. So the mean number of newspapers is 250 + 142 = 392. The standard deviation, though, is not quite as simple to calculate. Standard deviation measures spread and the spread will increase if either you *add* or *subtract* normal distributions. However standard deviations *do not add*. It can be shown that it is the variance, which is the square of the standard deviations, that add. In the newspaper example the standard deviation of the sales of both papers combined is:

$$\sigma = \sqrt{42^2 + 36^2}$$

$$= 55.32$$

This example has been illustrated in diagrammatic form in Figure 8, below.

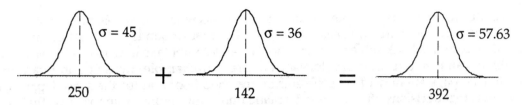

Figure 8

You will find this idea of adding normal distributions quite useful, particularly in inventory control (Unit 17, page 40)

Further reading

Introductory Statistics for Business and Economics, Wonnacott, (WILEY)

Statistics without Tears, Rowntree, (PELICAN)

A First Course in Statistics (2nd edition), Booth, (DP PUBLICATIONS)

Essential Statistics (3rd edition), Rees, (CHAPMAN & HALL)

Statistics For Management, Levin, (PRENTICE-HALL)

Quantitative Approaches in Business Studies, Morris, (PITMAN)

Decision analysis

Introduction

You may wonder why there is a chapter on decision analysis when the whole book is aimed at making correct decisions. There are two reasons for this. The first reason is that most of the techniques that you will meet in this book solve specific problems and do not take into account how the solution to one problem can create further problems elsewhere. For example, the solution to an inventory problem (Unit 17, page 40) may cause problems on the shop floor and for the sales department. The second reason is that decisions often have to be made under conditions of uncertainty, that is, knowledge about particular aspects of a problem are vague.

Many *strategic* decisions have to be made with incomplete knowledge. For example, a car accessory company, Marla Plc have developed a new car immobiliser and have to decide whether to market the product nationwide, to sell by mail order or to sell the patent to a large chain of motor accessory shops. The cost of distributing nationwide is very high but the potential profits could also be large. There is less risk with selling by mail order but the potential profits would also be less. The safe option is to sell the patent but in this case the chance of making large profits would be lost. How does Marla make their decision given that they have limited knowledge of the likely demand for the product?

There are very many decision analysis techniques, some involve quite complex mathematical models while others require a more subjective (non-quantitative) approach. Some techniques are only suitable where single stage decisions are involved; that is only one decision is required. However, in many cases the outcome of one decision leads to subsequent decisions. Techniques for solving both single and multi-stage decision problems will be now be provided.

Payoff tables

Where only single stage decisions are required, *payoff* tables can be used. A payoff represents the outcome of a decision given a particular state of nature. In the Marla example the state of nature is the level of demand that could occur; these will be defined as high, medium and low.

The various payoffs are usually written in a payoff table. Decisions can then be made according to a *decision rule*. There are many decision rules, some assume that all the outcomes are known with certainty, while others assume that a probability can be assigned to each one. The decision rules that do not require the use of probability are the

Maximax rule

Maximin rule

Minimax rule

and the **Hurwicz criterion**

To illustrate these rules the Marla example will be used. Imagine that expected payoffs have been evaluated for the first year according to the three decisions available to the company (nationwide distribution, mail order or sell patent. The payoffs, after costs have been deducted, are as follows:

Payoff table (£000's)

Decision	State of the market		
	High	medium	low
Nationwide	95	52	(26)
Mail order	48	24	19
Sell patent	25	25	25

This table shows that nationwide distribution will give the greatest payoff but there is the chance that a loss of £26,000 will be made.

The *maximax* rule chooses the 'best of the best'. The largest payoff for each decision is £95,000, £48,000 and £25,000 respectively and the best of these is £95,000, so the decision using this rule is to distribute nationwide. It is a decision rule used by decision makers who are prepared to take risks.

The *maximin* rule chooses the 'best of the worst'. The worst payoff for each decision is noted and the best is chosen. In the table above the worst payoffs are –26,000, £19,000 and £25,000 respectively. The best of these is £25,000 so the decision would be to sell the patent. This decision rule is for people who are adverse to risk taking.

The *minimax* rule minimises the maximum opportunity loss. The opportunity loss is the loss that occurs through not taking the best option. To work out the opportunity loss you have to subtract each payoff for a particular state of nature from the best that could be achieved given that state. For example, the best option given high demand is to distribute nationwide at £95,000 but if instead the mail order option was chosen a 'loss' of £47,000 would be made (£95,000 – £48,000). The remaining opportunity loss values can be seen in the table below.

Opportunity loss table (£000's)

Decision	State of the market		
	High	Medium	Low
Nationwide	0	0	51
Mail order	47	28	6
Sell patent	70	27	0

For each option the largest opportunity loss is £51,000, £47,000 and £70,000 respectively. The minimum of these is £47,000 so under this decision rule the mail order option would be chosen. This is a 'middle of the road' rule and would suit people who are neither risk takers or risk avoiders.

The *Hurwicz* criterion like the minimax rule, attempts to give a compromise between the cautious maximin rule and the optimistic maximax rule. However, unlike the minimax rule weights are assigned to the best and worst payoff for each decision option and the option with the highest weighted payoff is chosen.

The weighted payoff is calculated as:

$$\alpha \times \text{worst payoff} + (1 - \alpha) \times \text{best payoff}$$

The value of α (alpha) depends on the decision maker's attitude to risk. The smaller the value, the bigger risk he is prepared to take; when $\alpha = 0$ the decision will be the same as for the maximax rule.

Using $\alpha = 0.6$, which represents a slightly cautious decision maker, the weighted payoffs become:

Nationwide: $0.6 \times (-27) + 0.4 \times 95 = 22.4$

Mail order: $0.6 \times 19 + 0.4 \times 48 = 30.6$

Sell patent: $0.6 \times 25 + 0.4 \times 25 = 25$

So under this criterion and using $\alpha = 0.6$, the decision is to go for the mail order option.

Each of these decision rules assumes that each state of nature is equally likely. In reality some states are more likely than others and this allows probabilities to be assigned to each state. The availability of probabilities allows expected values (see page 60) to be calculated and two further decision rules follow. These are

Maximise expected monetary value (EMV)

Minimise expected opportunity loss (EOL)

Expected monetary value is the long run average return (or cost) of making a particular decision. For example, suppose that it is estimated that there is a 0.45 probability that the demand will be low and a 0.25 probability that demand will be high. This means that the probability that demand will be medium is 0.3 (1− 0.45 − 0.25). The EMV can now be worked out for each decision as follows:

Nationwide: $0.25 \times 95 + 0.3 \times 52 + 0.45 \times (-26) = 27.65$

Mail order: $0.25 \times 48 + 0.3 \times 24 + 0.45 \times 19 = 27.75$

Sell patent: $0.25 \times 25 + 0.3 \times 25 + 0.45 \times 25 = 25$

This suggests that, on average, choosing the mail order option would give you a slightly higher payoff at £27,750.

Please note: EMV calculations are a very useful method of comparing alternatives but the assumptions behind this method should perhaps be borne in mind. Expected values are based on what would be expected if the decision were repeated many times, that is, it is a long run average. One-off decisions cannot of course be repeated and the results obtained from using this technique in these circumstances should therefore be viewed with care. However the technique is so popular and useful that most decision makers ignore this reservation.

Expected opportunity loss is essentially the same technique as the EMV method except that the probabilities are applied to the opportunity loss table and the option that *minimises* the expected opportunity loss is chosen. For Marla's problem, the EOL values are

Nationwide: $0.25 \times 0 + 0.3 \times 0 + 0.45 \times 51 = 22.95$

Mail order: $0.25 \times 47 + 0.3 \times 28 + 0.45 \times 6 = 22.85$

Sell patent: $0.25 \times 70 + 0.3 \times 27 + 0.45 \times 0 = 25.6$

The decision that would minimise the EOL is again the mail order option. (The EMV and EOL decision rules should always agree).

Value of perfect information

If the state of the market were known *before* the decision had to be made, a perfect decision could be made every time. For example, if it was known that demand would be low, the best option would be to sell the patent and if demand was known to be high, the option to distribute nationwide would be chosen. The expected value given this perfect information would be:

$$0.25 \times 95 + 0.3 \times 52 + 0.45 \times 25 = 50.6$$

The difference between this value and that obtained earlier is:

$$50.6 - 27.75 = 22.85, \text{ or } £22,850$$

This is known as the value of perfect information and is the maximum amount that a decision maker would be prepared to pay for this information. You should note that this is the same figure as the minimum EOL calculated above.

Decision trees

Decision trees are similar to probability trees (see page 57) except that as well as probabilistic (or chance) branches there are also decision branches. Decision branches allow the decision maker to compare alternative options.

To illustrate this technique the Marla example will be used. In Figure 1 opposite, the square node at the start from which the three decision branches are drawn represent the point at which a decision has to be made. The round nodes represent the point at which chance takes over. The outcomes have been written at the end of each probabilistic branch.

The decision tree is drawn from left to right but to evaluate the tree you work from right to left. This is called the 'roll-back' method. You first evaluate the EMV at each chance node and then at the decision node you select the 'best' EMV (don't forget, 'best' can be lowest cost as well as largest profit).

Decision trees are normally used where multi-stage decisions are involved and the following example illustrates a typical problem.

The Delma oil company has acquired rights to conduct surveys and test drillings in a particular area. The area is considered to have potential and it is believed that there is a 70% chance that tests would indicate a commercially viable field. The cost of carrying out these tests will be £10m

Whether the tests show the possibility of ultimate success or not, or even if no tests are undertaken at all, the company could still pursue its drilling programme or alternatively it could sell its rights to drill in the area. However, if it carried out the drilling programme, the probability of success is as follows:

If 'successful' tests have been carried out, the probability of a viable field is put at 0.8, whereas if the tests are a 'failure' the probability of a viable field is only 0.25. If no tests have been carried out the probability of a viable field is put at 0.55. The cost of carrying out the drilling programme is reckoned to be £40m and the revenue obtained from a viable field is estimated to be £120m at today's prices. The revenue obtained from the sale of the rights will depend on the outcome of the tests (if carried out) and are as follows:

Prior tests show 'success'   £40m

Prior tests show 'failure'   £5m

Without prior tests   £20m

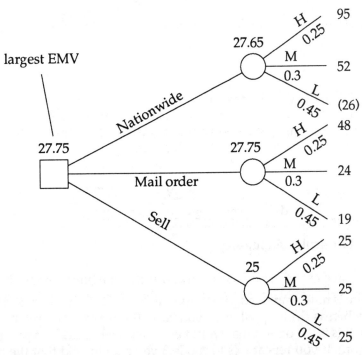

Figure 1

To solve this decision problem you would carry out the following three steps:

Step 1

Draw out the decision tree. This is shown in Figure 2. You will see that the decision nodes have been numbered 1, 2, and 3 while the chance nodes have been labelled as a, b, c and d. Also the cost of a decision has been written alongside each decision branch.

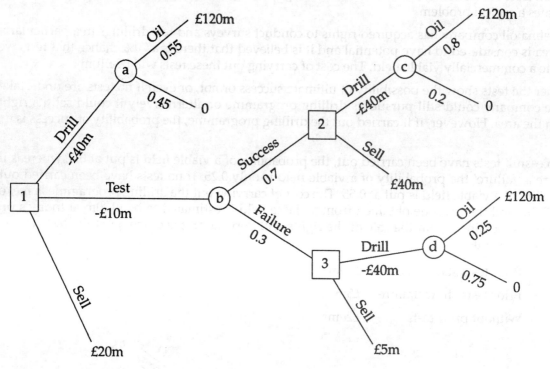

Figure 2

Step 2

Working from the right, the EMV at the chance nodes a, c and d are calculated as follows:

Node	EMV
a	$0.55 \times 120 + 0.45 \times 0 = £66m$
c	$0.80 \times 120 + 0.20 \times 0 = £96m$
d	$0.25 \times 120 + 0.75 \times 0 = £30m$

(The EMV at b cannot be calculated until step 3.)

Step 3

The roll-back technique is now employed. At decision node 2, the decision is to either drill or sell. Sell will give you £40m, whereas drilling will give you $96 - 40 = £56m$. The option that gives the largest EMV is to drill and so this is the option that would be taken. The value 56 is put above node 2 and the sell option is crossed out. If you repeat this for node 3 you should find that the best option here is to sell. The EMV at chance node b can now be calculated and you should find that this is £40.7m ($0.7 \times 56 + 0.3 \times 5$). You can now go to decision node 1 and compare the three decisions. You should find the following:

Drill: $66 - 40 = £26m$

Test: $40.7 - 10 = £30.7m$

Sell: £20m

The best decision is to test first. If the test gives successful results, only then should drilling start; *Otherwise* the rights should be sold for £5m. You will see this analysis summarised in Figure 3, below.

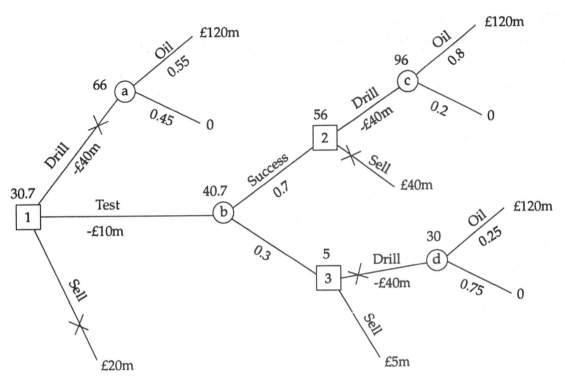

Figure 3

Sensitivity analysis

The major difficulty with decision analysis is estimating the probabilities and the expected returns. In many cases the probabilities are simply 'plucked from the air'. In any decision analysis, the sensitivity of the recommended decision to changes in any of the estimated values should be investigated. This is particularly true for cases where the EMV values for two or more decisions are similar.

For example, suppose that you wanted to see how much the probability of a successful test in the Delma Oil company could vary before the decision changed from 'test first' to 'drill without test'. You could try different values of the probability but the easiest method is to call the probability 'p' and the EMV at node b then becomes:

$$56 \times p + 5 \times (1 - p) = 51p + 5$$

The EMV at 1 is $\quad 51p + 5 - 10 = 51p - 5$

The decision will change when this expression is less than £26m. That is:

$$51p + 5 < 26$$

therefore: $\quad p < 0.608$

So the probability has to fall from 0.7 to 0.6 before the decision changes. This idea could be repeated for other probabilities but the algebra becomes more difficult when decision nodes are involved as well and when you want to change more than one probability at once. The easiest method in these cases is to use a spreadsheet to carry out the necessary calculations and comparisons.

Further reading

Decision Analysis, Gregory, (PITMAN)

Making Decisions, Lindley, (WILEY)

Decision making for Management Judgement , Goodwin and Wright, (WILEY)

Quantitative Techniques , Lucey, (DP PUBLICATIONS)

Quantitative Analysis , Stansfield, (LONGMAN)

Estimation

Introduction: samples and sampling

This chapter could be titled 'what happens when you take samples'. Sampling is an extensive and in many cases controversial technique. Whenever there is a general election in this country the question of sampling accuracy is raised and this was most evident in the 1992 election. However, sampling peoples views and intentions is notoriously difficult and even the best sampling plan can fail in these circumstances. Fortunately when sampling is done by measurement, the results tend to be much more reliable. Sampling in industry and business tends to be of the measurement kind and it will be this aspect of sampling that will be emphasized here.

However, before the question of 'what happens' is answered perhaps the question 'why take samples?' should be addressed first. The alternative to taking samples is to measure or test every member of the 'population'. (The word population in this context doesn't necessarily mean people, it is used to define all the items or things that are of interest, such as all television sets produced by a company in a day). It is impractical to measure or test every member of the population for the following reasons:

It would take too long. Measuring or testing can be time consuming and it is simply not always feasible to find the necessary time.

It is too expensive. Testing costs money as inspectors need to be employed and goods that are to be tested take up space and cannot be sold until the testing is complete.

Some tests are destructive. Sometimes goods have to be tested to destruction and if all the goods were tested there would be nothing left to sell!

The total population is unknown. There are occasions when the size of the population is so large as to be considered infinite (without limit). In other cases the size of the population is simply unknown. For example, does anyone know the number of fishes in the sea?

Statistical sampling requires that the chosen members of the population are selected in such a way that no bias is involved. For example, suppose you work for the toy manufacturer 'Real Toys'. You buy in various materials such as plastic granules that are used in the extruding process. These granules are delivered in 100 kg bags and each consignment is tested for fire resistance. Since this is destructive testing, the only option available to the company is to test a sample from each consignment, but how do you decide which bag or bags are to be tested? If you tested samples from just one bag you may be biasing the result, because this bag may not be typical of the rest of the batch. Perhaps this bag happens to be old stock or is different in some way. Whenever you take samples you must ensure that the samples are selected at *random*; that is every member of the population has an equal chance of being selected. To ensure this, one of two methods are used.

Either:

Random numbers are used to select the required number of samples. Random numbers are simply numbers that are guaranteed to be free of bias and are obtained from tables or from a computer (spreadsheets have a random number facility). To illustrate the use of random numbers imagine that you wanted to select 10 bags of granules from a batch of 100. You would first of all number each bag from 0 to 99 and then use a stream of two digit random numbers in the range 00 to 99. If the first random number was 23 then you would pick bag number 23 and so on. (A simpler method is to write the numbers 0 to 99 on cards, place these cards in a box, shuffle the cards, and pick 10 cards from the box).

Or:

Every *nth* item is chosen. So, for the granules, every 10th bag would be chosen. This is the simplest method and is quite satisfactory provided that no pattern is present. (For example, if there was something different about each 10th bag then this wouldn't be a satisfactory sampling plan).

Point estimates

The whole purpose of obtaining a sample from a population is to obtain estimates of various population parameters such as the mean, the standard deviation or proportion. These parameters can also be obtained for the sample and it is the purpose of this section to show how the population parameters and the sample parameters are related. However, before continuing, it is necessary to define the symbols that are to be used throughout this (and the next) chapter.

The convention is to use Greek letters for the population parameters and normal letters for the sample parameters. In addition when you are referring to an *estimate* of some population parameter you would normally put the '^' symbol above the Greek letter. The various symbols used are given below.

Parameter	Population	Population estimate	Sample
Mean	μ	$\hat{\mu}$	$\overline{X}$
Standard deviation	σ	$\hat{\sigma}$	S
Proportion	π	$\hat{\pi}$	P

The one exception to this rule is that the size of the population is usually referred to as 'N' and the sample size as 'n'.

You will probably not be surprised to learn that the 'best' (or *unbiased*) estimate of the population mean is $\overline{X}$ and the best estimate for the population proportion is P. To illustrate this, imagine that you have tested 10 samples of plastic granules for fire resistance and the temperature (in centigrade) that they each caught fire are as follows:

Sample No.	1	2	3	4	5	6	7	8	9	10
Temperature	510	535	498	450	491	505	487	500	501	469

The mean of these temperatures is 494.6°C with a standard deviation of 21.85°C. Therefore the best estimate of μ is 494.6°C. But what is the best estimate of the population standard deviation? It is *not* S, the sample standard deviation as S is an *underestimate* of the true figure. To understand this, imagine that the population of temperatures follows some probability distribution. This distribution has a few extreme values but most of them are clustered around the mean. The population standard deviation is a measure of spread and all values, including the extreme ones, contribute to this value. However, if a sample is chosen at random the sample is most unlikely to include any of the extreme values and therefore the spread and hence the standard deviation of the sample will be *less* than the population. You should also realise that as the sample gets larger, the standard deviation will get closer and closer to the population value since the chance of selecting an extreme value increases.

So how is σ calculated? Fortunately there is quite a simple formula relating S and σ, it is as follows:

$$\hat{\sigma} = s\sqrt{\frac{n}{n-1}}$$

Equation 1

This is known as Bessel's correction factor.

You will see that as n gets larger the factor under the square root gets closer to 1, which ties in with the discussion above. For 'large' samples, which is generally considered to be anything above 30, this correction is usually ignored.

For the plastic granules, the estimate of the population standard deviation is:

$$\hat{\sigma} = 21.85 \times \sqrt{\frac{10}{9}}$$

$$= 23.03$$

A word of warning: There is probably more confusion caused by this correction factor than almost anything else in statistics. You will find different authors using different terminology and even calculators use a different notation. The problem arises because it is possible to calculate the population estimate directly.

This can be done by amending the standard deviation formula as follows:

$$\sqrt{\frac{\Sigma(x - \bar{x})^2}{n}} \times \sqrt{\frac{n}{n-1}}$$

$$= \sqrt{\frac{\Sigma(x - \bar{x})^2}{n-1}} \qquad \textbf{Equation 2}$$

Unfortunately this is often referred to as the 'sample standard deviation', which is a little confusing. If you use a calculator to obtain the standard deviation, you may find that there are two values that can be obtained, one with the 'n' denominator and one with the 'n-1' denominator. If you are confused about the correct one to use, the golden rule is that the *estimate* of the population (that is, $\hat{\sigma}$) is the *larger* of the two values.

Sampling distribution of the means

Imagine that you took lots and lots of samples and calculated the mean of each. Each mean is an estimate of the population value and therefore the 'mean of the means' should be an even better estimate. If you now plotted the distribution of the means, what shape would you expect the distribution to be? The answer is that the shape would tend towards the *normal* curve. The degree of agreement with the normal curve depends on two factors:

❏ The distribution of the population values

❏ The sample size

If the population values are normally distributed, the 'sampling distribution of the means' would also be normal. If the population is not normally distributed the agreement with the normal distribution depends on the sample size; the larger the sample size, the closer the agreement. This very important result is known as the *central limit theorem*.

In addition, the spread of this sampling distribution depends on the sample size; the larger the sample size, the smaller the spread (that is, the standard deviation). The standard deviation of the sampling distribution is called the *standard error* as it measures the error that could arise in your estimate due to the spread of the sampling distribution. To avoid confusion with the standard error of the sampling distribution of a proportion, which will be discussed later (page 000), the standard error of the sampling distribution of the means will be referred to as **STEM** (the STandard Error of the Means). Is it necessary to collect many samples in order to calculate the value of STEM? Fortunately not, as there is a relationship between σ and STEM. This relationship is as follows:

$$\text{STEM} = \frac{\sigma}{\sqrt{n}} \qquad \textbf{Equation 3}$$

So the larger the sample size (n), the smaller the value of STEM, which makes sense.

These ideas are illustrated in Figure 1, on the following page. Two sampling distributions are shown, one for a sample size of 4 and one for a sample size of 16. The population distribution (assumed normal in this case) has been superimposed onto the diagram.

You will see that the mean of each sampling distribution is the same and equal to the population value. You would normally only take one sample and from Figure 1 you can see that the mean of a sample can lie anywhere within the relevant sampling distribution; although it is more likely to be near the centre than in the tails. This variation depends on the value of STEM, so the smaller this figure, the more reliable your estimate of the population mean will be.

Confidence intervals for a population mean using the normal distribution

Rather than simply quote the value of STEM, a much better idea of the reliability of your estimate is to specify some limits within which the true mean is expected to lie. These limits are called confidence limits or intervals.

Sampling distribution of the means

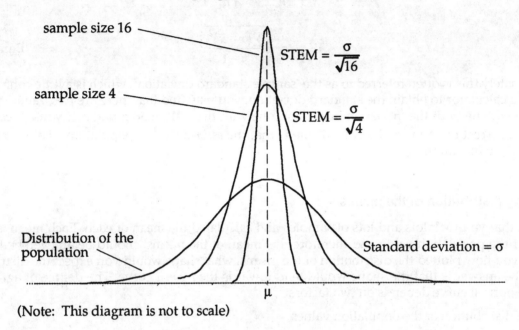

(Note: This diagram is not to scale)

Figure 1

When calculating confidence intervals it is necessary to decide what level of confidence you wish to use. The most common level is 95%, which means that you are 95% confident that the true mean lies within the calculated limits. Or put another way, there is a 5% chance that the true mean *doesn't* lie within these limits. Other limits are frequently used, such as 90%, 99% and 99.9%; but remember that as the confidence level gets closer to 100%, the interval gets larger and larger (at 100% it would be infinitely large).

The *normal distribution* (page 69) can be used to calculate these limits if the following conditions are met:

The population is normal and the standard deviation of the population (σ) is known.

or

The population is not normal but σ is known *and* the sample size is large (greater than 30)

If the population is normal then the sampling distribution for any sample size will be normal. However, if you do not have any evidence that the population is normally distributed, then for the central limit to apply, a large sample size is required.

Figure 2 on the following page, illustrates the Z values that enclose 95% of the standard normal distribution (see page 71). The values ±1.96 have been found from the normal table (appendix 3, page 250) by noting that the area (or probability) in either tail is .025 (0.05/2).

From your knowledge of the normal distribution, you will know that any normal distribution can be transformed into the standard normal distribution using the formula:

$$Z = \frac{X - \mu}{\sigma}$$

However, this formula is for individual 'X' values. For a sampling distribution of the means, the 'X' needs to be replaced by $\overline{X}$ and σ needs to be replaced by STEM. The formula then becomes:

$$Z = \frac{\overline{X} - \mu}{STEM}$$

If you rearrange this formula to make μ the subject, you will get:

$$\mu = \overline{X} \pm Z \times STEM$$

This is the equation you would use to calculate confidence intervals using the normal distribution.

For 95% confidence intervals the Z value is 1.96 and the formula becomes:

$$\mu = \overline{X} \pm 1.96 \times STEM$$

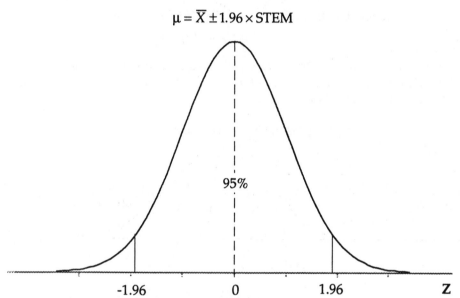

Figure 2 – 95% Confidence intervals

How would you use this formula? Imagine that you worked for the quality control unit of a sugar producer. One of your tasks is to weigh samples of 1 kg bags of sugar and from a sample of 6 bags you obtain a mean weight of 0.958 kg. You know from previous investigations that the weights of individual bags of sugar are normally distributed with a standard deviation of 0.056 kg. What is the 95% confidence interval for the true mean weight of bags of sugar?

From the discussion on point estimates (page 86), you know that the best estimate of the true mean is 0.958 kg. That is:

$$\hat{\mu} = 0.958 \text{ kg}$$

From this you can assume that the best estimate of the mean of the sampling distribution for a sample size 6 also has this value. The value of STEM is:

$$\frac{\sigma}{\sqrt{n}} = \frac{0.056}{\sqrt{6}}$$

$$= 0.02286$$

Therefore the 95% confidence interval for the true mean is:

$$0.958 \pm 1.96 \times 0.02286 \quad = 0.958 \pm 0.045$$
$$= 0.958 - 0.045 \text{ and } 0.958 + 0.045$$
$$= 0.913 \text{ and } 1.003 \text{ kg}$$

The 0.913 kg is the *lower* limit and 1.003 kg is the *upper* limit. It is usual to write this confidence interval as:

$$0.913, 1.003 \text{ (or } 0.913 \text{ to } 1.003\text{)}$$

This interval is summarised in the diagram below.

Notice that the interval includes 1 kg, so this may indicate that the process is producing bags of sugar with a mean weight of 1 kg. But more about this later (page 94).

If accuracy was really important you may want to calculate 99% confidence intervals. From the normal table, the value of Z for 0.005 (1% divided by 2) is 2.58, so the 99% confidence interval is:

$$0.958 \pm 2.58 \times 0.02286 \quad = 0.958 \pm 0.059$$
$$= 0.899, 1.017 \text{ kg}$$

The interval is wider, which was expected. Now there is only a 1% chance that the true mean will be outside these limits. If these limits are too wide the only way to reduce them (for the same confidence level) is to increase the sample size (see page 92).

Sampling distribution for a sample of size 6

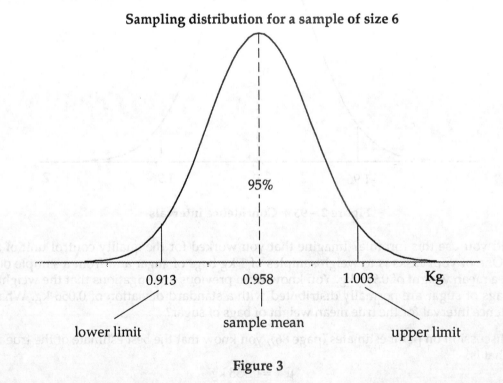

Figure 3

Confidence intervals for a population mean using the t-distribution

If the standard deviation of the population is *not* known, it could be *estimated* using either equations 1 or 2 (pages 86–87). However, in this case you would not generally be justified in using the normal table (but see below). The reason for this is that the uncertainty generated by estimating σ decreases the reliability of the confidence interval. To overcome this problem a different distribution is used, called the *'t-distribution'*. This distribution is symmetrical like the normal, but it is flatter. This 'flatness' increases the proportion of the distribution in the 'tails' and this means that the confidence interval, for the same confidence level, is wider. The amount of 'flatness' decreases with increase in 'n', the sample size. When 'n' is 50 there is virtually no difference between the two distributions and even for a sample size of 30 the difference is quite small. This similarity between the two distributions allows you to use the normal distribution for large samples. Many authors suggest that 30 is the cut-off figure. However, you should remember that the use of the normal distribution in these cases is an approximation.

Figure 4 below, shows the t-distribution for a sample size of 6 together with the normal distribution for comparison.

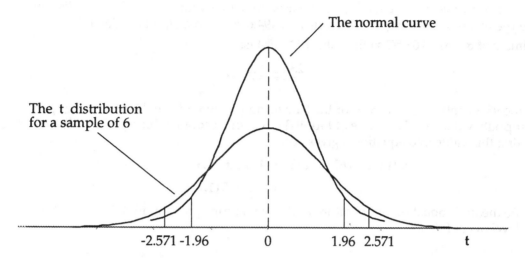

Figure 4 – Comparison of the normal and t-distributions

The t table is given in appendix 3 and an extract is given below.

Probability (α)

df	0.2	0.1	0.05	0.025	0.01	0.005	0.001	0.0001
1	1.376	3.078	6.314	12.706	31.821	63.657	318.309	3183.1
2	1.061	1.886	2.920	4.303	6.965	9.925	22.327	70.700
3	0.978	1.638	2.353	3.182	4.541	5.841	10.215	22.204
4	0.941	1.533	2.132	2.776	3.747	4.604	7.173	13.034
5	0.920	1.476	2.015	**2.571**	3.365	4.032	5.893	9.678
6	0.906	1.440	1.943	2.447	3.143	3.707	5.208	8.025

If you compare this table with the normal table, you will see some important differences. For a start, the numbers within the table are t-values and not probabilities. The other difference is the numbers in the first column. These numbers are the *'degrees of freedom'* (df) of the sample. Degrees of freedom can be thought of as the 'freedom' that you have in choosing the values of the sample. If you were given the mean of the sample of 6 values, you would be free to choose 5 of the 6 but not the sixth one. Therefore there are 5 degrees of freedom. *The number of degrees of freedom for a single sample of size 'n' is 'n-1'*. For a very large sample (shown as α in the table) the t and Z distributions are exactly the same. Since the t-distribution is a little easier to use, you might prefer to use this table when you want the Z value of one of the 'standard' probabilities. In the table supplied in this book these 'standard' probabilities are 0.2, 0.1, 0.05, 0.025, 0.01, 0.005, 0.001 and 0.0001.

To use this table you would first decide on the probability level. For a 95% confidence interval you would choose the 0.025 level since this represents 2.5% in each tail. For a sample size of 6, the degrees of freedom is 5, so the t value for 5 degrees of freedom at 95% confidence level is 2.571. This value has been highlighted in the table above and has also been shown in Figure 4. (Remember that the t-distribution is symmetrical about the mean of zero, so the equivalent value in the left hand side of the distribution is −2.571).

The formula for calculating confidence intervals using this distribution is the same as when the normal distribution was used except that 'Z' is replaced by 't' and is therefore:

$$\hat{\mu} = \overline{X} \pm t \times STEM \qquad \qquad \textbf{Equation 5}$$

The 'Real Toys' problem (see page 86) will be used to demonstrate the use of the t-distribution. In this example the mean of the sample of size 10 was 494.6 °C with a standard deviation of 21.85 °C. The best estimate of σ was 23.03 °C so the value of STEM is:

$$\frac{23.03}{\sqrt{10}} = 7.283$$

To find the 95% confidence interval for the true mean you would use the t table in appendix 3 to find the appropriate value of t. The value of t for 9 degrees of freedom, with a probability of 0.025 is 2.262. Substituting this value into equation 5 gives you:

$$494.6 \pm 2.262 \times 7.283 = 494.6 \pm 16.5$$

$$= 478.1, 511.1 \, ^\circ C$$

So the true mean combustion temperature of the whole consignment lies between 478.1 to 511.1°C at the 95% level of confidence.

Calculation of sample size

Since the value of STEM depends on the sample size, the width of the confidence interval for the same confidence level, can be reduced by increasing the value of 'n'. For the sugar example the *half* width of the interval, that is, the difference between the lower or upper limit and the sample mean, is 0.045 kg for a confidence level of 95% (see page 90). This was obtained by multiplying STEM by 1.96, that is:

$$\text{Half width of confidence interval} = 1.96 \times STEM$$

$$= 1.96 \times \frac{\sigma}{\sqrt{n}}$$

If you wanted to reduce this half width to say, 0.025 kg, then you need to calculate the value of n required to achieve this reduction. That is:

$$1.96 \times \frac{0.056}{\sqrt{n}} = 0.025$$

since σ = 0.056 (see page 89).

Re-arranging this equation gives:

$$\sqrt{n} = \frac{1.96 \times 0.056}{0.025}$$

$$= 4.3904$$

Squaring both sides of the equation gives:

$$n = 19.3$$

So a sample size of 20 would be required to achieve an accuracy of ± 0.025 kg.

This idea also applies when the t-distribution is used, but there is a problem in this case concerning the value of t to use. It is perhaps easier to explain this problem using an example. Suppose in the

'Real toys' example (page 86), it was required to reduce the half width from 16.5°C to 5°C. Proceeding as before you would note that the best estimate of σ is 23.03°C (page 87) and the half width is:

$$t \times \frac{23.03}{\sqrt{n}}$$

You now have two unknowns, n *and* t. Fortunately the sample size usually turns out to be quite large and the Z value can be used as an approximation. In the case of 95% confidence, the Z value is 1.96, so you can now proceed as before.

$$1.96 \times \frac{23.03}{\sqrt{n}} = 5$$

and therefore: n $= 81.5$

That is a sample size of approximately 82 is required. This is certainly a large sample and therefore the use of Z is justified. If you found that 'n' was small, you could repeat the analysis using the value of t appropriate to the new sample size. You would repeat this until no further change in 'n' occurred. However, this is rarely necessary.

Confidence interval of a proportion

Proportions (or percentages) occur quite frequently in the analysis of survey results. For example, the proportion of people who like a particular product or the proportion of students over the age of 25. You have also met proportions in quality control (Unit 2, page 6) when you solved problems concerning the proportion of defective items in a batch. From this you will realise that anything to do with proportions is really a *binomial* problem. However, provided n is large and the proportion is not too small or too large, the distribution can be approximated by the normal distribution (see page 75).

The standard error of the sampling distribution of proportions (STEP) is:

$$\text{STEP} = \sqrt{\frac{P(1-P)}{n}} \qquad \textbf{Equation 6}$$

Where P is the sample proportion. (This formula may look familiar to you – it is the standard deviation of the binomial distribution).

The calculation of a confidence interval for a proportion is the same as for a mean but in this case you only need to use the normal table, since the sample size must be large. That is:

$$\pi = P \pm Z \times \text{STEP} \qquad \textbf{Equation 7}$$

For example, a survey among 250 students revealed that 147 were female. What is the 90% confidence interval for the true proportion of female students?

The value of P is $\frac{147}{250} = 0.588$. That is, the survey suggested that 58.8% of the student population is female.

The value of STEP for this problem is:

$$\sqrt{\frac{0.588 \times (1 - 0.588)}{250}} = 0.03113$$

The value of Z for 90% confidence is 1.645, so the confidence interval becomes:

$$0.588 \pm 1.645 \times 0.03113 = 0.588 \pm 0.051$$
$$= 0.537, 0.639$$

That is, the true proportion lies somewhere between 53.7% to 63.9%.

Finite populations

The assumption that has implicitly been made in this chapter is that the population is infinitely large, or at least much larger than the sample. The reason for this is that all sampling is done *without* replacement. That is, you would not measure or test the same person or item twice. This has no effect when the population is large, but for small populations, the probability that an item will be selected will change as soon as one item has been selected. (See conditional probability, page 57). To overcome this problem, the standard error (either STEM or STEP) is modified. This is achieved by multiplying the value by the *Finite Population Correction Factor*, which is:

$$\sqrt{\frac{N-n}{N-1}}$$

Where N is the size of the population. For example in the sugar example STEM was 0.02286 (see page 89). If the size of the population was 100, then STEM becomes:

$$0.02286 \times \sqrt{\frac{100-6}{100-1}} = 0.02286 \times 0.9744$$

$$= 0.02228$$

Which is a *reduction*. (Since STEM is reduced, confidence intervals will also be reduced).

As 'N' gets larger relative to 'n', the correction factor approaches 1 and can therefore be ignored. For example, if you try N = 10,000 and n = 10, you should get a value of 0.9995.

Statistical process control

An extremely useful application of confidence intervals is in the area of quality control. Instead of testing quality after a product has been made, the idea now is to check quality *while* the product is being made. This change in philosophy has come from the Japanese although the ideas have been around for many years. The reasoning behind this approach is a simple one; if causes for poor quality can be detected *and* corrected during the process, then there should be less defective items produced. The method adopted is to measure or test samples of items during production. These samples are analysed and based on this analysis the following may happen:

> The process is deemed *in control* and is allowed to continue.

or   The process is considered *out of control* and is stopped and the problem rectified

or   There is some evidence that the process is *going* out of control. This acts as a warning to the operator of the process.

If the sampling distribution of the means can be assumed normal, then confidence intervals can be used to help determine whether a process is in or out of control. For example, suppose a process is designed to manufacture metal rods of diameter 10.0 mm with a standard deviation 0.5 mm. A sample of 5 metal rods from this process gave a mean of 10.6 mm. Is this value consistent with a population mean of 10.0 mm? To solve this problem you could calculate a confidence interval using the sample mean of 10.6 mm and then see if the value 10.0 mm was inside or outside the interval. However a better approach is to calculate a confidence interval for the *population* mean of 10.0 mm. This will give you the interval within which a sample mean is expected to lie. The advantage of this method is that the confidence interval need only be calculated once. For the metal rods, the value of STEM is:

$$\frac{0.5}{\sqrt{5}} = 0.2236$$

and if you use the 95% level of confidence the confidence interval is:

$$10.0 \pm 1.96 \times 0.2236 \quad = 10.0 \pm 0.44$$

$$= 9.56, 10.44$$

That is, a sample mean could lie anywhere between 9.56 and 10.44 mm, at the 95% level of confidence. Since your sample mean is 10.6 mm you could conclude that the process is out of control. However, there is still a 5% chance that a sample mean could be outside these limits, so it may be this high sample mean is due to random fluctuations rather than any *assignable* cause. To be on the safe side you might like to calculate a higher limit, such as the 99% confidence interval, as then there would only be a 1% chance that a sample mean could be outside these limits.

Statistical process control or **SPC** uses this idea of two limits. The 95% interval is used to represent *warning* limits and the 99.8% interval is used for *action* limits. If a sample mean is outside one of the warning limits but inside the action limits you may want to check the process but not to stop it; whereas if it is outside one of the action limits you would almost certainly conclude that there was a problem.

SPC involves taking samples at regular intervals and *plotting* the means on a chart. The advantage with this is that any non-random trend in the data can be observed. A slowly decreasing mean can more easily be spotted on a chart than from a set of figures. The graphical display that is used is quite an ingenious but simple one. The normal curve is rotated through 90 degrees and the warning and action limits are drawn in. This is shown in Figure 5, below.

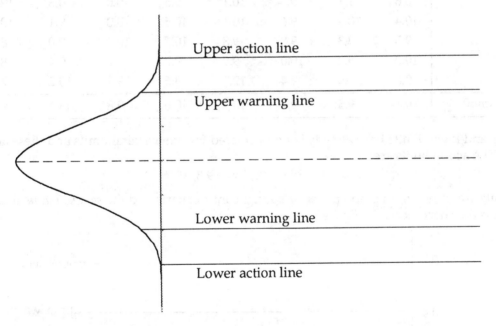

Upper action line

Upper warning line

Lower warning line

Lower action line

Figure 5

However the curve itself is not really required and if this is removed you get the **control chart for means** shown in Figure 6.

The central horizontal line can be used to represent time or sample number and the sample means are plotted at regular intervals. This forms a permanent record of the performance of the process and any pattern in the points can be immediately observed.

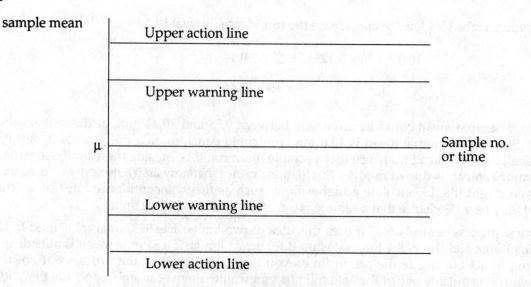

Figure 6 – Control chart for means

Suppose you sampled the rod making process every hour for 8 hours and you obtained the following results:

Sample No.	1	2	3	4	5	6	7	8
	10.6	9.1	9.7	10.1	9.5	10.0	10.8	12.6
	10.4	10.4	9.6	10.1	10.5	10.0	9.1	10.4
	9.5	9.3	9.8	9.8	10.7	10.1	9.0	8.7
	10.0	9.2	10.0	9.9	9.7	9.2	9.4	8.5
	10.0	9.5	9.4	12.1	9.6	9.7	10.2	7.3
Mean (mm)	10.1	9.5	9.7	10.4	10.0	9.8	9.7	9.5

The upper and lower limits have already been calculated for the warning limits and these are 9.6 and 10.4 mm. The action limits are:

$$10 \pm 3.09 \times 0.2236 = 9.3, 10.7$$

These limits are drawn onto graph paper or special control charts and the *sample means* then plotted. The result is the chart shown in Figure 7.

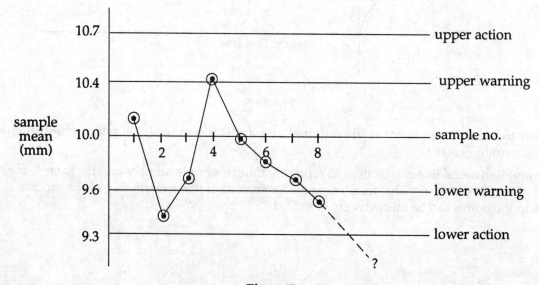

Figure 7

Sample number 2 is outside the warning limit but you would probably not stop the process at this point. You may decide though, to take another sample sooner than you otherwise would have done. The next sample indicates that the process is in control and in fact all the remaining samples, on their own, do not give any cause for concern. However from sample number 4 there is a gradual drift downwards and the dotted line has been drawn to show what might happen next. The process would probably be stopped after the mean for sample number 8 had been plotted.

In practise the design of the charts is slightly different to the description given here. There are two reasons for this. The first is that the users of the charts are not statisticians and therefore they need a procedure that is free of such terms as standard deviation or standard error.The second reason is that the mean and the standard deviation of the process is often unknown and must be found from sample data. To calculate the limits for the mean chart the following procedure is followed:

1. Collect sets of samples (at least 20) from a process that you *know* is in control.

2. Calculate the mean and *range* of each sample. The range is the difference between the largest and smallest value and is a crude measure of the spread of the sample.

3. Work out the 'mean of means'($\hat{\mu}$) and the mean range ($\overline{R}$).

4. Use the following formula to calculate the approximate values of the control limits:

$$\hat{\mu} \pm A \times \overline{R}$$

Where A is a constant that depends on the type of limit (warning or action) and the sample size. The value of A can be found from tables.

A *range* chart can also be produced, using a similar procedure. A range chart is like the mean chart except that the range for each sample is plotted instead of the mean. The range chart is useful because it gives warning of increased variability in the data. Normally only the upper limits are plotted for the range chart and they are found from:

$$D \times \overline{R}$$

Where D is a constant that is again found from tables.

To illustrate this procedure, suppose the mean range of many samples from the rod making process was 1.65 mm. The value of the constants 'A' and 'D' can be found from special tables, an extract of which is given below.

Sample size	Mean chart		Range chart	
	Action	Warning	Action	Warning
3	1.054	0.668	2.98	2.17
4	0.750	0.476	2.57	1.93
5	**0.594**	**0.377**	**2.34**	**1.81**
6	0.498	0.316	2.21	1.72

The values of the constants A and D for a sample size 5 have been highlighted in the table and the calculations of the limits are as follows:

Mean chart:

Action: $10.0 \pm 0.594 \times 1.65 \quad = 9.0, 11.0$

Warning: $10.0 \pm 0.377 \times 1.65 \quad = 9.4, 10.6$

If you compare these limits with those calculated before you will see that they are slightly wider.

Range chart:

Action: $2.34 \times 1.65 \quad = 3.9$

Warning: $1.81 \times 1.65 \quad = 3.0$

The range chart is shown in Figure 8 where you will see that the range for each sample has been plotted. The range was obtained by subtracting the largest measurement from the smallest to give the following values:

Sample No.	1	2	3	4	5	6	7	8
Range	1.1	1.3	0.6	2.3	1.2	0.9	1.8	5.3

The sample range number 8 exceeds the action limit, which again indicates that the process should be stopped.

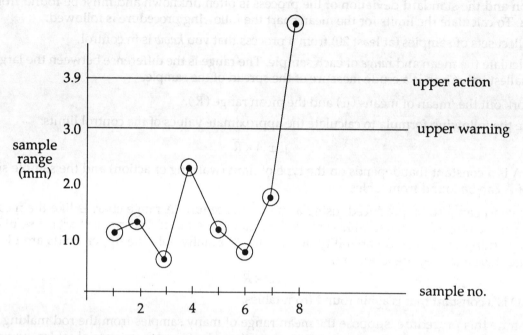

Figure 8 Control chart for the range

Further reading

Introductory Statistics for Business and Economics, Wonnacott, (WILEY)

A First Course in Statistics (2nd edition), Booth, (DP PUBLICATIONS)

Essential Statistics (3rd edition), Rees, (CHAPMAN and HALL)

Statistics For Management Levin, (PRENTICE-HALL)

Statistical Process Control, Oakland, (HEINEMANN)

Quantitative Techniques, Lucey, (DP PUBLICATIONS)

Quantitative Analysis, Stansfield, (LONGMAN)

Hypothesis testing

Introduction

The light bulbs manufactured by 'Bright Lights' are designed to last for 1000 hours on average. How can the company be sure that the average lifetime of a large batch of bulbs really is 1000 hours?

The mean lifetime could be found by testing a sample of bulbs and constructing a confidence interval within which the true mean is likely to lie (see Unit 6, page 13). If the interval does contain 1000 hours, then you could assume that the true mean really is 1000 hours.

Alternatively, you could construct a confidence interval for the supposed true mean of 1000 hours and see if the sample mean was contained within this interval. (See Unit 7, page 15).

However, there is a third approach. This approach makes the *hypothesis* that any departure from the supposed true mean by the sample mean is simply due to chance effects. It is then a matter of calculating the probability that this sample result could have occurred by chance. This is the general idea of hypothesis testing – it assumes that the hypothesis is true and then tries to disprove it. This hypothesis is known as the *null hypothesis*. If the null hypothesis is rejected an *alternative hypothesis* is accepted. The null hypothesis is called 'H_0' and the alternative hypothesis 'H_1'.

The null hypothesis is tested at a particular *significance level*. This level relates to the area (or probability) in the tail of the distribution being used for the test. This area is called the *critical region* and if the **test statistic** lies in the critical region, you would infer that the result is unlikely to have occurred by chance. You would then reject the null hypothesis. For example, if the 5% level of significance was used and the null hypothesis was rejected, you would say that H_0 had been rejected at the 5% (or the 0.05) significance level, and the result was *significant*.

As the probability level decreases, the chance that H_0 has been rejected in error decreases. At the 5% level of significance, there is a 5% chance that the null hypothesis had been rejected incorrectly. At the 1% level, this probability has been reduced to 1%. However, there is always some chance that an error has been made. This is known as a *type 1* error. Of course, there is also a chance that the null hypothesis has been accepted incorrectly and this error will increase as the significance level decreases. This is known as a *type 2* error. It is not possible to minimise both the type 1 and type 2 errors and judgement has to be used regarding the correct level of significance to use. If the consequences of making a type 1 error are serious (for example, in medical research), you would probably test at the 0.1% or even the 0.01% level of significance. However, in many applications you will find the 5% level quite satisfactory.

These ideas apply to all types of hypothesis tests. The precise form of each hypothesis and the calculations necessary to test H_0 depend on the test being carried out. There are very many tests that can be applied to samples. The most important group are *parametric* tests. These tests compare sample statistics with the population parameters and make assumptions about the form of the sampling distribution. *Non-parametric* (or distribution-free) tests are more general and do not insist on such stringent conditions. They can also be used where the data can only be ordered (ordinal data) rather than measured. However non-parametric tests are less discriminating; that is, the results tend to be less reliable.

Whatever the test, the steps for checking the hypothesis are the same. This is:

Step 1. Set up the null and alternative hypotheses and determine (usually from tables) the boundaries of the critical region. These boundaries are called the *critical values*.

Step 2. Calculate the test statistic

Step 3. Decide whether to accept or reject H_0

Hypothesis tests involving a single sample mean

There are two tests that can be used for a single mean. The first is the Z-*test*, which uses the normal distribution, and is used when the standard deviation of the population is known. The other is the *t-test*, which uses the t-distribution, and is used when the standard deviation is not known.

The Z-test for a single sample mean

The normal distribution can be used to solve problems involving single means, provided that either of the two conditions apply:

(a) The population is normal and the standard deviation of the population (σ) is known; or

(b) The population is not normal but σ is known *and* the sample size is large (greater than 30).

These are the same conditions that were required when using the normal distribution to calculate confidence intervals (page 88).

The formula for '**Z**' is also the same as that used in the derivation of the formula for confidence intervals. That is;

$$Z = \frac{\overline{X} - \mu}{STEM}$$

Where $\overline{X}$ is the mean of the sample, μ is the mean of the population and STEM is the standard error of the sampling distribution of the means and is given by:

$$STEM = \frac{\sigma}{\sqrt{n}}$$

'n' is the sample size.

Suppose that the distribution of the lifetime of all bulbs made by Bright Lights is normal and that the standard deviation of the population is known to be 120 hours. A sample of 15 bulbs was tested and the mean lifetime was found to be 1100 hours, is this consistent, at the 5% level of significance, with the supposed true mean of 1000 hours?

Step 1: Set up H_0 and H_1 and decide on the critical values

The null hypothesis in this case is that the true mean lifetime is 1000 hours. The alternative hypothesis can be one of three statements. These are:

> The true mean is *not* equal to 1000 hours

or The true mean is greater than 1000 hours

or The true mean is less than 1000 hours.

Using symbols, the null and alternative hypotheses become:

$$H_0: \mu = 1000 \text{ hours} \qquad H_1: \mu \neq 1000 \text{ hours} \quad \text{or}$$

$$H_1: \mu > 1000 \text{ hours} \quad \text{or}$$

$$H_1: \mu < 1000 \text{ hours}$$

(The ':' is the mathematical shorthand for 'such that')

The first form of the alternative hypothesis is used for a *two tailed* (or a two sided) test and the other two forms are used for *one tailed* tests. The two tailed test is used when you have no reason to suppose that the true mean could be either greater than or less than the value given by the null hypothesis. The one tailed test is used when you are more interested in one side of the supposed mean than the other. The golden rule when carrying out hypothesis tests is that H_0 and H_1 are set up *before* the test is carried out (and preferably before the data is collected). You may find the diagrams below helpful in clarifying the situation.

In Figure 1 the critical values of ± 1.96 mark the boundaries of the *two* critical regions at the 5% significance level. These values are found from the normal table in appendix 3, page 250. If the test statistic (Z) is either greater than the right hand critical value or less than the left hand value, then H_0 is rejected. If Z lies in between the two critical values then H_0 is accepted – *or you should really say that you do not have sufficient information to reject H_0.*

The left hand diagram of Figure 2 illustrates the case where the alternative hypothesis is of the 'less than' kind. There is only one critical region in this case and you would reject H_0 if Z was *less* than the critical value of *–1.645*. The reason that the critical value is different than for the two tailed case is that the area in the one tail is now the full amount (5% in this example) and not half as it was before. The right hand diagram is for the 'greater than' case and the same reasoning applies here as in the left hand diagram. That is, H_0 would be rejected if Z was *greater* than 1.645.

Two tailed test at the 5% significance level

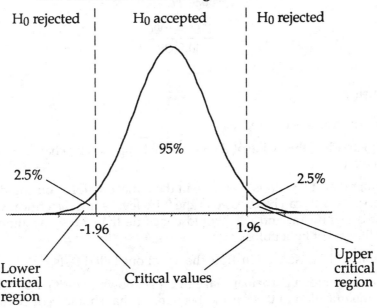

Figure 1

One tailed tests for the 5% significance level

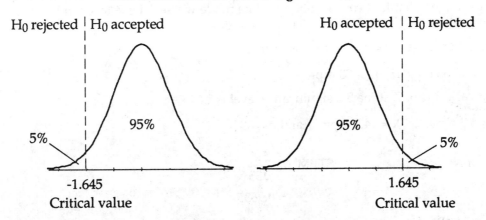

Figure 2

The light bulb example would be a two tailed test because there is nothing in the wording of the problem that suggests that you are more interested in one side of the mean. So the null and alternative hypothesis for this example are:

$$H_0: \mu = 1000 \text{ hours} \quad H_1: \mu \neq 1000 \text{ hours}$$

and the critical values are ± 1.96

Step 2:: Calculate the test statistic

In this problem, $n = 15$, $\mu = 1000$, $\sigma = 120$, and $\overline{X} = 1100$.

Therefore:
$$\text{STEM} = \frac{120}{\sqrt{15}}$$
$$= 30.9839$$

and:
$$Z = \frac{1100 - 1000}{30.9839}$$
$$= 3.23$$

This is your test statistic.

Step 3: Decide whether to accept or reject H_0

It is now necessary to decide if this value of Z could have happened by chance or if it is indicative of a change in the population mean.

Since Z (3.23) is greater than 1.96 and is therefore in the critical region, you could reject H_0 at the 5% level of significance. (In fact H_0 can be rejected at the 0.1% level since the critical value at 0.1% (0.001) is 3.091). The result is significant and you would conclude that there has almost certainly been a change in the mean lifetime of light bulbs.

The following example will be used to illustrate the use of one tailed tests.

The mean fuel consumption for a particular make of car is known to be 33 mpg with a standard deviation of 5.7 mpg. A modification to this car has been made that should reduce fuel consumption. 35 cars are fitted with this device and their fuel consumption is recorded over 12 months. At the end of this period the mean fuel consumption of the 35 cars is found to be 34.8 mpg. Is there any evidence, at the 5% level of significance, that the fuel consumption has been improved?

This is a one tailed test since is hoped that the modification will improve the fuel consumption – there is nothing to suggest that fuel consumption will be made worse. The Z test can be used without assuming normality because the sample is 'large' (over 30).

The null and alternative hypotheses for this problem are:

$$H_0: \mu = 33 \text{ mpg} \quad H_1: \mu > 33 \text{ mpg}$$

And the critical value of Z at the 5% significance level is 1.645

$$\sigma = 5.7 \text{ mpg} \qquad X = 34.8 \text{ mpg} \qquad \text{and } n = 35$$

Therefore:
$$\text{STEM} = \frac{5.7}{\sqrt{35}}$$
$$= 0.9635$$

and the test statistic:
$$Z = \frac{34.8 - 33.0}{0.9635}$$
$$= 1.868$$

Since 1.868 is greater than the critical value of 1.645, you would reject the null hypothesis. That is, there is a *significant* difference between mean the fuel consumption before and after the modification has been fitted. You would conclude that the modification appears to have improved the fuel consumption of this particular make of car.

It is usually a good idea to draw a diagram when carrying out hypothesis tests. The diagram for this problem is shown below.

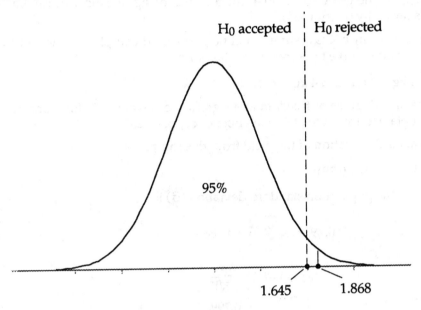

Figure 3

This diagram clearly shows that the test statistic is in the critical region and H_0 should therefore be rejected. You may have noticed that H_0 would *not* have been rejected if the test had been two tailed. (Compare this diagram with Figure 1). This is why it is so important to ensure that you are justified in using a one tailed test as the chance of rejecting H_0 is greater in the one tailed case. In fact there are many statisticians who believe that one tailed tests can never be justified

The t-test for a single sample mean

As in the case of confidence intervals (page 90), the normal distribution is not applicable when the standard deviation of the population has to be estimated from the sample. In this case the t-distribution has to be used. The formula for the *t statistic* is:

$$t = \frac{\overline{X} - \mu}{\text{STEM}}$$

Which is identical to the expression for Z. The formula for STEM is also the same, except that the standard deviation used is the estimate obtained from the sample. That is:

$$\text{STEM} = \frac{\hat{\sigma}}{\sqrt{n}}$$

The same considerations apply concerning the critical region, except that the critical value is obtained from the t-distribution on n-1 degrees of freedom (Appendix 3, page 251). For example, the critical value on 7 degrees of freedom at the 5% significance level is ± 2.365 for a two tailed test and ± 1.895 for a one tailed test.

The following example may help you understand the differences between the Z and t tests.

A tomato grower has developed a new variety of tomato. This variety is supposed to give good crops without the need for a greenhouse. One of the supposed attributes of this tomato is that the average yield per plant is 4 kg of fruit. A gardening magazine decides to test this claim and grows 8 plants in controlled conditions. The yield from each plant is carefully recorded and is as follows:

Plant:	1	2	3	4	5	6	7	8
Yield	3.6	4.2	3.3	2.5	4.8	2.75	4.2	4.6

Do these data support the grower's claim at the 5% level of significance? (It can be assumed that the yield per plant is normally distributed).

This is a one tailed test since it is assumed that no one would complain if the yield was greater than stated. The null and alternative hypotheses are therefore:

$$H_0: \mu = 4 \text{ kg} \qquad H_1: \mu < 4 \text{ kg}$$

The critical value on 7 degrees of freedom at a significance level of 5% for a one tailed test is –1.895. (This figure was obtained from the t table in appendix 3, page 251).

The mean and standard deviation of the yield from this sample is:

$$\overline{X} = 3.74 \qquad S = 0.7919$$

The best estimate of the population standard deviation ($\hat{\sigma}$) is:

$$0.7919 \times \sqrt{\frac{8}{7}} = 0.8466$$

and:

$$\text{STEM} = \frac{0.8466}{\sqrt{8}}$$

$$= 0.2993$$

The test statistic is therefore:

$$t = \frac{3.74 - 4}{0.2993}$$

$$= -0.869$$

Since –0.869 is *greater* than –1.895, you cannot reject H_0. (You may find it easier to ignore the negative signs and just compare 0.869 with 1.895, in which case 0.869 is *less* than 1.895). Alternatively you could draw a diagram as shown in Figure 4, below.

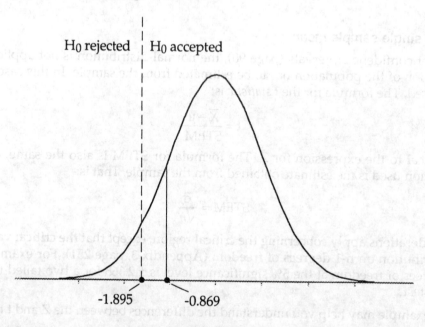

Figure 4

This diagram confirms that the test statistic is not in the critical region, and therefore it is not possible to reject H_0. That is, it hasn't been possible to disprove the grower's claim.

(Note: In practise the *experimental design* for this example would be a little more involved than has been suggested here)

Comparison of two sample means

The two tests you have met so far were concerned with testing a mean of a single sample against the population mean. However, you will often have two samples to consider and you will need to decide if both samples could have come from populations with identical means. The same questions arise; that is:

Is the population normally distributed? If not, is the sample size large?

Is the population standard deviation known.

You also need to consider if the two samples are independent. A different test is applied for cases where the samples are related to each other in some way. A further problem arises when the standard deviation has to be estimated from the two samples.

Hypothesis test of two independent sample means

If sample 1 is represented by subscript '1' and sample 2 by subscript '2', then the null hypothesis will be that the two means (μ_1 and μ_2) are equal and the alternative hypothesis can be either one or two sided. That is:

$$H_0: \mu_1 = \mu_2 \qquad H_1: \mu_1 \neq \mu_2 \quad \text{or}$$

$$H_1: \mu_1 > \mu_2 \quad \text{or}$$

$$H_1: \mu_1 < \mu_2$$

The test statistic is:

$$z \text{ or } t = \frac{(\overline{X}_1 - \overline{X}_2) - (\mu_1 - \mu_2)}{SE(\overline{X}_1 - \overline{X}_2)}$$

and will follow either a normal or t-distribution, depending on whether the standard deviation of the populations are known or have to be estimated from the samples.

The formula for the standard error of the *difference* between the two means $SE(\overline{X}_1 - \overline{X}_2)$ also depends on whether the standard deviations are known.

The Z-test for two sample means

When the standard deviation of the population is known the normal distribution can be used. The standard error of the difference between the two means is:

$$SE(\overline{X}_1 - \overline{X}_2) = \sqrt{\frac{\sigma_1^2}{n_1} + \frac{\sigma_2^2}{n_2}}$$

For example, suppose a 'best buy' magazine decided to test two similar kettles from different manufacturers. One of the tests involved the time taken to boil a litre of water. After each test the kettles were allowed to cool and the experiment repeated. This was done 10 times for both kettles. The mean times were 80 seconds and 95 seconds for kettle 1 and kettle 2 respectively. From previous analysis by the manufacturers it was known that the distribution of heating times was normally distributed and the standard deviation for kettle 1 was 10.2 seconds and 15.5 seconds for kettle 2. Is there any difference between the boil times of the two kettles?

The null and alternative hypotheses are:

$$H_0: \mu_1 = \mu_2 \ (\text{or } \mu_1 - \mu_2 = 0) \quad H_1: \mu_1 \neq \mu_2 \ (\text{or } \mu_1 - \mu_2 \neq 0)$$

This is a two sided test because there is no reason to suppose that one kettle would boil faster than the other.

Since no significance level has been provided you would assume 5% and if the test statistic is significant at this level you would try 1% and so on. The critical value at the 5% level is ± 1.96 and at the 1% level of significance it is ± 2.58.

The standard error is:
$$\sqrt{\frac{(10.2)^2}{10} + \frac{(15.5)^2}{10}} = 5.8676$$

and the test statistic is:
$$Z = \frac{(80 - 95) - 0}{5.8676}$$
$$= -2.556$$

Therefore, since -2.556 is *less* than -1.96, the test statistic lies in the critical region and H_0 can be rejected at the 5% level. That is, there appears to be a difference between the boiling times of the two kettles.

The t-test for two sample means

In practise it is likely that the standard deviations of the two populations will have to be estimated from the samples. When this is the case, a further assumption is necessary. That is:

The population standard deviations are equal.

(If there is any doubt about this, a test can be applied to the sample – see the Further reading section, page 115)

If it is assumed that the standard deviations are equal, then

$$\sigma_1 = \sigma_2 = \sigma$$

And the standard error of the difference of the two means becomes:

$$SE\left(\overline{X}_1 - \overline{X}_2\right) = \sigma\sqrt{\frac{1}{n_1} + \frac{1}{n_2}}$$

The best estimate of σ ($\hat{\sigma}$) can be obtained by 'pooling ' the two sample estimates (S_1 and S_2) as follows:

$$\hat{\sigma} = \sqrt{\frac{n_1 S_1^2 + n_2 S_2^2}{n_1 + n_2 - 2}}$$

The test statistic is as follows:

$$t = \frac{\left(\overline{X}_1 - \overline{X}_2\right) - \left(\mu_1 - \mu_2\right)}{SE\left(\overline{X}_1 - \overline{X}_2\right)}$$

And is based on the t-distribution on $(n_1 + n_2 - 2)$ degrees of freedom. (The reason for the '-2' is that 1 degree of freedom is removed from each sample by having to estimate the standard deviation of each sample).

For example, an engineer is trying to decide which cutting tool should be bought for his company's machines. He has reduced the choice to two and he has decided to purchase the one that requires less sharpening. To enable the mean time between sharpening to be found, each tool is fitted to an identical machine and times between sharpening recorded. After several days the results (in hours) were as follows:

| Tool 1: | 4.7 | 6.2 | 3.9 | 4.5 | 2.9 | 5.1 |
| Tool 2: | 3.8 | 4.9 | 5.1 | 6.3 | 6.5 | |

Which tool should he buy?

This is a two tailed test because there is no reason to suppose that one tool is any better than the other. Therefore the null and alternative hypotheses are:

$$H_0: \mu_1 - \mu_2 = 0 \quad H_1: \mu_1 - \mu_2 \neq 0$$

The critical value of t on 9 degrees of freedom at 5% is ± 2.262.

The mean and standard deviation of the two samples are:

Tool 1: $\overline{X}_1 = 4.55; \quad S_1 = 1.0161$

Tool 2: $\overline{X}_2 = 5.32; \quad S_2 = 0.9887$

The best estimate of σ is:

$$\hat{\sigma} = \sqrt{\frac{6 \times (1.0161)^2 + 5 \times (0.9887)^2}{6 + 5 - 2}}$$

$$= \sqrt{\frac{6.1948 + 4.8876}{9}}$$

$$= 1.1097$$

($n_1 = 6$ and $n_2 = 5$)

And the standard error of the difference of the two means is:

$$SE(\overline{X}_1 - \overline{X}_2) = 1.1097 \times \sqrt{\frac{1}{6} + \frac{1}{5}}$$

$$= 1.1097 \times 0.6055$$

$$= 0.6719$$

Therefore the test statistic is:

$$t = \frac{4.55 - 5.32 - 0}{0.6719}$$

$$= -1.146$$

Since −1.146 is greater than −2.262, the test statistic is *not* in the critical region. H_0 cannot be rejected and it appears that there is no significant difference between the mean sharpening times of the two tools. Choice of cutting tool cannot therefore be made on times between sharpening.

Hypothesis test for samples that are not independent

This test is often referred to as the *paired t-test* and you will understand the reason for this name from the following example.

A pharmaceutical company has developed a vitamin supplement that is supposed to improve the IQ of children. However, this claim has been challenged by a rival company who insist that there is no evidence to link IQ with vitamin intake. In order to settle the matter the Drug Advisory Council decided to carry out a test on 12 children. These children were first given an IQ test and then asked to take the recommended daily dose of the vitamin for the next 6 months. At the end of the 6 months, they were tested again. The IQ before and after taking the vitamin supplement was as follows:

Child:	1	2	3	4	5	6	7	8	9	10	11	12
Before:	110	121	95	80	130	100	105	85	95	100	82	135
After:	105	115	98	90	132	105	105	90	96	94	85	130

Do these data support either case?

The data is *not* independent because each member of the 'before' sample is related to a member of the 'after' sample by the attributes of the child. This choice of design is deliberate because it eliminates variation within the sample. In the example here, each sample has a mixture of bright and not so bright children but since the data is *paired* you can compare like with like. To do this the *difference* between each pair is calculated. This difference represents the change in IQ score for the same child and if the vitamin supplement had no effect you would expect the true average difference to be zero. A one sample *t-test* could be performed on the sample mean to see if it is significantly different from zero.

The test statistic is:

$$t = \frac{\overline{X}_D}{SE_D}$$

Where $\overline{X}_D$ is the mean of the differences and SE_D is the standard error of the differences and is given by:

$$SE_D = \frac{\hat{\sigma}_D}{\sqrt{n}}$$

Where $\hat{\sigma}_D$ is the best estimate of the population standard deviation of the differences.

Before the vitamin problem is solved you need to decide on the alternative hypothesis. The company who developed the supplement believe that IQ will be improved and the rival company believe that the IQ will not be improved. However, since it is the Drug Advisory Council who have instigated the test and don't appear to be on either side, then a two tailed test is appropriate. That is:

$$H_0: \mu_D = 0 \quad H_1: \mu_D \neq 0$$

Where μ_D is the true mean difference

The critical value of t at the 5% significance level and on 11 (12 – 1) degrees of freedom is 2.201.

The differences (after – before) are as follows:

Child:	1	2	3	4	5	6	7	8	9	10	11	12
Diff:	–5	–6	3	10	2	5	0	5	1	–6	3	–5

The average difference ($\overline{X}_D$) is 0.5833 and the standard deviation (S_D) is 4.9237.

Therefore:
$$\hat{\sigma}_D = 4.9237 \times \sqrt{\frac{12}{11}}$$
$$= 5.1427$$

and
$$SE_D = \frac{5.1427}{\sqrt{12}}$$
$$= 1.4846$$

The test statistic is:
$$t = \frac{0.5833}{1.4846}$$
$$= 0.393$$

Since 0.393 is less than 2.201 you cannot reject H_0 and therefore you would conclude that on the evidence of this data the vitamin supplement doesn't increase a child's IQ.

Hypothesis test of a proportion

Testing a sample proportion against some expected or hypothesised value (π) is another important test. The test given here is based on the normal approximation to the binomial and therefore 'n' should be large and π should not be too large or too small.

The standard error of the sampling distribution of a proportion (STEP) was given by equation 6, page 93 as:

$$\sqrt{\frac{P(1-P)}{n}}$$

However, for hypothesis testing it is the *population parameter,* π that must be used. With this substitution, the equation for STEP becomes:

$$STEP = \sqrt{\frac{\pi(1-\pi)}{n}}$$

The Z statistic is similar to that used for the test on a mean and is:

$$Z = \frac{P - \pi}{STEP}$$

The following example illustrates how the test would be carried out.

A trade union is considering strike action and intends to ballot its large membership on the issue. In order to gauge the likely result of the ballot, a survey was conducted among a random sample of members. Of the 60 people surveyed, 34 were in favour of a strike. Would the ballot give the required two thirds majority for a strike?

For a strike to be called, at least 66.7% of the membership must agree. Anything less would not be good enough. The null and alternative hypothesis should therefore be:

$H_0: \pi = 0.667$ $H_1: \pi < 0.667$

The cut-off point for the decision is a proportion of 0.667 and the test will determine whether the sample proportion (P) of $\frac{34}{60} = 0.567$ is significantly *less* than 0.667.

The critical value for a one tailed test at the 5% level is –1.645.

And:
$$STEP = \sqrt{\frac{0.667 \times (1 - 0.667)}{60}}$$
$$= 0.06084$$

and the test statistic,
$$Z = \frac{0.567 - 0.667}{0.06084}$$
$$= -1.644$$

Since –1.644 is greater (just) than –1.645, H_0 cannot be rejected. That is, it appears that the majority would be two thirds and a strike would be called. However, the critical value and test statistic are almost the same, and therefore the result is hardly conclusive. (Don't forget that the survey result is only a 'snapshot' of people's opinion at one instant in time. Some people may not have been entirely honest with their answers and others may change their opinion before the ballot.)

Hypothesis test of two proportions

If it can be assumed that the normal approximation is applicable to both proportions then the difference between the two proportions ($\pi_1 - \pi_2$) is also normally distributed. The null hypothesis will be:

$H_0: \pi_1 = \pi_2 = \pi$

and H_1 can be either one or two sided.

The estimate of the population proportion π, can be found from a weighted average of the two sample proportions P_1 and P_2.

That is:

$$\hat{\pi} = \frac{n_1 P_1 + n_2 P_2}{n_1 + n_2}$$

The standard error of the difference between the two proportions is:

$$SE(\pi_1 - \pi_2) = \sqrt{\frac{\hat{\pi}(1-\hat{\pi})}{n_1} + \frac{\hat{\pi}(1-\hat{\pi})}{n_2}}$$

And the test statistic is:

$$Z = \frac{(P_1 - P_2) - (\pi_1 - \pi_2)}{SE(\pi_1 - \pi_2)}$$

P_1 and P_2 refer to the two sample proportions.

For example, it was thought that there were more households in council tax band D in the North of England than in the South of the country. In order to discover if this was true, a random sample of 50 households were surveyed in one town in the North of England and 60 households were surveyed in a similar size town in the South of England. The number of households in this band was 19 in the North and 17 in the South. Is there a significant difference, at the 5% level of significance, between the two towns?

This is a one tailed test because it is required to find out if the proportion in the North (π_N) is greater than the proportion in the South (π_S). The null and alternative hypothesis is therefore:

$$H_0: \pi_N = \pi_S = \pi \qquad\qquad H_1: \pi_N > \pi_S$$

The critical value at 5% significance level is 1.645 (from the normal table in appendix 3, page 250).

The two proportions are: $\quad P_N = \dfrac{19}{50} = 0.38,\ $ and $\ P_S = \dfrac{17}{60} = 0.283$

And the estimate of the population proportion is:

$$\hat{\pi} = \frac{50 \times 0.38 + 60 \times 0.283}{50 + 60}$$

$$= 0.3271$$

The standard error is: $\qquad SE(\pi_1 - \pi_2) = \sqrt{\dfrac{0.3271(1-0.3271)}{50} + \dfrac{0.3271(1-0.3271)}{60}}$

$$= \sqrt{0.004402 + 0.003668}$$

$$= 0.08984$$

The value of the test statistic is: $\qquad Z = \dfrac{(0.38 - 0.283) - 0}{0.08984}$

$$= 1.080$$

Since 1.080 is less than 1.645, H_0 cannot be rejected and it appears that the proportion of households in band D is not significantly different in the two areas.

The χ^2 hypothesis test

Is it possible to compare several proportions rather than just two? The short answer is yes, but a different kind of test has to be used. To use this new test you have to group the data into categories by *counting* the number of data items that have specific properties. The test statistic is then calculated using the following formula:

$$\sum \frac{(O-E)^2}{E}$$

Where 'O' represents the observed count and 'E' represents the expected count. The formula simply says 'find the difference between the observed and expected frequency of one category, square this value to remove any negative signs and then divide by the expected frequency for that category. Repeat this for all categories and sum the individual answers'.

This test statistic follows the χ^2 distribution (pronounced *chi square*). The shape of this distribution depends on the degrees of freedom of the data. For example, for 4 degrees of freedom you would get the following shape.

The χ^2 distribution (on 4 degrees of freedom)

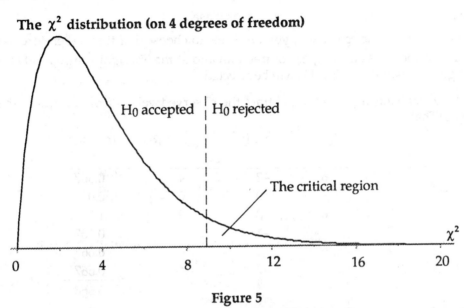

Figure 5

The area under the curve is again 1 but only one tail is used for the critical region – the upper tail. The area representing 5% has been indicated and H_0 would be rejected if the test statistic was in this region.

The critical value of χ^2 is found from the χ^2 table that you will find in appendix 3, page 252. An extract of the table is given below:

Probability (α)

df	0.995	0.99	0.9	0.1	0.05	0.025	0.01	0.005	0.001
1	0.000	0.000	0.016	2.706	3.841	5.024	6.635	7.879	10.828
2	0.010	0.020	0.211	4.605	5.991	7.378	9.210	10.597	13.816
3	0.072	0.115	0.584	6.251	7.815	9.348	11.345	12.838	16.266
4	0.207	0.297	1.064	7.779	**9.488**	11.143	13.277	14.860	18.467

For example, the critical value on 4 degrees of freedom at the 5% (0.05) significance level is 9.488. This value has been highlighted in the table above.

Two applications of the χ^2 test will be illustrated here. The first is called the 'goodness of fit' test. The second is the 'contingency table' test or the 'test of association'.

The 'goodness of fit' test

Suppose you threw a six sided die 36 times. You would *expect* the faces numbered 1 to 6 to appear the same number of times, that is 6. However you might *observe* a rather different frequency. For example, you might get the following:

Face	1	2	3	4	5	6
Frequency	4	6	9	5	4	8

Is this observed frequency due to chance effects or does it indicate that the die is biased towards the face numbered 3 and 6? The null hypothesis is that the die is fair and the alternate hypothesis is that it is biased, that is:

H_0: Die is fair $\qquad\qquad$ H_1: Die is biased

Since the sum of the frequencies is fixed, you are 'free' to choose 5 of them; therefore the degrees of freedom is 5. The value of χ^2 on 5 degrees of freedom and at the 5% significance level is 11.070. If the test statistic is greater than this value, H_0 will be rejected.

To calculate the χ^2 statistic you need to subtract the observed values from 6, square the result and then divide by 6. That is:

O	E	(O – E)	(O – E)²	$\dfrac{(O-E)^2}{E}$
4	6	–2	4	0.667
6	6	0	0	0.0
9	6	3	9	1.5
5	6	–1	1	0.167
4	6	–2	4	0.667
8	6	2	4	0.667
				3.668

The sum of these values is 3.668 and this is compared with the critical value of 11.070. H_0 cannot be rejected and you would have to assume that the die was fair. The diagram below demonstrates that the test statistic is not in the critical region.

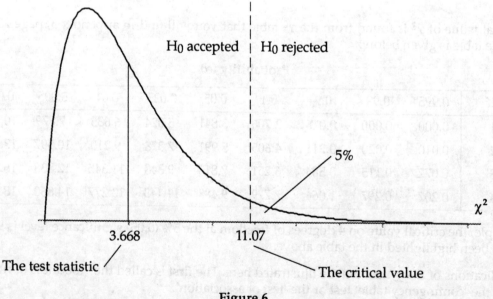

Figure 6

This is quite a simple application of the goodness of fit test since the expected values follow a uniform distribution (that is, each 'category' has the same expected value). However, the test can be applied to any situation where it is possible to calculate the expected values. The binomial (Unit 2, page 6), the Poisson (Unit 3, page 8) and the normal distributions (Unit 4, page 9) are obvious examples where these expected values could be calculated. In these examples you might want to discover whether a set of data follows one of these distributions. The degrees of freedom are found from the formula:

$$v = n - 1 - k$$

Where 'n' is the number of pairs of observed and expected frequencies and 'k' is the number of population parameters estimated from the sample. For both the binomial and the Poisson the value of k is 1, since in the case of the binomial the probability 'p' has to be estimated and for the Poisson the mean has to be estimated. For the normal distribution both the mean and the standard deviation have to be estimated, so k is 2 in this case.

The χ^2 test of association

The personnel manager of a company believes that monthly paid staff take more time off work through sickness than those staff who are paid weekly (and do not belong to the company sickness scheme). To test this theory, the sickness records for 531 employees who have been in continuous employment for the past year were analysed. The table shown below was produced, which placed employees into 3 categories according to how many days they were off work through sickness during the past year. For example, 95 monthly paid employees were off sick for less than 5 days.

Type of employee	Number of days off sick		
	Less than 5 days	5 to 10 days	More than 10 days
Monthly paid	95	47	18
Weekly paid	143	146	112

This is known as a *contingency* table. The null and alternative hypothesis are:

H_0:   There is no *association* between type of employee and number of days off sick.

H_1:   There is an association between type of employee and number of days off sick.

In order to calculate the χ^2 test statistic it is necessary to determine the expected values for each category. To do this you first have to work out the row and column totals as follows:

Type of employee	Number of days off sick			Total
	Less than 5 days	5 to 10 days	More than 10 days	
Monthly paid	95	47	18	160
Weekly paid	143	146	112	401
Total	238	193	130	561

You now need to apply some basic ideas of probability (see Unit 1, page 3) to the problem. If an employee was chosen at random, the probability that he was monthly paid would be $\frac{160}{561}$ and the probability that he would have been off sick for less than 5 days is $\frac{238}{561}$.

Therefore, using the multiplication rule for two probabilities, the probability that the person is both monthly paid *and* in the 'less than 5 days' category is $\frac{160}{561} \times \frac{238}{561}$.

Since there are 561 employees in total, the *expected* number of employees with both these attributes is:

$$\frac{160}{561} \times \frac{238}{561} \times 561 = \frac{160 \times 238}{561}$$
$$= 67.9$$

This could be written as:

$$\text{Expected value} = \frac{\text{Row Total} \times \text{Column Total}}{\text{Grand Total}}$$

and is applicable for all cells of a contingency table. The rest of the expected values can now be worked out and a table set up similar to the one used for the 'goodness of fit' test (page 112).

O	E	(O – E)	$(O-E)^2$	$\dfrac{(O-E)^2}{E}$
95	67.9	27.1	734.41	10.816
47	55.0	–8.00	64.0	1.164
18	37.1	–19.1	364.81	9.833
143	170.1	–27.1	734.41	4.318
146	138.0	8.00	64.00	0.464
112	92.9	19.10	364.81	3.927
				30.522

The sum of the χ^2 values is 30.522 and this is the test statistic for this problem. The critical value depends on the degrees of freedom of this table. As you know, degrees of freedom relates to the number of values that you are free to choose. If, for example, you choose the value for the top left hand cell, the bottom left hand cell is determined since the two cells must add to 238. Likewise you could choose the next cell along, but then all other cells are determined for you. So, for this problem, there are 2 degrees of freedom. Fortunately, there is a formula for calculating the degrees of freedom and is:

(number of columns – 1) × (number of rows – 1)

In the table above, there are 3 columns (excluding the total column) and 2 rows, so the degrees of freedom are:

$$(3 - 1) \times (2 - 1) = 2$$

The critical value for 2 degrees of freedom at the 5% significance level is 5.991 and at the 0.1% significance level it is 13.816. Therefore, since the test statistic is greater than 13.816, H_0 can be rejected and you could conclude that there does seem to be an association between staff category and the number of days off sick.

It is possible to be more specific about this association by looking at the individual χ^2 values and also the (O – E) column. The two largest values χ^2 values are 10.816 and 9.883. These both relate to the monthly paid staff and it suggests that this group of employees have a higher frequency in the 'less than 5 days category' than expected but a lower frequency in the 'more than 10 days' category.

The χ^2 test for association is a very important and useful test in the area of statistics in particular and decision making in general. However there are a few problems that you need to be aware of.

Low expected values

The test statistic follows the χ^2 distribution provided the expected values are not too small. The guideline that is normally adopted is that the expected value for any cell should be greater than 5. If any expected values are less than 5 it is possible to combine categories until this minimum expected value is achieved. Of course there must be at least 3 rows or 3 columns to be able to do this.

Two by two tables

The X^2 distribution is a continuous distribution, whereas the sample data is discrete. Normally the sample size is sufficient to avoid making a continuity correction, but this will be needed for 2×2 tables. The correction required is to *subtract* 0.5 from the *absolute* value of the difference between the observed and expected values. For example, if the difference was –2.7, the corrected value would be –2.2 (*not* –3.2)

Tables of percentages

The χ^2 test is applied to tables of frequencies *not* percentages. If you are given a table of percentages you will need to convert it to frequencies by multiplying each percentage by the total frequency. If you are not given the total frequency then it is not possible to use this test.

Further reading

Introductory Statistics for Business and Economics, Wonnacott, (WILEY)

A First Course in Statistics (2nd edition), Booth, (DP PUBLICATIONS)

Essential Statistics (3rd edition), Rees, (CHAPMAN AND HALL)

Statistics For Management, Levin, (PRENTICE-HALL)

Statistics (3rd edition), Owen and Jones, (PITMAN)

Quantitative Approaches in Business Studies, Morris, (PITMAN)

Quantitative Techniques, Lucey, (DP PUBLICATIONS)

Quantitative Analysis, Stansfield, (LONGMAN)

Correlation and regression

Introduction

The statistical analysis that you have covered so far has been concerned with the characteristics of a single variable. However, it also might be of interest to look at two variables simultaneously. For instance you might suspect that the cost of production is dependent on the quantity produced and you would like to test this hypothesis and obtain a relationship linking the variables. To carry out this analysis you would need to collect the data in pairs, and typical data is shown below:

Units produced (000's)	1	2	3	4	5	6
Production costs (£000's)	5.0	10.5	15.5	25.0	16.0	22.5

This gives you a sample of paired or *bivariate* data. A glance at this data should reveal that high production does seem to cost more although the highest cost is not paired with the highest production. This casual observation of bivariate data is not normally sufficient to discover if the variables are really related and more detailed analysis is often required.

The techniques introduced in this section will enable you to obtain answers to the following questions.

(i) Is there an association between the variables?

(ii) How strong is this association?

(iii) What is the relationship between the variables?

The technique of correlation allows answers to (i) and (ii) to be obtained and regression supplies the answer to (iii); that is *correlation is concerned with the degree of association between the variables and regression attempts to describe the nature of the relationship between the variables*. The assumption will be made that the relationship between the variables is a linear one although problems of non-linearity will be discussed later (page 125).

Before correlation and regression analysis is carried out, it is important that the data is represented graphically as this will allow you to observe any association between the variables and to identify any 'rogue' data (outliers).

Scatter diagrams

A scatter diagram is simply a way of representing a set of bivariate data by a scatter of plots. One variable is plotted on the X axis and the other on the Y axis. Normally the X variable is the one you have control over (the *independent* variable) and the Y variable is the variable that you are interested in (the *dependent* variable).

Examples of scatter diagrams are given in Figure 1 opposite. The first diagram indicates a *positive correlation* because as the number of deliveries increases so apparently does the delivery time. The second diagram indicates a *negative correlation* because as the air temperature increases the heating cost falls. The third diagram suggests that no correlation exists between salary and age of employees. The fourth diagram suggests that the quantity produced and the efficiency of a machine are correlated but not linearly.

When categorising scatter diagrams you may find it easier to draw a closed loop around the points. This loop should be drawn so that it encloses all the points but at the same time making the area within the loop as small as possible. If the loop looks like a circle, this suggests that there is little, if any, correlation, but if the loop looks more like an ellipse then this suggests that there is some correlation present. An ellipse pointing upwards would represent a positive correlation and one pointing downwards would represent a negative correlation. If you try this with diagrams 1 to 3 above you will see that this agrees with the statements already made. A loop around the points in diagram 4 would clearly show the non-linear nature of the association.

The closer the ellipse becomes to a straight line, the stronger the correlation. If the ellipse became a straight line you would say that you have perfect correlation. (Unless the straight line was horizontal, in which case there can be no correlation since the dependent variable has a constant value). An example of a perfect positive correlation would be that between the number of electrical units used and the cost of electricity. (Analysis in this situation would be pointless since the relationship between cost and units used is already known precisely).

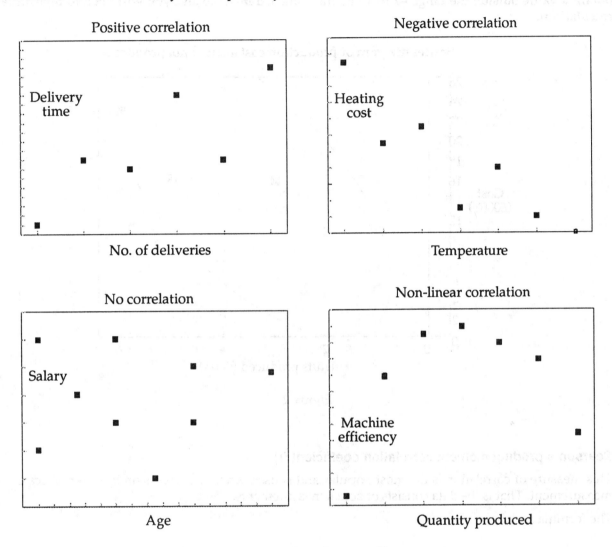

Figure 1 – Examples of scatter diagrams

The scatter diagram of the production cost data already provided is shown in Figure 2 on the following page. A closed loop has been drawn around the points and from this you should be able to make the following observations:

(i)   There is a positive correlation between volume and cost.

(ii) The loop is a fairly narrow ellipse shape suggesting that, for the range of data provided, the association is reasonably strong (but not perfect).

(iii) If the point representing 4000 units was omitted the ellipse would be narrower.

(iv) There is no evidence of non-linearity in the data.

Although these observations are valid the sample size is rather small to make definite conclusions. In practise a larger sample size would be advisable (at least twelve pairs) and the cost of 4000 units would be checked. Sometimes these 'rogue' results suggest that other factors are influencing the dependent variable and further investigation is called for (see Multiple regression, page 126).

Correlation

The technique of correlation measures the strength of the association between the variables. There are two widely used measures of correlation. These are Pearson's product moment correlation coefficient and Spearman's rank correlation coefficient. Both give a value between −1 and 1 so that −1 indicates a perfect negative correlation, +1 a perfect positive correlation and zero indicates no correlation. (If you obtain a value outside the range −1 to 1 you have made a mistake and you will need to repeat the calculation).

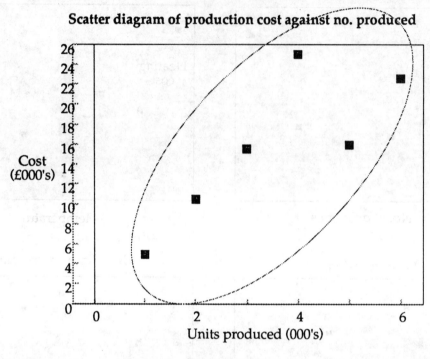

Scatter diagram of production cost against no. produced

Figure 2

Pearson's product moment correlation coefficient (r)

This measure of correlation is the most popular and is used when the data is on the interval scale of measurement. That is the data consists of actual measurements.

The formula for **r** is:

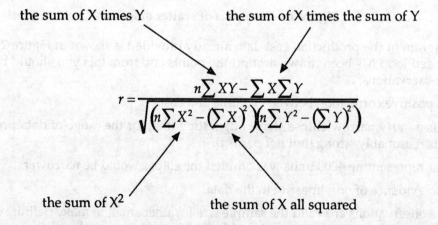

the sum of X times Y   the sum of X times the sum of Y

$$r = \frac{n\sum XY - \sum X \sum Y}{\sqrt{\left(n\sum X^2 - \left(\sum X\right)^2\right)\left(n\sum Y^2 - \left(\sum Y\right)^2\right)}}$$

the sum of X²   the sum of X all squared

This formula looks daunting at first sight but it is quite straight forward to use as you will see by applying it to the data on production volume and cost.

| Units produced | Costs | | | |
X	Y	XY	X²	Y²
1	5.0	5.0	1	25.0
2	10.5	21.0	4	110.25
3	15.5	46.5	9	240.25
4	25.0	100.0	16	625.00
5	16.0	80.0	25	256.00
6	22.5	135.0	36	506.25
$\Sigma X = 21$	$\Sigma Y = 94.5$	$\Sigma XY = 387.5$	$\Sigma X^2 = 91$	$\Sigma Y^2 = 1762.75$

Substituting these values into the formula for **r** gives:

$$r = \frac{6 \times 387.5 - 21 \times 94.5}{\sqrt{\left(6 \times 91 - (21)^2\right)\left(6 \times 1762.75 - (94.5)^2\right)}}$$

$$= \frac{340.5}{\sqrt{105 \times 1646.250}}$$

$$= 0.8190$$

This value is close to +1 which supports the assessment made from the scatter diagram that there is a fairly strong positive relationship between cost of production and production volume. However since the sample size is so small, a very high value is necessary for the correlation to be significant. You will now see how the size of the sample can be used to decide whether the value of r is significantly different from zero.

Significance of r

(This section assumes a knowledge of hypothesis testing – see Unit 8, page 18)

Don't forget that the analysis above involved a sample of data. Just as with hypothesis testing, samples are used to provide information on the population. Large samples should be more reliable than small ones so you should have more faith in a correlation coefficient of 0.8 if it had come from a sample of say 20 rather than 6.

The correlation coefficient **r** is normally assessed using a t test. As with any hypothesis test you should set up a null and alternative hypothesis:

H₀: There is no linear correlation, **r = 0**

H₁: There is some linear correlation, **r ≠ 0**

The test statistic is:

$$t = \sqrt{\frac{r^2(n-2)}{1-r^2}} \quad \text{on (n-2) degrees of freedom}$$

Substituting the value of **r** and **n** into the formula gives:

$$t = \sqrt{\frac{(0.819)^2 \times (6-2)}{1-(0.819)^2}}$$

$$= 2.855$$

From the t-tables in appendix 3 (page 251) the critical value at 5% level of significance (two tailed test) and 4 degrees of freedom is 2.776. Since the test statistic is greater (just) than the critical value you would reject the null hypothesis and conclude that there appears to be some correlation between production volume and cost.

Although it is reasonable to believe that an increase in production volume would *cause* an increase in costs, a significant correlation doesn't necessarily imply a causal relationship. For example, it might be found that car sales are related to the sales of beer, yet no one would believe that beer sales actually cause people to buy cars. In this case there is probably a third factor, such as level of disposable income that affects both variables.

Spearman's rank correlation coefficient (R)

Data does not always consist of actual measurements. For example, in market research, data may consist of opinions on a particular product. This kind of data is called ordinal data and a non-parametric test must be used. Ordinal data has the property that although they do not have actual numerical values, they can be ranked. The formula for Spearman's rank correlation coefficient (R) is:

$$R = 1 - \frac{6\sum d^2}{n(n^2 - 1)}$$

Where d is the difference in rank between pairs and n is the number of pairs. Like the product moment correlation coefficient, the value of **R** lies between +1 and –1.

To illustrate the method consider the production cost data. The data will be ranked so that the lowest cost (£5000) has a rank of 1 and the highest (£22,500) a rank of 6. Similarly for production volume.

No. of units	1	2	3	4	5	6	Total
Cost	1	2	3	6	4	5	
Difference	0	0	0	–2	1	1	0
Diff squared	0	0	0	4	1	1	6

$$R = 1 - \frac{6 \times 6}{6 \times 35}$$
$$= 0.829$$

This agrees with the previous calculation that there is a strong positive correlation between production volume and cost.

Linear regression

The technique of linear regression attempts to define the relationship between the dependent and independent variables by the means of a linear equation. This is the simplest form of equation between two variables and fortunately many situations can at least be approximated by this type of relationship.

The scatter diagram of production cost against production volume has been reproduced in Figure 3 below. You will see that a line has been drawn through the data and this line represents the linear relationship between the two variables. However, since the relationship is not perfect it is possible to draw several different lines 'by eye' through the diagram, each of which would look reasonable. However each line would represent a slightly different relationship as the gradient and/or intercept on the Y axis would be different. To decide how good a particular line is, you could find the difference between each point and the line. These differences are often referred to as the 'errors' between the actual value and that predicted by the line.

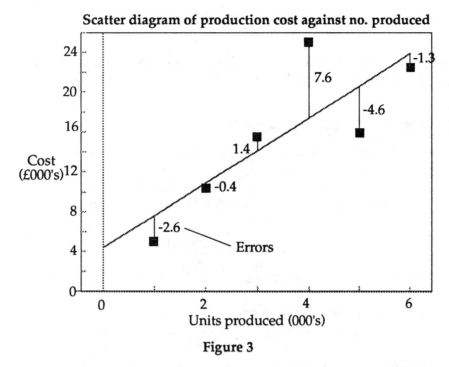

Figure 3

These errors have been represented by vertical lines on the diagram. Note that the errors below the line are negative and those above the line are positive. If you add these errors you will find that the total error is zero. Does this prove that the line is a good one? Unfortunately not, because the zero value is only obtained by adding positive and negative values. Many more lines could be found that also would give a total error of zero. The errors could be added, ignoring the sign but it can be shown that the best line or the *'line of best fit'* is obtained when the sum of the squares of the errors is minimised. Squaring the errors not only removes the minus sign but it also gives more emphasis to the large errors.

The method of least squares

Linear regression involves finding that line that minimises the sum of squares of the errors. The theory behind 'the method of least squares' is beyond the scope of this book but the application of the theory is straight forward. The most important part is to ensure that the Y variable is the dependent variable – so, for example, the production cost depends on the number of units produced.

The linear regression model is given in the form:

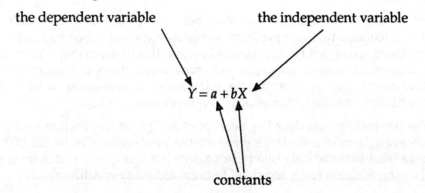

The values of 'a' and 'b' that minimise the squared errors are given by the following equations:

$$b = \frac{n\sum XY - \sum X \sum Y}{n\sum X^2 - (\sum X)^2}$$

$$a = \frac{\sum Y}{n} - b \frac{\sum X}{n}$$

You will probably realise that there are many similarities between the formula for **b** and that for **r**, the product moment correlation coefficient (page 000). Hence for the production cost example you can note that:

$$\sum X = 21, \sum Y = 94.5, \sum XY = 387.5 \text{ and } \sum X^2 = 91$$

Substituting these values into the equations for 'a' and 'b' give:

$$b = \frac{6 \times 387.5 - 21 \times 94.5}{6 \times 91 - 21^2}$$
$$= 3.2429$$

and:

$$a = \frac{94.5}{6} - \frac{3.2429 \times 21}{6}$$
$$= 4.3999$$

The regression equation for this data is therefore:

$$Y = 4.4 + 3.24X$$

This suggests that for every 1 unit (1000) rise in production volume, the production cost would rise by, on average 3.24 units (£3,240) and that when nothing is produced (X = 0), the production cost would still be £4400. This probably can be explained by factory overhead costs that are incurred even when there is no production.

Coefficient of Determination

Before a regression equation can be used effectively as a predictor for the dependent variable, it is necessary to decide how well it fits the data. One statistic that gives this information is the Coefficient of Determination. This measures the proportion of the variation in the dependent variable explained by the variation in the independent variable. It is given by r^2, which is the square of the product moment correlation coefficient. In the example of production costs the value of r is 0.8190 (see page 119) so $r^2 = 0.671$ which means that .67 or 67% of the variation in production cost is explained by the production volume.

Analysis of the errors

The errors in regression analysis are the differences between the actual value of the dependent variable and the value calculated by the regression. Whenever you carry out regression analysis it is a good idea to plot these errors, which can be easily done if you are using a computer. The errors should be small and should show no pattern; a pattern such as a string of negative errors followed by a string of positive ones might suggest that the relationship is non-linear or that an important explanatory variable has been omitted. (See Multiple regression, page 126).

The errors for the production cost data has been plotted against production cost and is shown in Figure 4 on the next page, where the large error for the production cost of £25,000 is clearly seen. There are four negative errors and only two positive ones but apart from this there is no obvious pattern. However the sample size is really too small to draw too many conclusions.

GRAPH OF ERRORS
against production cost

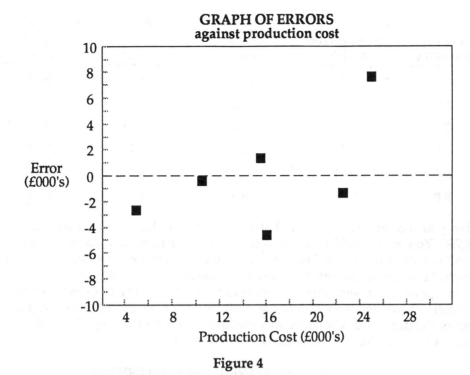

Figure 4

Prediction and estimation using linear regression

You could use the linear regression formula you worked out to estimate the production cost given a particular value of the production volume. For example suppose you wanted to produce 2500 units. From the equation on the opposite page you would substitute 2.5 for X. That is:

$$Y = 4.4 + 3.24 \times 2.5$$
$$= 12.5$$

So 2500 units would cost about £12,500 on average.

However you might be concerned about the accuracy of this figure. Unless the regression was perfect there will be some uncertainty with any estimate using the regression equation. You will recall that with univariate data, confidence intervals were obtained for the mean value (see Unit 6, page 13) to take account of the scatter of values around the mean; the larger the scatter, the larger the confidence interval. For bivariate data the scatter is around the regression line rather than a single value but the same principles would apply, except that the calculations are likely to be more involved. You also would expect that the confidence interval would be larger if you tried to predict the vale of Y outside the range of the data. The formula for the confidence interval for an estimated value of Y ($\hat{Y}$) is quite complicated and is as follows:

$$\hat{Y} \pm t_p \times \hat{\sigma}_e \sqrt{\frac{1}{n} + \frac{X_0 - \overline{X}}{\sum \left(X - \overline{X}\right)^2}}$$

where t_p is the critical t value for p% confidence interval and with (n-2) degrees of freedom, n is the number of pairs of observations, $\overline{X}$ is the mean value of X and X_0 is the value of X you wish to use for your confidence interval.

$\hat{\sigma}_e$ is the standard error of the Y estimate (that is the standard deviation of the residuals) and is given by:

$$\hat{\sigma}_e = \frac{\sum \left(Y - \hat{Y}\right)^2}{n - 2}$$

You would normally use a computer (see next page) to calculate confidence intervals. The table below has been calculated using a spreadsheet.

No. of Units (X_0) (000's)	Estimated cost (£000's)	95% half width	95% confidence interval Lower limit	Upper limit
0.0	4.4	12.28	−7.88	16.68
1.0	7.64	9.55	−1.91	17.19
2.5	12.51	6.24	6.27	18.75
3.5	15.75	5.39	10.36	21.14
5.0	20.61	7.17	13.45	27.78
6.0	23.86	9.55	14.31	33.41

From this table you should be able to see that for 2500 units, the cost will be somewhere between £6,270 to £18,750. You also should notice that the confidence interval is lowest at X_0 of 3.5 and becomes larger either side of this value. The value 3.5 is the mean of the X values and the confidence interval will always be at a minimum at this point. (The regression line always passes through the mean of X and Y). The upper and lower confidence intervals have been drawn on the graph in Figure 5 below and this clearly shows that the width of the confidence interval increases as you get further away from the mean of the data. You will notice that the lower limit on the graph has not been allowed to go below zero as a negative cost is meaningless in this context.

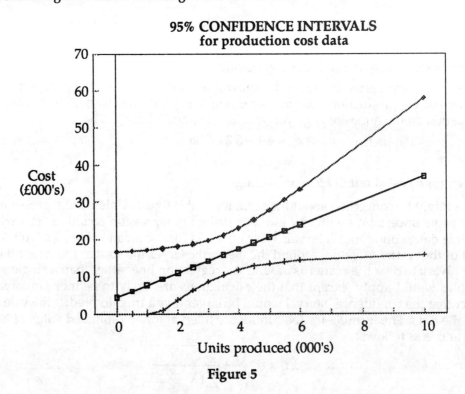

95% CONFIDENCE INTERVALS
for production cost data

Figure 5

Computational aids in correlation and regression analysis

Calculating the correlation coefficient and the regression coefficients can be tedious, particularly for large quantities of data. Most scientific calculators (e.g the Casio FX series) can be used to obtain the ΣX, ΣX^2, etc and for a couple of pounds more a calculator containing the linear regression function can be purchased.

However, as you have seen above, calculating confidence intervals for regression estimates is quite involved even using advanced calculators. For this calculation and indeed for all regression work a computer software package is recommended. The most widely available and easy to use is a spreadsheet (for example LOTUS 1-2-3).

You probably will have used a spreadsheet elsewhere on your course so you will understand the basic operation such as the graph option. You can use the graph option to obtain scatter diagrams quickly and easily. To do this it is necessary to choose the XY graph option and to plot symbols only.

To carry out a regression analysis with a spreadsheet you would use the DATA REGRESSION option. Do ensure that your output-range is large enough for the output (at least 4 columns by 10 rows). An example of the output is shown below:

Qty X	Cost Y		
1	5.0	Regression Output:	
2	10.5	Constant	**4.4**
3	15.5	Std Err of Y Est	4.752442
4	25.0	r Squared	0.670732
5	16.0	No. of Observations	6
6	22.5	Degrees of Freedom	4
		X Coefficient(s)	**3.242857**
		Std Err of Coef.	1.136051

The values of 'a' and 'b' have been highlighted and you will see that these agree with the values already obtained. You also will notice that r squared has been calculated as has the standard error of the Y estimate (Std Err of Y Est). For the confidence interval calculation you will need to write your own formula (see the book by Soper in the further reading section on the next page). Alternatively use a statistical package such as MINITAB.

Non-linearity

The most important assumption that is made when carrying out regression analysis is that of linearity. A scatter diagram will indicate if this assumption is valid, provided that you don't intend to extrapolate beyond the range of the data. Where non-linearity cannot be assumed then it is either necessary to use non-linear regression or to try to 'straighten' the data using a suitable transformation. The latter technique is the easiest and involves carrying out some mathematical manipulation on either the X or Y (or both) variables. A very common transformation is the logarithmic (or log) transformation and is applied where the relationship is likely to take the form:

$$Y = a\,b^X$$

This looks complicated but it can be made linear by taking logs of both sides of the equation. That is:

$$\log Y = \log a + X \log b$$

If log Y is plotted against X a linear relationship should be observed.

For example suppose the following data relates to sales (£m) of a particular make of car.

Year (X)	1987	1988	1989	1990	1991
Sales (Y)	6.5	3.2	2.2	1.3	.75

If you assign the numbers 1 to 5 for the years 1987 to 1991 and plot this, you will get the scatter diagram shown in Figure 6, opposite.

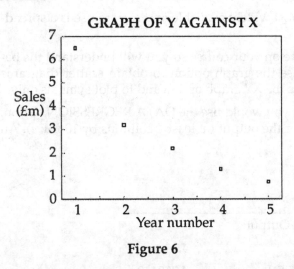

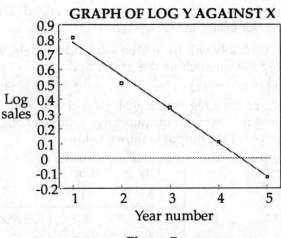

Figure 6   Figure 7

Although a straight line could be fitted to this data it wouldn't be a very good fit because the relationship is clearly non-linear. Also a linear relationship would suggest that at some point in the future negative sales would result! To see whether a log transformation would straighten the data, the log of the Y values are found (a spreadsheet is very useful here) and then log Y is plotted against X.

This has been done in Figure 7 above, using log to the base 10.

A regression has been carried out (again using a spreadsheet) and the regression line fitted to the graph. Notice how close to a straight line the data has become. The correlation coefficient is very high at 0.996. From the regression analysis the constant (**log a**) is 1.009971 and the X coefficient (**log b**)is −0.22669. The inverse of these figures gives you a and b, so that **a** = 10.23 and **b** = 0.593. The relationship is therefore:

$$Y = 10.23 \times 0.593^X$$

This suggests that in year 6 the sales will be

$$10.23 \times 0.593^6 = £0.445m$$

Multiple regression

There are many instances where more than one factor is responsible for the variation in the dependent variable. For instance, production cost may be thought to be related to the production volume, age of machinery, the utilisation of the equipment and skill of the operator. The technique of multiple regression allows a single equation to be found that would incorporate some or all of these factors. A statistical software package such as MINITAB is normally used to obtain this equation, although a spreadsheet can again be used.

Further reading

A First Course in Statistics, DJ Booth, (DP PUBLICATIONS)

Introductory Statistics for Business and Economics, Wonnacott, (WILEY)

Statistics For Management, R Levin, (PRENTICE-HALL)

Quantitative Techniques, T Lucey, (DP PUBLICATIONS)

MINITAB Handbook, Ryan, Joiner, (PWS -KENT)

Statistics with Lotus 1-2-3, J Soper, (CHARTWELL-BRATT)

Quantitative Analysis, E Stansfield, (LONGMAN)

Spreadsheets for Business Students, C West, (DP PUBLICATIONS)

Statistics (3rd edition), Owen and Jones, (PITMAN)

Quantitative Approaches in Business Studies Morris (PITMAN)

Time series analysis

Introduction

Many variables have values that change with time. For example the weekly sales of ice cream, the monthly unemployment figures and the daily production rates for a factory. The changing value of such variables over a period of time is called a time series.

A time series can be likened to a set of bivariate data (see Correlation and regression, page 116) where the dependent variable is the variable of interest (for example sales) and the independent variable is time. However linear regression analysis requires that the relationship between the dependent and independent variables should be linear, which as you will see, rarely occurs.

The analysis of a time series will tell you about the behaviour of the variable over this time period. If you make the assumption that the future will behave exactly like the past then the analysis will allow you to make a prediction of the future value of this variable. This method is only suitable for the immediate future (up to about five periods ahead) and if you want to forecast further you will need to use other techniques, such as judgemental or causal methods. There are very many forecasting techniques and in particular there are many time series analysis methods. You will only meet two methods here, the decomposition model and exponential smoothing, but these two techniques are easy to understand and probably the most popular.

The decomposition model

This model assumes that a time series is made up of several components. These components are:

- ❒ Trend
- ❒ Seasonality
- ❒ Cyclic behaviour
- ❒ Randomness

The trend represents the long run behaviour of the data and can be increasing, decreasing or constant. Seasonality relates to periodic fluctuations that repeat themselves at fixed intervals of time. Cyclic behaviour represents the ups and downs of the economy or of a specific industry. It is a long term fluctuation and for practical purposes is usually ignored. Randomness is always present in a time series and represents variation that cannot be explained. Some time series (for example share prices) have a very high random component and the forecasts of these series will be subject to a high degree of error.

Examples of time series are shown in graph form in Figures 1 and 2 opposite. You should notice that both series show a marked seasonal component since the pattern repeats themselves at regular intervals. In the case of the Star petrol station, the highest sales always occurs on a Saturday and the lowest on a Monday. The time series for the quarterly sales of a sun cream by Mace Skin Care plc shows a peak in quarter 3 and a trough in quarter 1. You also should notice that the sales of the sun cream appears to have increased rapidly during the three year period.

Isolating the trend

To isolate the trend you need to remove the seasonal fluctuations. In the case of the petrol sales the pattern repeats itself every week, so perhaps the average sales each week would be a useful calculation? Well, yes and no. The average would certainly smooth the variation from day to day but it also would eliminate most of the data! An average for each of the three weeks would reduce the quantity of data from twenty one values to three. However why use Monday to Sunday as a week? Why not

Tuesday to Monday or Wednesday to Tuesday? If you think along these lines you will see that many more than three averages can be obtained. This is called moving averages since the average is moved by one time period each time. The calculations for the first three averages are shown in the table below. Notice that the first average has been placed alongside Thursday, this is because Thursday is the middle of the week that starts on Monday.

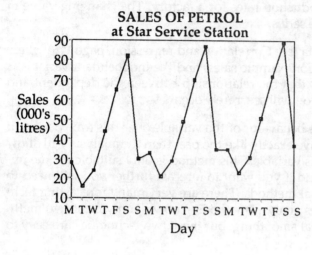

Figure 1

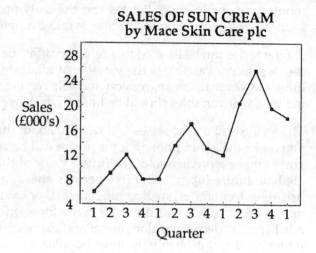

Figure 2

Day	Petrol sales (000's litres)	Moving average
Monday	28	
Tuesday	16	
Wednesday	24	
Thursday	44	(28+16+24+44+65+82+30)/7 = 41.3
Friday	65	(16+24+44+65+82+30+33)/7 = 42.0
Saturday	82	(24+44+65+82+30+33+21)/7 = 42.7
Sunday	30	
Monday	33	
Tuesday	21	

The complete moving average has been superimposed on the original time series graph and is shown in Figure 3 opposite.

There is no doubt that the moving average has smoothed the data and therefore this second series should represent the trend. You can see from the graph that there is a slight upward movement to this trend.

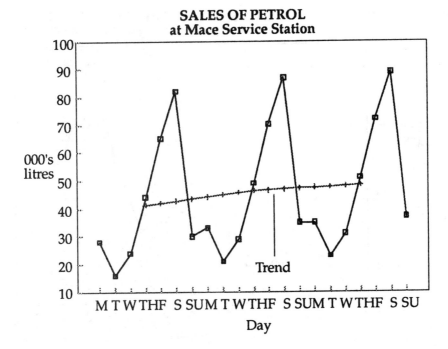

Figure 3

Isolating the trend – an even series

The Star Petrol Station example illustrated the case where the moving average was based on an odd number of periods (seven days). However with the sun cream series there is an even number of periods (four quarters). The problem with this is that the middle of the year falls between quarter two and three. This wouldn't be very helpful since the original data relates to a specific quarter. (How would you plot a value between two quarters and what would this value mean?). To get around this problem, centred moving averages are used. The moving averages are worked out as before, placing the averages between periods. Pairs of averages are then taken and the average of the averages can be written down alongside a specific period. The table below illustrates the calculations.

Year	Quarter	Sales	Moving average	Centred moving average
	1	6		
	2	9		
			8.75	
	3	12		(8.75+9.25)/2
			9.25	
	4	8		(9.25+10.38)/2
			10.38	
	1	8		
	2	13.5		

This procedure has been completed and the centred moving averages plotted. Figure 4 clearly shows the rapidly rising trend values.

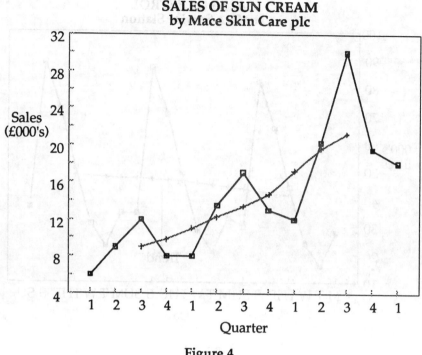

SALES OF SUN CREAM
by Mace Skin Care plc

Figure 4

Isolating the seasonal component

There are two models that will allow you to isolate the seasonal component. The first is the additive model and is applicable if the seasonal swings are a constant difference from the trend. The second is the multiplicative model and is applicable if the seasonal swings are a percentage of the trend; that is the seasonal swing will depend on the value of the trend at that point.

In equation form the additive model is: $$Y = T + S + C + R$$

and the multiplicative model is: $$Y = T \times S \times C \times R$$

where Y is the variable of interest, T is the trend, S is the seasonal component, C is the cyclic component and R is the random element.

In the Star Petrol Station example the seasonal swings about the trend appear reasonably constant (see Figure 3), so an additive model is probably appropriate here.

In the sun cream example the seasonal swings about the trend are increasing (see Figure 4), so the multiplicative model is probably the better model. However it is not always so clear cut and sometimes both models are tried and the results compared. To show this, both models will now be applied to the sun cream example.

To obtain the seasonal differences, the additive model can be rearranged as: $S + C + R = Y - T$

So the value of the variable minus the trend value at that point will give you the seasonal difference plus the cyclic and random components. The cyclic component can only be isolated when values of the variable Y are available over many years (at least twenty), which is rare. Usually the cyclic component is ignored and its effect (if any) forms part of the random element.

For quarter 3 of 1990 the estimate of the seasonal difference is $12 - 9 = 3$. This tells you that sales for quarter 3 in 1990 is 3 units (£3000) above the trend. For quarter 4 of 1990 the seasonal difference is -1.81 ($8 - 9.81$), which means the sales are 1.81 below the trend. You can see the complete table below, giving the centred moving averages and the remaining values of the seasonal differences.

Year	Quarter	Sales (£000's)	Centred moving aver- age	Seasonal dif- ference
1990	1	6.00		
	2	9.00		
	3	12.00	9.00	3.00
	4	8.00	9.81	–1.81
1991	1	8.00	11.00	–3.00
	2	13.50	12.25	1.25
	3	17.00	13.38	3.63
	4	13.00	14.72	–1.72
1992	1	12.00	17.19	–5.19
	2	20.25	19.63	0.63
	3	30.00	21.19	8.81
	4	19.50		
1993	1	18.00		

If you look at these figures you will notice that for the same quarter number the seasonal difference varies. This is the random element. This variation can best be observed in a table similar to the one below, which also allows the average seasonal difference to be calculated.

Quarter	1	2	3	4	
1990			3.00	–1.81	
1991	–3.00	1.25	3.63	–1.72	
1992	–5.19	0.63	8.81		
Average	–4.09	0.94	5.15	–1.77	Sum = 0.22
Adj. Av.	–4.15	0.88	5.09	–1.82	Sum = 0.00

The use of an average value helps to remove some of the random component. These averages should sum to zero since they should cancel out over the year. In the example above you will see that:

$$-4.09 + 0.94 + 5.15 - 1.77 = 0.22,$$

which is clearly not zero.

If each average is reduced by

$$\frac{0.22}{4} = 0.06$$

then you will get the adjusted figures above and you should check that their sum is now zero.

The calculations for the multiplicative model are similar except that S is called the seasonal factor and is worked out by *dividing* Y by T. The table of seasonal factors is shown below.

Year	Quarter	Sales (£000's)	Centred mov- ing average	Seasonal factor
1990	1	6.00		
	2	9.00		

	3	12.00	9.00	1.333
	4	8.00	9.81	0.815
1991	1	8.00	11.00	0.727
	2	13.50	12.25	1.102
	3	17.00	13.38	1.271
	4	13.00	14.72	0.883
1992	1	12.00	17.19	0.698
	2	20.25	19.63	1.032
	3	30.00	21.19	1.416
	4	19.50		
1993	1	18.00		

In this model a seasonal factor above 1.0 represents sales above the trend and a value below 1.0 represents sales below the trend. The table below is again used to calculate the adjusted average factors.

Quarter	1	2	3	4	
1990			1.333	0.815	
1991	0.727	1.102	1.271	0.883	
1992	0.698	1.032	1.416		
Average	0.713	1.067	1.340	0.849	Sum = 3.969
Adj. Av.	0.718	1.075	1.351	0.856	Sum = 4.000

Each average was adjusted by multiplying its value by 1.0078 (4.0/3.969), since the sum of the averages should in this case be 4.0. Some people prefer to quote the seasonal factors as percentages, so 0.718 would be 71.8% and 1.075 would be 107.5%.

Analysis of errors

Once you have isolated the trend and seasonal components it is a good idea to see how well the model fits the data. This is particularly important when you are not sure whether the additive or multiplicative model is the correct model to use.

For the additive model $Y = T + S$, so the Y variable can be predicted by adding the trend to the relevant adjusted average seasonal difference. For the multiplicative model $Y = T \times S$, so the prediction is made by multiplying the trend and adjusted average seasonal factor. In both cases the difference between the actual value and predicted value gives you the error in the prediction. For the sun cream example, the errors for both models have been calculated and can be seen below.

Year	Qtr	Sales	T	Additive			Multiplicative		
				S	Pred. sales	Error	S	Pred. sales	Error
1990	1	6.00							
	2	9.00							
	3	12.00	9.00	5.09	14.09	−2.09	1.351	12.15	−0.15
	4	8.00	9.81	−1.82	7.99	0.01	0.856	8.40	−0.40
1991	1	8.00	11.00	−4.15	6.85	1.15	0.718	7.90	0.10
	2	13.50	12.25	0.88	13.13	0.37	1.075	13.17	0.33
	3	17.00	13.38	5.09	18.46	−1.46	1.351	18.06	−1.06
	4	13.00	14.72	−1.82	12.90	0.10	0.856	12.60	0.40
1992	1	12.00	17.19	−4.15	13.04	−1.04	0.718	12.35	−0.35
	2	20.25	19.63	0.88	20.51	−0.26	1.075	21.10	−0.85
	3	30.00	21.19	5.09	26.28	3.72			
	4	19.50							
1993	1	18.00							

The errors should be small and show no pattern. Even with small quantities of data the easiest way to look at the errors is by means of a graph. Figures 5 and 6, below show that the multiplicative model gives the smallest errors and is therefore the better model, which is what was expected.

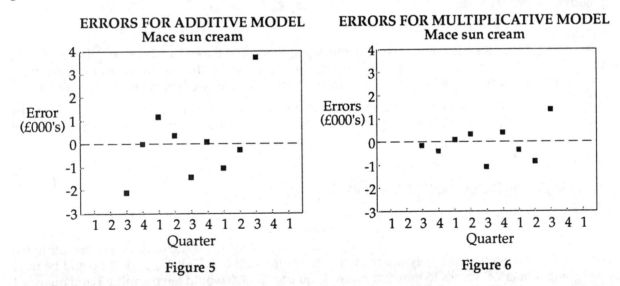

ERRORS FOR ADDITIVE MODEL
Mace sun cream

ERRORS FOR MULTIPLICATIVE MODEL
Mace sun cream

Figure 5   **Figure 6**

Apart from a graphical display of the errors, it is possible to analyse them statistically. Two statistics are normally calculated, the mean absolute deviation (MAD) and the mean square deviation (MSE). The formulae for these are:

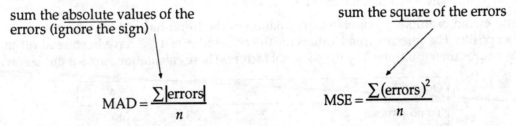

sum the <u>absolute</u> values of the errors (ignore the sign)

sum the <u>square</u> of the errors

$$MAD = \frac{\sum |errors|}{n} \qquad MSE = \frac{\sum (errors)^2}{n}$$

The MAD statistic is simply the mean of the absolute errors (or deviations), while MSE is the mean of the squared deviations. Both statistics are valid but you will find that many statisticians favour the

MSE statistic. One reason for this is that squaring puts more emphasis on large errors. For the sun cream example you will find that the values of MAD and MSE for both models are:

	MAD	MSE
Additive	1.13	2.55
Multiplicative	0.56	0.48

Both statistics support the conclusion that the multiplicative model is better since they are both lower than the additive values.

One problem of checking the accuracy of the models in this way is that the same data is used to check the model as was used to create it in the first place. A way around this problem is to use half the data to create the model and the other half to test it. This is only possible if a reasonably large amount of data is available.

Seasonally adjusted series

I am sure that you have heard the phrase 'seasonally adjusted' when economic time series are mentioned by the media. A common example is unemployment. If a series is seasonally adjusted it means that the seasonal component has been removed, leaving the trend component. By seasonally adjusting unemployment figures, for example, it is easy to tell what is happening to this important economic variable.

For the multiplicative model the series is de-seasonalized by dividing the value of the Y variable by the seasonal factor. That is:

$$T \times R = Y/S$$

However as you can see the random component is still there so the trend will not be quite as smooth as that calculated by moving averages. To illustrate this the series for the sun cream example has been de-seasonalized and plotted with the actual data and trend. You can see this in Figure 7 opposite.

However the advantage of using the seasonal factors in this way is that all values of the series can be seasonally adjusted, including the most recent values. Moving averages, by their very nature, cannot do this.

Forecasting using the decomposition model

One purpose of time series analysis is to use the results to forecast future values of the series. The procedure for this is to extrapolate the trend or seasonally adjusted series into the future and then apply the seasonal component to the forecast trend. There are various methods of extrapolating the trend. If the trend is approximately linear then linear regression (see Unit 13, page 28) could be used by assigning numerical values to time (for example quarter 1 1990 would have a value 1 and quarter 1 1993 would have a value 13). However, you will often find it easier to extrapolate by eye ('eyeballing') since other factors can then be considered, if necessary. If there is doubt about the future behaviour of the trend, you could make two or three different extrapolations to give different forecasts (say an optimistic and a pessimistic one).

For the sun cream example, a possible extrapolation of the trend has been made and can be seen in Figure 7 opposite. The forecast trend values for the remainder of 1993 have been read off this graph and these figures then multiplied by the seasonal factors. These calculations are set out below.

Quarter	2	3	4
Trend forecast	28	33	38
Seasonal factor	1.075	1.351	0.856
Forecast sales (£000's)	30.1	44.6	32.5

Exponential smoothing

The moving average method is a means of smoothing a time series. You saw how to use the method to remove the seasonal variations when applying the decomposition method to a time series. However moving averages can be applied to any time series where there is some unwanted random fluctuation. By smoothing such a series the underlying trend can be seen more clearly.

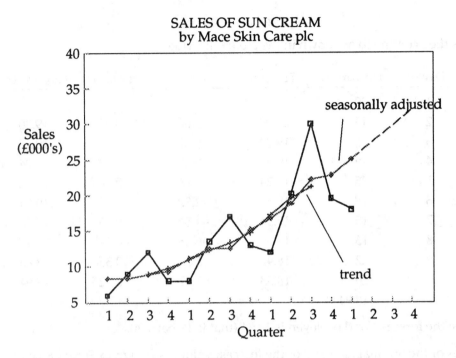

SALES OF SUN CREAM
by Mace Skin Care plc

Figure 7

Unfortunately moving averages in themselves are not very useful for forecasting. As you have seen, the problem with this method is that the moving average series ends before the original time series does and it would need extrapolating if a forecast were to be made. In addition the method of moving averages gives equal weight to all the data, which may not be desirable.

To overcome these problems the technique of exponential smoothing is often used where a short term forecast is required (that is the next period). The formula for this technique is very simple. It is:

Next forecast = Last forecast + α × error in last forecast

Where α (alpha) is a smoothing constant. This constant takes a value between 0 and 1 so that the next forecast will simply be the last forecast plus a fraction of the last error. The error in the last forecast is the actual value minus the forecast.

To illustrate this technique imagine that you are responsible for ensuring that the Small Brewery company has sufficient barrels available to store its beer. Full barrels are sent out and empty ones returned. You need to know how many barrels will be returned the next day to plan production. If insufficient barrels are available, beer is wasted whereas if more barrels than expected are returned you may have lost sales.

There are two problems with exponential smoothing. The first is what value of alpha to use. This can only be found by trial and error and you may even have to change the value in the light of experience. It is usually found that a value between 0.05 and 0.3 gives the smallest values of MAD or MSE. For the Small Brewery company, a value of 0.1 has been chosen.

The second problem is how to get the first forecast since a last forecast is required. Some people choose a suitable value while others prefer a warm up period. Once several forecasts have been made the starting value becomes less important anyway, but let us suppose that you have decided to use the warm up method. You are to use the last ten days for this purpose and therefore your first proper forecast will be for day eleven. The number of barrels returned over the last ten days are:

Day	1	2	3	4	5	6	7	8	9	10
No. of barrels	20	13	19	19	25	17	15	13	22	20

If you take the forecast for day two as the actual for day one then the error is –7 (13 – 20) and the forecast for day three becomes:

$$20 + (0.1 \times -7) = 19.3$$

The process is then continued as shown in the table following.

Day	No. barrels	Forecast	Error	$\alpha \times$ error	Next forecast
1	20				
2	13	20.00	–7.00	–0.70	19.30
3	19	19.30	–0.30	–0.03	19.27
4	19	19.27	–0.27	–0.03	19.24
5	25	19.24	5.76	0.58	19.82
6	17	19.82	–2.82	–0.28	19.54
7	15	19.54	–4.54	–0.45	19.08
8	13	19.08	–6.08	–0.61	18.47
9	22	18.47	3.53	0.35	18.83
10	20	18.83	1.17	0.12	18.94
11	18.94				

As you can see the forecast for day eleven is 18.94 (that is 19 barrels).

The time series of the original data and of the forecast values is shown in Figure 8 below. Also shown is the forecast using an alpha of 0.5 and you will see that a value of 0.1 gives a smoother series. This is generally true, the smaller the value of alpha the greater the smoothing effect.

In terms of accuracy using the sample data, an alpha of 0.1 gives an MSE of 17.96, while for alpha of 0.5 the MSE value is 23.21.

NUMBERS OF RETURNED BARRELS
Best Brewery Ltd

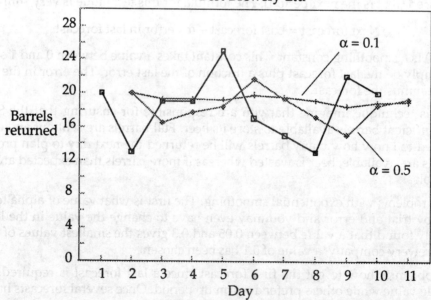

Figure 8

Simple exponential smoothing is a very useful and easy to use short term forecasting technique. However it will lag behind a series that is undergoing a sharp change such as a series that has a seasonal component or a steep trend. It can still be used on seasonal data however, provided the series has been de-seasonalized first.

Further reading

Introductory Statistics for Business and Economics, Wonnacott, (WILEY)

A First Course in Statistics (2nd edition), Booth, (DP PUBLICATIONS)

Essential Statistics (3rd edition), Rees, (CHAPMAN AND HALL)

Statistics (3rd edition), Owen and Jones, (PITMAN)

Business Forecasting in a LOTUS 1-2-3 environment, Lewis, (WILEY)

Quantitative Approaches in Business Studies, Morris, (PITMAN)

Spreadsheets for Business Students, West, (DP PUBLICATIONS)

Managerial Decisions with the Microcomputer, Bridge, (ALLAN)

Statistics with Lotus 1-2-3, Soper, (CHARTWELL-BRATT)

MINITAB Handbook, Ryan, Joiner, (PWS-KENT)

Network analysis

Introduction

Whenever a large or complex project is undertaken a great deal of planning is necessary. Building a house is a good example as there are many tasks or activities that have to be completed, some of which can proceed at the same time while others have to wait until preceding tasks are completed. Without careful planning, you might find that materials for a particular activity are not delivered on time or an electrician is not available when he is required. Delays in the project would result and you would find that the cost is far higher than it should be.

Network analysis is the collective name of a set of techniques that are used to plan projects where there are a number of interdependent activities. The four main techniques are:

> Critical path analysis
>
> Resource scheduling
>
> Cost scheduling
>
> PERT analysis

Critical path analysis

This technique allows the time of the project and the slack (or *float*) of individual activities to be determined. If an activity has zero float you would say that it was *critical* because any delay in that activity would delay the entire project.

Before critical path analysis (or CPA) is used it is first necessary to make a list of all the activities, their durations and which activities must immediately precede them. Rather than use house building as an example you may find it easier to consider a rather simpler project such as building a garage. Assuming that you have obtained planning permission and bought the materials you will probably want to employ a bricklayer for the walls. Before the walls are built you will need to dig the foundations and lay the base. Once the walls are built other tasks can start such as building the roof and fitting the window frames. A possible list with details of the immediate preceding activities and the duration in days is shown below.

Activity	Description	Immediate preceding activities	Duration (Days)
A	Obtain bricklayer	–	10
B	Dig the foundations	–	8
C	Lay the base	B	1
D	Build the walls	A and C	8
E	Build the roof	D	3
F	Tile the roof	E	2
G	Make window frames	–	3
H	Fit the window frames	D and G	1
I	Fit glass to frames	H	1
J	Fit the door	E	1
K	Paint the door and window frames	I and J	2
L	Point the brickwork	D	2

Once this list has been completed, it is necessary to display it on a diagram. A project can be displayed using either the *activity-on-arrow* method or the *activity-on-node* approach. The basic diagram for each method is shown below. In the activity-on-arrow method the activity is represented by the line between two nodes; the nodes represents the start and end of an activity. In the activity-on-node approach the node represents the activity and the lines the dependencies between activities. Both methods have their devotees and I shall use the activity-on-node method as this is a little easier to draw and avoids the use of dummy activities.

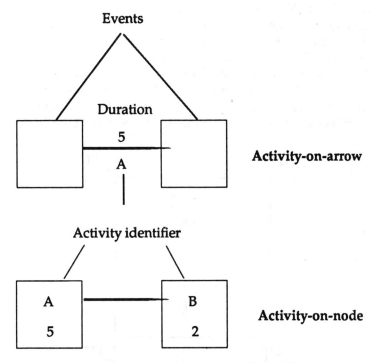

Figure 1 – Network methods

Activity-on-node

The basic diagram for the garage problem is shown below. You will see that the name of each activity is displayed in the box together with the duration. You will also see that there are start and end nodes. This is to ensure that every activity has at least one line entering and one line leaving its node.

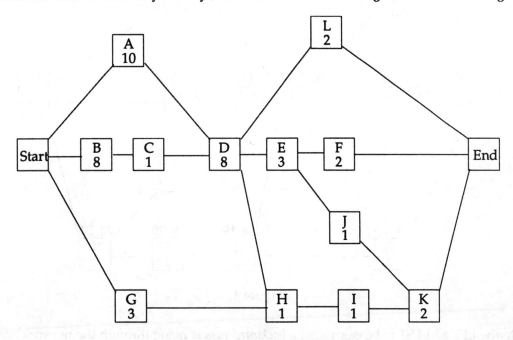

Figure 2 – The garage problem

For this method you need to display 4 additional pieces of information on each node. They are the earliest start time of the activity (EST), the latest start time (LST), the earliest finish time (EFT), and the latest finish time (LFT). This information will be displayed as in Figure 3.

In order to calculate the EST and EFT a *forward pass* is made through the network. If the start is at time zero then the EST of activities A, B and G is zero and their EFT is 10, 8 and 3 respectively. The EST of activity C must be 8 since it can start as soon as B is completed. However what about activity D? This activity cannot start until both A and C are completed and as A is completed later than C then activity A determines the EST of D, which must be 10. This is the general rule when calculating the EST – *if there are two or more choices the EST is the larger of the EFT's of the preceding activities*. From this you will see that the EST of K must be 22 and not 20. If this forward pass is continued you should get the diagram in Figure 4. From this diagram you will see that the project will take 24 days in total.

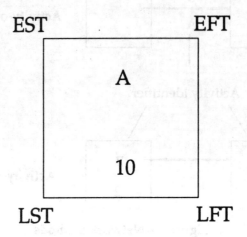

Figure 3

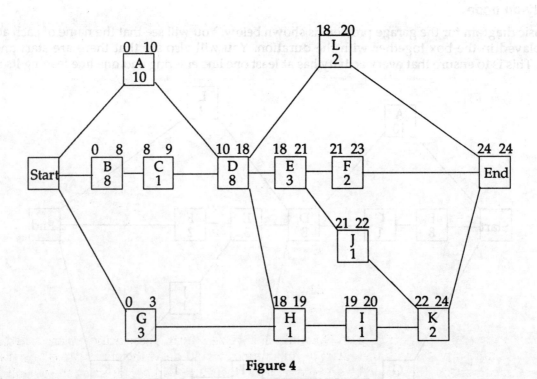

Figure 4

To enable the LFT and LST to be calculated a *backward pass* is made through the network, starting at the END node. The LFT of activity F, K and L must be 24 since the project is only complete when all these activities have been completed. The LST of F, K and L must all be 22 days since the duration of all three activities are 2 weeks. To calculate the LFT of all other activities involves a process similar to that for the forward pass, with one difference, which is *that when there is a choice the smallest value is chosen.* This can be seen at E where the LST of F and J is 22 and 21 respectively. To enable J to be completed at its LFT it must have started by time 21. The completed network is shown in Figure 5.

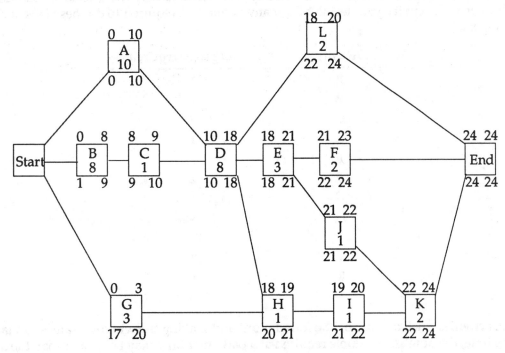

Figure 5 – The completed network

Calculation of the floats

The float is the difference between the EST and LST (or between the EFT and LFT) for each activity. Using the network above the floats are as follows.

Activity	EST	LST	Float
A	0	0	0
B	0	1	1
C	8	9	1
D	10	10	0
E	18	18	0
F	21	22	1
G	0	17	17
H	18	20	2
I	19	21	2
J	21	21	0
K	22	22	0
L	18	22	4

From this you can see that activities A,D,E,J and K have zero float. These activities are called *critical* activities because any delay in their start or finish times would delay the entire project by the same amount. The other activities could be delayed by up to their float without affecting the overall project time. For example activity B (dig foundations) could be delayed by one day but this activity would then become critical. You will notice that the critical activities form a path through the network – this is called the *critical path*. However it is possible to have more than one critical path as you will see when crashing is looked at (see page 144).

Resource scheduling

Activities of a project often involve resources of one kind or another. In the garage building example, labour is the obvious resource since each activity requires people to do the work. Perhaps you have asked a friend or neighbour to help and the two of you intend to help the bricklayer and do the less skilled jobs. For each activity you decide how many people are required to do these jobs and you get the following list.

Activity	No. of people required
A	0
B	2
C	2
D	1
E	1
F	2
G	1
H	1
I	1
J	2
K	1
L	1

Since some activities, such as digging the foundations and making the window frames can take place at the same time, the number of people required at a particular time may be greater than the availability. However it may be possible to delay non-critical activities such as making the window frames sufficiently to avoid this problem. The critical path network cannot easily solve this problem because this network is designed to show the order in which activities take place rather than when they take place. A better chart to use is the *Gantt* chart. A Gantt chart is like a bar chart that has been turned on its side. The horizontal axis is time and each activity is represented by a bar, the start of the bar is initially the EST and the end of the bar is the EFT. The float of an activity is represented by a dotted line. The Gantt chart for the garage project is shown in Figure 6, below.

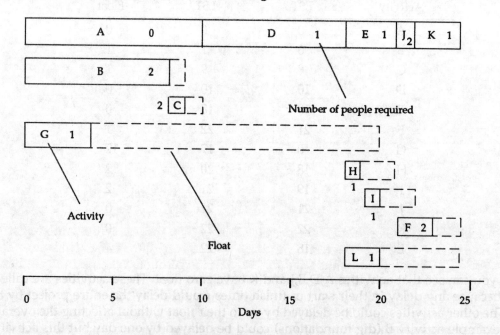

Figure 6 – The Gantt chart

142

You will see that the bars representing the critical activities have all been placed on one line – this is because each activity follows one another on the critical path. The non-critical activities should however be placed on separate lines so that their floats can be clearly shown. The number of people required has been added to each bar and if you add up the total number of people required each day you should find that this exceeds 2 on several occasions. The figures are given in the table opposite.

Day	Number of people required
0-3	3
4-8	2
9-10	0
11-18	1
19-20	3
21	1
22	4
23	3
24	1

You might find this easier to see on the *resource histogram* in Figure 7, below.

Resource histogram

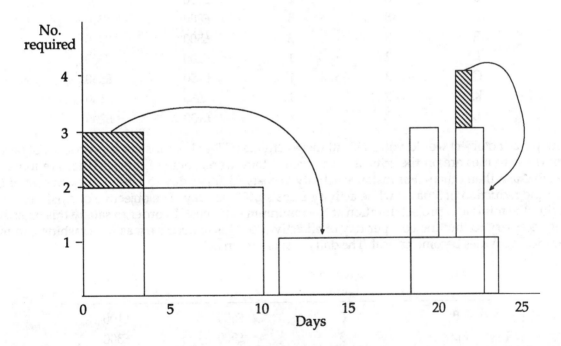

Figure 7 – The resource histogram

From this histogram you will see clearly the peaks and troughs in the resource requirements. If a peak could be moved into a trough the net result would be a smoother histogram which is the point of the exercise. A perfectly smooth histogram would mean that the resource is being fully utilised and no further savings would be possible. In the case of the garage it would be possible to delay the start of activity G (make window frames) until day 9 since G has a float of 17 days. This would mean that from the start of the project until day 12 two people would be required all the time. (The smoothing is shown using shading on the histogram). The peaks at the end of the project is not so easy to solve. If the start of activity F (tile the roof) was delayed by its float of one day, the peak of four people during day 22 could be reduced by one. So three people are required for much of the latter part of the project. The alternative to increasing the number of people is to extend the project. For example if the critical activities J (fitting the door) and K (painting) were delayed for three days the project would be delayed by this amount of time but you would then find that the project could be completed with 2 people for the entire 27 days.

Cost scheduling

A very important resource in network analysis is money. This resource is usually so important that a separate technique has been devised to solve problems posed by financial considerations. This technique is called *crashing*.

It is usually desirable to reduce the time a project takes because there are often financial advantages in doing so. For example, the Department of Transport pays a bonus to contractors who complete a road building or repair project early. (And a penalty is charged if the project time is over-run). It is often possible to speed up the completion of an activity at a extra cost. This cost may be because a machine is hired or because more people are employed. In the garage building example it would be possible to dig the foundations much quicker if a mechanical digger (JCB) was used. The reduced duration is called the crashed duration and the increased cost is called the crashed cost. In the garage example it has been assumed that activities B, D, E, F, G, K and L could be crashed. The data for the crashing is given below.

Activity	Normal duration (days)	Crash duration (days)	Normal cost	Crash cost
B	8	2	£100	£700
D	8	5	£800	£1700
E	3	2	£500	£900
F	2	1	£200	£400
G	3	1	£150	£550
K	2	1	£30	£130
L	2	1	£100	£200

If money was no object would you crash all these activities? The short answer is probably not because not all the activities are on the critical path. Even if they were, some of the activities are more economic to crash than others. For instance activity D costs £300 per day to crash (an extra cost of £900 and a time reduction of 3 days) while activity E costs £400 per day. The objective of crashing should be to find the minimum project duration at the minimum extra cost. In order to satisfy this objective it is first necessary to find the cost per day of *all* activities. This is necessary as the crashing can make non-critical activities become critical. The daily cost is shown below.

Activity	Time reduction (days)	Extra cost	Cost/day
B	6	£600	£100
D	3	£900	£300
E	1	£400	£400
F	1	£200	£200
G	2	£400	£200
K	1	£100	£100
L	1	£100	£100

The next step is to write down all the paths through the network together with their durations. (Path GHIK can be ignored because it has a relatively short duration). There are 8 major paths, which are:

Path	Duration
ADEJK	24
BCDEJK	23
ADEF	23
ADHIK	22
BCDEF	22
BCDHIK	21
ADL	20
BCDL	19

Path ADEJK must be reduced first because it is the longest path through the network and therefore the critical path. Activities D, E and K can be crashed but of the three K is the cheapest. If K is crashed by one day then not only will the duration of path ADEJK be reduced by one but so will paths BCDEJK, ADHIK and BCDHIK. The project duration has now been reduced by one day at a cost of £100 but path ADEF is now critical, in addition to ADEJK. These two paths must now be crashed together. Both D and E are common to these two paths and since D is the cheapest, this will be crashed by three days at a cost of £900. Finally E is crashed by one day to reduce the project duration to 19 weeks at an extra cost of £1400. No further crashing is worthwhile because it is not possible to crash both critical paths (only F has any crashing capability left). You might find it easier to write the necessary steps in a table similar to the one below.

Path	Duration	Step 1	Step 2	Step 3
ADEJK	24	23	20	19
BCDEJK	23	22	19	18
ADEF	23	23	20	19
ADHIK	22	21	18	18
BCDEF	22	22	19	18
BCDHIK	21	20	17	17
ADL	20	20	17	17
BCDL	19	19	16	16
Activities crashed		K-1	D-3	E-1
Extra cost		£100	£900	£400
Cumulative extra cost		£100	£1000	£1400

Is it worthwhile reducing the project time by 5 days at an extra cost of £1400? It may be that you are paying someone by the day to help you and any reduction in time would save you this 'overhead' charge. For example, suppose you were paying this person £150 per day. It would be worthwhile crashing K because for an expenditure of £100 you would save £150; a net gain of £50. However it wouldn't be worthwhile crashing D because for each day saved it has cost you £150 (£300 – £150).

PERT analysis

So far it has been assumed that all activity times are known with certainty. In practise most times will be an estimate and therefore the overall project time will be subject to error. You could of course analyse two networks; the first network using optimistic times for each activity and the second using pessimistic times. You would then have a range of times within which the project would be expected to finish.

145

An alternative is to use the PERT technique. This approach is useful where some or all of the activities have been carried out in the past and a good deal of information on their durations is available. In addition to being able to obtain an optimistic time (t_o) and a pessimistic time (t_p), a most likely time (t_m) is also required. The most likely time is the time that occurs most frequently but it is not necessarily the mean time. The equations for calculating the mean activity time ($\bar{t}$) and the standard deviation of the activity times (σ_t) are based on the beta distribution (this is a mathematical distribution that needn't concern you) are:

$$\bar{t} = \frac{t_o + 4t_m + t_p}{6}$$

$$\sigma_t = \sqrt{\frac{t_p - t_o}{6}}$$

These formulae are applied to all activities where the three time estimates can be obtained and critical path analysis is then carried out using the mean times.

To illustrate this method imagine that you can give the activities B, E and F an optimistic, a pessimistic and a most likely estimate as shown in the following table.

Activity	t_o	t_p	t_m
B	4	12	8
E	1	5	4
F	1	5	3

So B (dig the foundations) could possibly be done in 4 days but if you had poor weather this activity could take as long as 12 days. However from past experience the majority of times would indicate a duration of 8 days. Substituting these values into the formulae gives:

$$\bar{t} = \frac{4 + 4 \times 8 + 12}{6}$$

$$= 8$$

$$\sigma_t = \sqrt{\frac{12 - 4}{6}}$$

$$= 1.15$$

This calculation has been repeated for activities E and F and the results are as follows:

Activity	$\bar{t}$	σ_t
B	8	1.15
E	3.67	0.82
F	3	0.82

The amended project duration can be found by repeating the critical path analysis procedure using these mean times (see page 140). You should find that the *mean* project duration hasn't changed at 24 days but activity F has now become critical as well as activities A, D, E, J, and K. (There are now two critical paths, which are A, D, E, F and A, D, E, J, K).

In addition to the project time it is possible to find the standard deviation associated with this mean duration time. The procedure is to add the *variance* for activities on the critical path (the variance is the square of the standard deviation). Where there are two or more critical paths the larger of the variance totals is used. In the garage example activities E and F are critical and the sum of these variances is $0.82^2 + 0.82^2 = 1.3448$. The standard deviation is the square root of this value which is 1.16.

If it is now assumed that the distribution of project times is normally distributed you can apply the ideas of Unit 4 (page 9) to your data. In the garage example you may want to find out the probability that the project time will be greater than 26 days. The diagram in Figure 8, below illustrates the problem.

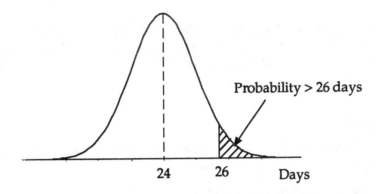

Figure 8

To obtain this probability, the value of **Z** is found from:

$$Z = \frac{X - \mu}{\sigma}$$

$$= \frac{26 - 24}{1.16}$$

$$= 1.72$$

From normal tables (see appendix 3 page 250), this value of Z is equivalent to a probability of 0.0427 or about 4.3%.

If you feel by now that this result bears no resemblance to reality, you will probably be right! The assumptions made will probably never be met in practise so the final result is of little real meaning. However the actual process of forcing people to come up with different estimates of an activity's duration is a useful exercise in its own right and is likely to make the overall result more accurate.

Further reading

Introduction to Management Science, Cook and Russell, (PRENTICE)

Quantitative Approaches in Business Studies, Morris, (PITMAN)

Quantitative Techniques, Lucey, (DP PUBLICATIONS)

Quantitative Analysis, Stansfield, (LONGMAN)

Critical Path Analysis & other Project Network techniques., Lockyer & Gordon, (PITMAN)

Inventory control

Introduction

Holding stock is a very expensive business particularly where the goods are of high value. However even for small value items the cost can be high if the quantities involved are large enough. How much stock should a company hold? Before this question can be answered, you will need to understand the type of costs involved in holding stock.

Costs of holding stock

There are many costs associated with holding (or not holding) stock. Some of these are:

Warehouse costs

money tied up in stock (interest charges)

damage while in storage

deterioration while in storage

obsolescence

ordering costs

delivery costs

cost of any 'stock-outs'

Warehouse costs include things like rental charges, heating and wages. Money that is tied up in stock could be earning money (or reduce overdraft charges). A certain proportion of goods will be damaged while in the warehouse or may be stolen and certain products deteriorate (for example food) while other items may become obsolete if stored too long (last years computer will be worth less than the latest version). In addition to the costs directly associated with the holding of stock there is also the cost of ordering and delivery. Most large companies will have a buying department and this means that there must be a cost associated with ordering. Even if only telephone and postage were costed, each order would still cost a finite amount. Finally there is a cost of a 'stock-out'. If the computer game store 'Game World' sells computer games and reckons to make, say £30 on a sale of a particular game, then for each sale that cannot be fulfilled the company will lose this profit. Not only will they lose this sale but they may lose future sales because potential customers may decide to go to stores that always have adequate stock.

If the case for and against holding stock can be resolved on cost alone then it is a matter of minimising the total cost associated with an inventory policy. There are many inventory control models that do this, some are quite simple deterministic models while others can accommodate uncertainty or handle many different goods at the same time. For particularly complex inventory control systems, simulation may be used to arrive at the best policy. (See Unit 20, page 48).

All models will tell you *how much to order* and *when to order*. The simplest model is the Economic Order Quantity model, which will now be described.

Economic Order Quantity (EOQ) Model

The assumptions that have to be made before this model can be used are as follows:

Demand is known and constant.

Lead (delivery) time is constant.

Only one item is involved.

Stock is monitored on a continuous basis and an order is made when the stock level reaches a *re-order* point.

When an order arrives, the stock level is replenished instantaneously.

Stock-outs do not occur

Figure 1, below may help you picture the general problem. An order quantity Q arrives and is used up at a constant rate, until the stock level reaches zero, at which point a new order arrives.

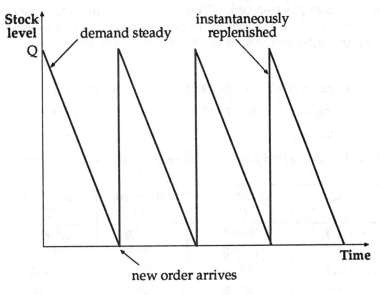

Figure 1

For small values of Q more frequent ordering will be necessary and hence order costs will be high, while large values of Q will increase the quantity in store and therefore increase the storage costs. The problem is to determine the value of Q that minimises the sum of the order and storage costs.

If the cost of placing an order is represented by the letter **c**, then the total order cost is simply the number of orders made multiplied by c. If D is the demand over a specified time period then the number of orders made must be $\dfrac{D}{Q}$ and the order cost is:

$$C \times \frac{D}{Q}$$

To calculate the storage cost it is assumed that the cost of holding one unit in stock for a specified time period is known. This cost is represented by **h**. As the amount in stock varies the average stock level is required and you will see from Figure 2 that this must be $\dfrac{Q}{2}$.

Hence the storage cost is:
$$h \times \frac{Q}{2}$$

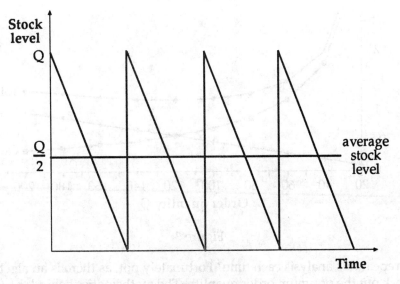

Figure 2

Imagine that you work for 'Game World' and you have been asked to decide on the best inventory control policy for a particular computer game. You are told that the demand is fairly constant at 5000 units p.a and it costs £14.40 to place an order. You are also told that the storage cost of holding one unit of the game per annum is £10. In order to investigate how inventory costs vary with order size you decide to work out the order and storage costs for different order quantities.

For an order size of 20:

$$\text{Order cost} = £14.4 \times 5000/20 \qquad = £3600 \text{ p.a}$$
$$\text{Storage cost} = £10 \times 20/2 \qquad = £100 \text{ p.a}$$
$$\text{Total cost} \qquad = £3700 \text{ p.a}$$

These calculations have been repeated for order quantities from 40 to 200 and are shown in the table below:

Q	Order cost (£)	Storage cost (£)	Total cost (£)
20	3600.0	100.0	3700.0
40	1800.0	200.0	2000.0
60	1200.0	300.0	1500.0
80	900.0	400.0	1300.0
100	720.0	500.0	1220.0
120	600.0	600.0	1200.0
140	514.3	700.0	1214.3
160	450.0	800.0	1250.0
180	400.0	900.0	1300.0
200	360.0	1000.0	1360.0

From this table it appears that an order quantity of 120 gives the lowest total costs at £1200 p.a. This can best be seen in the graph in Figure 3, below. You will also probably notice that the total cost curve is fairly flat around the minimum so that departing from the order size of 120 does not incur much additional cost.

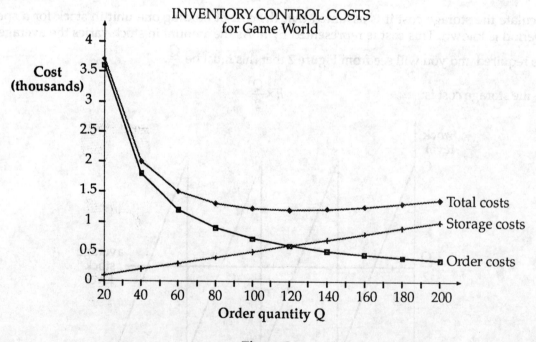

Figure 3

Is it necessary to repeat this analysis each time? Fortunately not, as there is an algebraic formula that can be used to work out the optimum order quantity. The mathematics behind the formula is beyond the scope of this book but you will see from the analysis that at minimum cost the order cost equals storage costs. This is generally true so:

$$c.\frac{D}{Q} = h.\frac{Q}{2}$$

Multiplying both sides by 2Q and rearranging gives you:

$$Q^2 = 2c.\frac{D}{h}$$

That is:

$$Q = \sqrt{\frac{2cD}{h}}$$

This formula is known as the economic order quantity or **EOQ**.

All you have to do to use this formula is simply to substitute the values for c, D, and h. That is:

$$Q = \sqrt{\frac{2 \times 14.40 \times 5000}{10}}$$

$$= \sqrt{14400}$$

$$= 120$$

Time between orders and the re-order level

In the 'Game World' problem the number of orders per year at the EOQ of 120 is 5000/120 = 41.67. If the company works for 300 days a year this means that the time between orders should be 300/41.67 = 7.2 days on average.

From Figure 1, page 149, you will see that a new order arrives just as the stock level reaches zero. For this to happen an order must have been placed sometime previously. In practise an order is placed when the stock reaches a predetermined level. To calculate this level all that is required is the lead (or delivery) time. If the lead time is say 4 days then during this time a certain amount of stock will have been sold. With a demand of 5000 a year, the daily sales will be approximately 5000/300 = 16.7, that is about 17 games. In 4 days about 68 games will be sold and therefore an order will need to be placed when the stock is down to this level. This re-order level is shown in Figure 4, below.

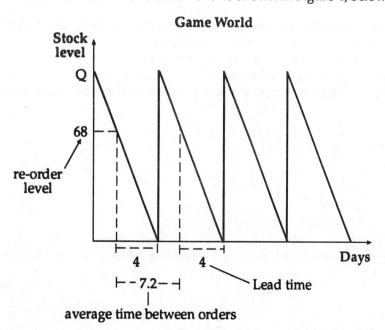

Figure 4

Discounts

The EOQ is not always the cheapest quantity to purchase. It is often found that discounts are given by the manufacturer or supplier if a certain minimum quantity of goods are bought. In these cases it is necessary to add the cost of the goods to the order and storage costs in order to arrive at the cheapest policy.

For example, suppose you can purchase these games for £50 each but if you order in quantities of 500 or more a 5% discount is given. At the EOQ (120), the product cost is:

$$5000 \times £50 = £250,000$$

and the storage and order cost is £1200 (see page 150)

The total cost is therefore $250,000 + 1200 = £251,200$ p.a

If 500 is purchased at a time, the order and storage will change and the unit cost will fall to £50 – £2.50 = £47.50, so:

Order cost:	$£14.40 \times \dfrac{5000}{500} = £144.0$
Storage cost:	$£10 \times 500/2 = £2500$
Product cost:	$5000 \times £47.50 = \underline{£237,500}$
Total cost:	$= £240,144$

By ordering in quantities of 500 a saving of £11,056 p.a (£251,200 – £240,144) can be realised.

Uncertainty in demand

The EOQ model assumes that the demand for the product is known and constant. This assumption is unlikely to be valid in practise, and the demand is likely to fluctuate from day to day. Rather than scrap this model completely it is possible, with further assumptions, to compensate for this variability.

Assuming that you are operating a re-order level system (that is, the stock level is continuously monitored) any fluctuation in demand *before* the next order is placed is unimportant. This is because any increase in demand will simply mean that an order is placed earlier than expected. However once an order has been placed any increase in demand is more serious and could result in a stock-out. To prevent this happening a buffer (or safety) stock is purchased. The stock level diagram now looks like Figure 5 below.

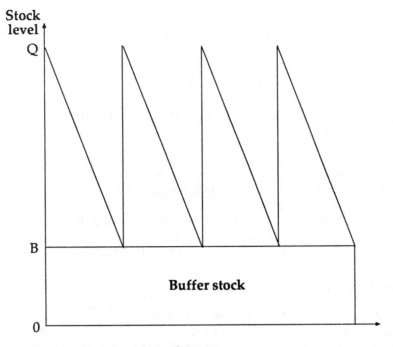

Figure 5

It is now a matter of calculating the size (B) of the buffer stock. However before this can be done an assumption needs to be made regarding the *distribution* of demand. The simplest assumption is to say that the demand is normally distributed. In the case of Game World, you may have decided that the demand for games is normally distributed with a mean of 17 games per day and a standard deviation of 4 games. During the 4 days lead time the mean demand will be 4 × 17 = 68 games and the standard deviation will be:

$$\sigma = \sqrt{4^2 + 4^2 + 4^2 + 4^2}$$
$$= 8$$

(Don't forget to add *variances*)

The use of the normal distribution means that it is possible for the demand to reach very high levels since the tails of the distribution in theory have no end. (see page 69). However in practise a limit is set such as 5% and the demand is found that is only exceeded for this percentage of times. In the case of Game World the demand that is exceeded on only 5% of occasions is denoted by X in Figure 6 below.

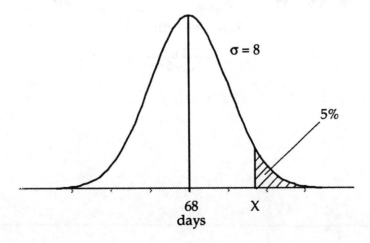

Figure 6

The normal equation is:

$$Z = \frac{X - 68}{8}$$

From the normal table (see appendix 3, page 250), the value of Z for a probability of 0.05 (5%) is 1.645 so

$$X = 1.645 \times 8 + 68$$
$$= 81.2$$

This means that on 5% of occasions the demand could exceed 81 units. The buffer level to ensure that a stock-out only occurs on 5% of occasions is therefore 81 – 68 = 13 units. In practise this would be rounded up to 15 or even more. To ensure that this buffer stock is maintained at the correct level the re-order level will need to be set at 81 units (The value of 'X' in Figure 6). The storage cost will now be increased by £130 p.a since 13 units are permanently in stock.

The Economic batch quantity model (EBQ)

The economic order quantity assumes that when an order arrives stock is replenished instantaneously. You will notice that in Figure 1, page 149, this is represented by a vertical line. However in certain situations this assumption does not hold and goods are received gradually over a period of time.

A good example of this situation is where a product is manufactured in stages. Figure 7 below illustrates a simple example where a product goes through two stages, A and B. This could be the production of a drivegear for a car. Stage A grinds the gear to size while stage B cuts the teeth.

If it is assumed that D units of these completed drivegears are required per day and that stage A is a faster operation than B, then it is not necessary for stage A to operate continuously on this product. In practise stage A would be capable of producing different gears while stage B might be dedicated to one particular gear. The problem then becomes one of determining the batch quantity, **Q**. Similar costs apply as to the EOQ model since the set-up cost of stage A, (**c**) is equivalent to the order cost and the stock of part finished gears also incurs a storage cost (**h**). However, while production of quantity Q is taking place during stage A, the second stage (B) is using some of this production. The net build-up of stock is represented by the sloping line in Figure 8, on the following page. You will also notice that the maximum stock level is less than Q for the same reason.

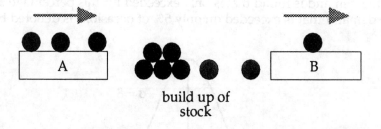

build up of stock

Figure 7

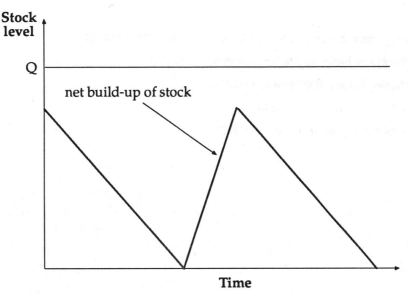

Figure 8

Using **r** to represent the rate of production of stage A, the total set-up cost and storage cost is as follows:

Set-up cost:
$$C \times \frac{D}{Q}$$

Storage cost:
$$h \times \frac{Q}{2} \times \left(1 - \frac{D}{r}\right)$$

And the formula for the **EBQ** is:

$$Q = \sqrt{\frac{2cD}{h\left(1 - \frac{D}{r}\right)}}$$

To illustrate this formula, suppose that the rate of production of stage A is 2000 per day and 500 finished gears are required. The set up cost of stage A is £250 and the storage cost is 33p per gear per day.

Hence: $c = £250$, $h = £0.33$, $D = 500$, and $r = 2000$

and:
$$Q = \sqrt{\frac{2 \times 259 \times 500}{0.33 \times \left(1 - \frac{500}{2000}\right)}}$$

$$= 1005$$

That is one production run of stage A will be required approximately every two days. The daily set-up cost will be £125 (£250 every two days).

The daily storage cost will be:
$$= 0.33 \times \frac{1005}{2} \times \left(1 - \frac{500}{2000}\right)$$

$$= £124.36$$

Section 2

Further reading

Introduction to Management Science, Cook and Russell, (PRENTICE-HALL)

Quantitative Approaches in Business Studies, Morris, (PITMAN)

Quantitative Techniques, Lucey, (DP PUBLICATIONS)

Quantitative Analysis, Stansfield, (LONGMAN)

Inventory Control and Management, Waters, (WILEY)

Linear programming

Introduction

The dream of any production manager must be that the resources required for production are limitless. However, this is never the case and availability of resources impose constraints on what and how much can be produced. For instance the labour resource is usually fixed as is machine hours. Frequently raw material is in short supply and this imposes yet another constraint upon production. For production of one product these constraints impose no real problem – the company will just produce as much as it can until one constraint is reached. For example, imagine that you are the production manager at the Just Shirts company and you are currently making just one type of shirt, the Regular Fit shirt. Each shirt takes one machine-hour to make (that is, a shirt can be made in one hour by one machinist or half an hour by two machinists) and requires five square metres of cotton (including wastage). If the supply of labour and material was limitless, production would just continue until the market had been saturated. However suppose that your workforce numbered twenty and worked an eight hour day. This would give you $20 \times 8 = 160$ machine-hours of labour per day. Perhaps there is a world shortage of cotton and you are restricted to 600 square metres a day. So how many shirts could you make each day? Since each shirt takes one machine-hour to make, the available labour would allow you to make 160 shirts each day. However the cotton availability would only allow you to make 120 shirts (600/5) so this restricts how much you could produce, unless the cotton resource could be increased.

You may not be very happy having your workforce idle some of the time but there can be no argument about the quantity of shirts to produce. However the problem becomes much more difficult if you decide to make another type of shirt as well – say the Deluxe Fit shirt. This shirt requires more stitching and consequently the time taken to produce this shirt is doubled to two man-hours. The amount of cotton used has also increased to six square metres. Obviously the price charged for this type of shirt must be greater to reflect the increased cost of production. The price is made up of two components – cost and profit. In accounting terms it is usual to refer to 'contribution to profits' since cost is made up of a fixed and a variable component. If the contribution to profits for the Regular shirt is £5 and for the Deluxe shirt it is £8 what quantity of each type of shirt should be made to maximise profits?

If you repeat the earlier calculations you should find that the most deluxe shirts you could make each day would be 80 (160/2), so if you made only deluxe shirts your daily profit would be £640 (80×8). Making only Regular shirts would yield a daily profit of £600 (5×120), so obviously it is better to make only Deluxe shirts rather than the Regular brand. However, is there a combination of Regular and Deluxe shirt production that would give you a higher profit than £640? The answer to this problem could be solved by trial and error but imagine a situation where you were making 100 different shirts and there were many constraints that had to be considered! Fortunately there is a mathematical technique that can solve problems where there is a defined objective (for example maximise profits or minimise costs) and where there are a series of linear constraints. This technique is called linear programming.

Linear programming formulation

Linear programming is concerned with the management of scarce resources. It is applicable where two or more activities are competing for these limited resources. The first thing that you have to do is to write down the objective and constraints in mathematical form. For example with the Just Shirts company, the objective is to maximise profits and if you say that you are going to make **R** Regular shirts and **D** Deluxe shirts, the total profit will be:

$$5R + 8D \text{ which is to be maximised.}$$

The number of man-hours of labour used to make **R** Regular shirts is **R** and for the Deluxe variety it is **2D**. The total man-hours used is therefore R + 2D and this sum must be less than or equal to the available man-hours, which is 160. Mathematically this is written as:

$$R + 2D \ \leq 160$$

Similarly for the cotton resource:

$$5R + 6D \ \leq 600$$

You should indicate that you are only interested in positive values of R and D and the two constraints $R \geq 0$ and $D \geq 0$ will do this for you.

When the problem has been written in this form it is often called the *L.P formulation*. So for the Just Shirts problem the formulation is:

$$\text{Max } P \ = 5R + 8D$$

subject to

$$R + 2D \ \leq 160$$
$$5R + 6D \ \leq 600$$
$$R, D \ \geq 0$$

There are many values of R and D that will satisfy these inequations. For instance, R = 40 and D = 20 would satisfy all the constraints so this is feasible combination. The problem is which combination will give the largest profit? There are many computer packages on the market that will solve linear programming problems but for two variable problems there is an alternative.

Graphical solution of linear programming problems

If for the moment you replace the inequality signs by equalities, the two main constraints become:

$$R + 2D \ = 160 \qquad \text{(labour)}$$

and: $$5R + 6D \ = 600 \qquad \text{(cotton)}$$

Since these equations contain only two variables, R and D, they can be represented as straight lines and plotted on a graph. Two points are required to plot a straight line and it is convenient to find where they cross the axes. To do this it is simply a matter of letting R = 0 and calculating D and then letting D = 0 and calculating R. This has been done below:

constraint	R	D
labour:	0	80
	160	0
cotton:	0	100
	120	0

These two lines can now be plotted on a graph (see Figure 1 opposite) and they mark the boundaries of the inequations. The *region* satisfying each inequation will be one side of the boundary. This region can be found by choosing a point one side of the boundary and substituting the values of R and D into the inequation. For example the point 'p' (R = 40 and D = 20) satisfies the inequation R + 2D since 80 (40 + 2 × 20) is less than 160. So the region below the line R + 2D = 160 satisfies the equivalent inequation. You also will find that the region below the line 5R + 6D = 600 also satisfies the appropriate inequation. You also should see that in this example the origin (R = 0, D = 0) also satisfies both inequalities, and the origin is normally the best point to choose (except where the line passes through the origin).

To identify the required region it is normal to shade the *unwanted* region, that is the region not satisfying the inequality. The reason for this is for clarity but you are at liberty to shade the wanted region if you so wish. The region that satisfies all inequalities is called the *feasible region* and any point within this region will satisfy all the constraints. The graph for the Just Shirts example is shown in **Figure 1** below and you should be able to identify the feasible region as OABC.

Any point within the feasible region will satisfy all constraints but which point or points give the largest profit? Fortunately this can be found quite easily.

Finding the optimum – the isoprofit/cost method

The point 'P' in Figure 1 is in the feasible region and the profit for this combination is:

$$P = 5 \times 40 + 8 \times 20$$
$$= £360$$

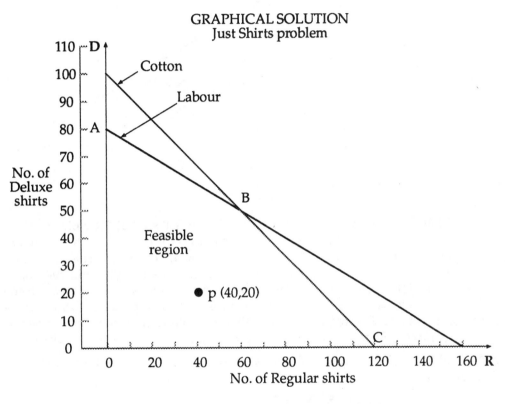

GRAPHICAL SOLUTION
Just Shirts problem

Figure 1

However there are other combinations of R and D that give the value of 360 since:

$$5R + 8D = 360$$

Thus the profit equation is just another straight line and can be plotted in the same way as the constraints.

That is if R = 0, then D = 45 and if D = 0 then R = 72

This line obviously passes through the point 'p' (see Figure 2, below).

GRAPHICAL SOLUTION
Just Shirts problem

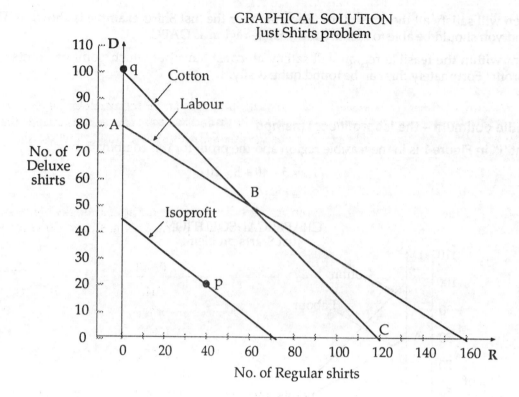

Figure 2

Can this figure of 360 be increased? If you try say a value of 500 so that 5R + 6D = 500 you will get another straight line that is parallel to the first one. The reason for this is that the gradient of the line stays the same – it is only the intercept on the axes that change. If you place a ruler on the original line and very carefully move it away from the origin and parallel to the line you will eventually find that the ruler leaves the feasible region completely. However as the line is moving away from the origin the profit is increasing and you will find that the point **B** is the point that is furthest away from the origin, yet still within the feasible region. The fact that the optimum point is at a corner point of the feasible region is no fluke – *the optimum value will always be found at a corner point of the feasible region.*

The values of R and D at point B can be read off the graph above. You should find that R = 60 and D = 50 and this gives a profit of:

$$5 \times 60 + 8 \times 50 \ = £700$$

which is £60 per day more than if deluxe shirts were made only. You may find it surprising that at the optimum solution more Regular shirts are made than Deluxe ones – this is because the Deluxe version uses proportionately more resources.

You found the value of R and D from the graph but for greater accuracy it is recommended that the relevant equations are solved algebraically. This is particularly important when the graph shows that fractional values are involved or when it is difficult to decide which point is optimal. The method of simultaneous equations is used to solve for R and D and is as follows:

$$R + 2D \ = 160 \qquad\qquad \text{equation (1)}$$
$$5R + 6D = 600 \qquad\qquad \text{equation (2)}$$

Multiply (1) by 5 and subtract (2) from (1) gives:

$$5R + 10D = 800$$
$$\underline{5R + \ 6D \ = 600}$$
$$4D = 200$$

so: $$D = 50$$

If D = 50 is now substituted back into (1) you get:

$$R + 100 = 160$$

$$R = 60$$

which is the solution found from the graph.

A word of warning – even if you use simultaneous equations to solve for the two variables you must still draw the graph first. Without drawing the graph you could quite easily solve pairs of equations outside the feasible region. Also the optimum point could be on either axis (for example point A or C in the graph above).

Finding the optimum – an alternative method

Since you now know that the optimum point must be at a corner point of the feasible region, you could work out the value of the two variables at every such point. This has been done for the Just Shirts problem and is as follows:

	R	D	Profit
Point A	0	80	£640
Point B	60	50	£700
Point C	120	0	£600

These figures agree with those that have been calculated earlier and confirm that point B gives the greatest profit.

For feasible regions that have few corner points, this method is probably the quickest. However, it is necessary for you to understand the idea of isoprofit lines as this concept is important when looking at sensitivity analysis.

Tight and slack constraints

If you substitute the optimal values of R (60) and D (50) back into the constraints you will get the following:

Labour: $60 + 2 \times 50 = 160$

Cotton: $5 \times 60 + 6 \times 50 = 600$

Since these values correspond the maximum quantity of both resources available, the resources are *scarce* and are called *tight* constraints. Where a constraint has not reached its limit it is referred to as a *slack* constraint. For example, if it was not possible to make more than 70 Deluxe shirts, the constraint would be written as D < 70. This constraint would be slack because the optimal solution has not reached this limit.

Sensitivity analysis

Linear programming is a deterministic model, that is, all variables are assumed to be known with certainty. So the quantity of cotton available each day was assumed to be exactly 600 square metres and the contribution to profits of the Regular shirt was assumed to be exactly £5. Of course in reality you will never be 100% certain about the value of many of the parameters in a L.P model and the purpose of sensitivity analysis is to ask 'what-if' type questions about these parameters. For example, what if more cotton can be purchased, or what if the profit of a Regular shirt increased to £6.

Sensitivity analysis in linear programming is concerned with the change in the right hand side of the constraints (normally the resources) and changes to the objective function coefficients (that is the profit/costs of each variable).

Changes to the right hand side of a constraint

Both the labour and cotton resource are tight constraints and an increase in either of these resources will increase the profit made. The reason for this is that as the right hand side of a tight constraint increases, the constraint *and* the optimum point move *away* from the origin.

This can be demonstrated by re-solving the simultaneous equations with the right hand side of the labour constraint increased by one to 161. That is:

$$R + 2D = 161$$

$$5R + 6D = 600$$

solving these two equations simultaneous as before gives:

$$R = 58.5 \text{ and } D = 51.25$$

(don't worry about the fractional values for the time being.)

and the new profit will be £702.5, an increase of £2.50. This £2.50 is called the *shadow price* of the labour resource. It is defined as the change in the value of the objective function if the right hand side of the labour constraint is increased (or decreased) by one unit.

So if it were possible to employ more labour or to work overtime, there is potentially a larger profit to be made. However this assumes that the direct costs do not increase. If for instance overtime rates increase costs by more than £2.50 per hour, then it wouldn't be economic to increase production in this way. However, assuming it is worthwhile, how many more man-hours should be worked? As the labour constraint moves away from the origin there comes a point where it moves outside the cotton constraint, this is at point 'q' on Figure 2, page 160. This means that the labour resource ceases to become scarce and further increase of this resource will just add to the surplus of labour. At point q, R = 0 and D = 100, so if these values are substituted into the labour equation you will get:

$$0 + 2 \times 100 = 200$$

So the labour resource can increase by 40 man-hours (200-160), which means a possible

$$40 \times 2.50 = £100$$

extra profit can be made each day.

If you repeat this procedure for the cotton constraint you should find that the shadow price of the cotton resource is £0.50 per square metre and that this resource can be increased to 800 square metres per day.

Changes to the objective function coefficients

The objective function for the Just Shirts example is:

$$\text{Max } P = 5R + 8D$$

where 5 (in £) is the profit per Regular shirt and 8 is the profit per Deluxe shirt.

If it were possible to reduce costs then profits per shirt would rise and vice versa, but would the production of 60 Regular shirts and 50 Deluxe shirts remain the optimal solution? To answer this question it is necessary to consider what would happen to the isoprofit line following a change in the profit coefficients.

The gradient of the isoprofit line can be found by rearranging the objective function into the form

$$Y = MX + C$$

where M is the gradient and C is the intercept on the D axis. That is:

$$D = -\frac{5}{8}R + \frac{P}{8}$$

The gradient is therefore $-\frac{5}{8}$ but any change in either profit coefficients will change this. The graph in Figure 3 shows the isoprofit line with a gradient of $-\frac{2}{8}$, that is, the profit of the Regular shirt has been decreased to £2.

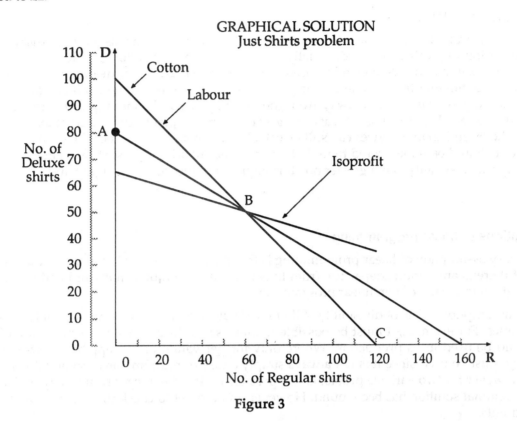

GRAPHICAL SOLUTION
Just Shirts problem

Figure 3

The optimum solution has changed and is now at point A. In this solution you would make 80 Deluxe shirts but no Regular ones. Although you could find the optimum point each time a change in the profit coefficient was made, it would be much easier if you knew the value of the profit that would cause a change in the optimal solution. To do this consider what happens as the isoprofit line changes from a gradient of $-\frac{5}{8}$ to $-\frac{2}{8}$. At some point it must become parallel to the labour constraint line and at this point the same profit will be obtained at both points A and B. (In fact all points along the line AB would give the same profit – this is known as multiple optimal solutions).

To find the profit of the Regular shirt that would make the isoprofit line parallel to the labour constraint, you need to work out the gradient of this line. Rearranging the equation

R + 2D = 160 into Y = MX + C form will give you a gradient of $\frac{1}{2}$. So you need to find the value of the Regular profit that will give this gradient. This can be done with the help of some elementary algebra:

Let x be the unknown value of the profit, then the gradient of the isoprofit line is $-\frac{x}{8}$ and:

$$-\frac{x}{8} = -\frac{1}{2}$$

This gives x = 4, so if the profit of a Regular shirt falls below £4 the optimum solution changes to R = 0 and D = 80.

The same argument can be applied if the profit on a Regular shirt increases. Then the isoprofit line will become parallel to BC and since the gradient of the cotton line is $-\frac{5}{6}$ the above equation becomes:

$$-\frac{x}{8} = -\frac{5}{6}$$

This gives x = 6.67, so if the profit of a Regular shirt rises above £6.67 the optimum solution changes to R = 120 and D = 0.

If you apply the same procedure to the Deluxe shirt you will find that the profit range within which the optimal solution will remain unchanged is from £6 to £10.

Minimisation problems

The Just Shirts example was a maximisation problem because a solution was required that maximised the contribution to profits. However, equally important are minimisation problems in which some objective, for example cost, is to be minimised. The general procedure for dealing with minimisation problems is no different from maximisation problems. A feasible region will still be obtained but instead of moving your *isocost* line away from the origin, you will be moving it towards the origin. There must have to be, of course, at least one greater than or equal to constraint otherwise you will arrive at the origin! Shadow prices can still be calculated although sometimes they can be difficult to interpret. It should be remembered though, that any shadow price represents a saving in cost and if the appropriate inequality was a greater one this implies a reduction in the right hand side of the constraint.

Assumptions of linear programming

The primary assumption of linear programming is that the objective function and constraints must be linear. If there is any serious departure from linearity this technique is not valid and consideration must be given to the use of non-linear programming.

Another assumption is one of divisibility. All units of output and resources must be able to take fractional values. For example, it must be possible to make say a third of a shirt or a fraction of a man-hour could be used in its production. Where only integer values are acceptable, *integer linear programming* must be used since it is not always simply a case of rounding any fractional values up or down. However for two variable problems it is possible to find the integer solution by trial and error once the optimal solution has been found. However don't forget to check that your solution satisfies all constraints.

Multivariable linear programming

The Just Shirt problem was a two variable problem and could be solved using the graphical method. However in practise most L.P problems will contain many variables and many constraints. Since a graph is only a two dimensional device it is not possible to solve these problems by the graphical method. For these larger problems the SIMPLEX algorithm or some derivative is used. The mathematics behind this algorithm is beyond the scope of this book but the procedure simply tests each corner point of the feasible region until the optimum point is found. Since an algorithm is a procedure that repeats itself, it is easily programmed for a computer.

Further reading

Introduction to Management Science, Cook and Russell, (PRENTICE-HALL)

Quantitative Approaches in Business Studies, Morris, (PITMAN)

Quantitative Techniques, Lucey, (DP PUBLICATIONS)

Quantitative Analysis, Stansfield, (LONGMAN)

The transportation and assignment algorithms

The Transportation algorithm

Imagine that you are the distribution manager of the BAZ oil company and each day you receive orders from your depots for bulk delivery of heating oil. On one particular day 4 depots request delivery of 24,500 litres in total and your 3 refineries have 40,500 litres available. Therefore you have no difficulty in meeting the order, but the problem is that you are not sure which refinery should supply which depot. The refineries are in different parts of the country and the cost of delivery from a refinery to a depot varies considerably. The cost in £ per litre from a refinery to a depot is given in the table below together with the availability (in 00's of litres) at each refinery and the requirement (again in 00's litres) at each depot.

Refinery / Depot	A	B	C	Required
P	5	13	7	60
Q	6	4	8	35
R	5	22	20	50
S	3	9	4	100
Available	175	80	150	

Cost per litre for delivery from refinery A to Depot P

Figure 1

Clearly you want the total delivery cost to be as low as possible so you wouldn't consider delivering oil from refinery B to depot R, unless there was no other option. However, the costs for delivering to depot Q are very similar so the answer is not so obvious in this case. You could try a 'trial and error' approach, which would probably work for a small problem like this. But suppose that you had 200 depots to deliver to? Even if you could come up with a reasonable solution in this case, how would you know if you had the optimal (that is the cheapest) solution? Another approach would be to use linear programming (see Unit 18, page 42). This could be done if you had access to a computer package (there are 15 variables and 9 constraints for this problem) but there is a simpler method. This is the *transportation* algorithm. The method consists of three steps, which are:

1. **Find an initial feasible solution**

2. **Test to see if the solution is optimal**

3. **If not optimal, improve the solution and repeat step 2.**

Step 1: (Find an initial feasible solution)

A feasible solution is one where all the requirements at the destinations are met and all supply at the origins are allocated. This means that:

total supply = total requirements

This is not the case with the BAZ problem since total supply exceeds total requirements by 160 units (405 − 245). However, any *unmatched* supply/demand problem can be made to match by the use of a dummy destination or origin. In the BAZ case a dummy depot is required that will 'soak' up the excess capacity. The 'transportation cost' for the this dummy depot will be zero.

The table in Figure 1 above, can now be modified to incorporate this dummy depot. To avoid too much clutter in the table, the transportation costs are usually placed in the top right hand corner of each cell as shown in Figure 2 below.

Depot / Refinery	A	B	C	Required
P	5	13	7	60
Q	6	4	8	35
R	5	22	20	50
S	3	9	4	100
Dummy	0	0	0	160
Available	175	80	150	405

Figure 2 – Basic transportation table

Each cell in the table can be used to represent a *route* from a refinery to a depot. It is now necessary to add quantities to each route so that a feasible solution can be found. There are various methods of obtaining an initial feasible solution, which range from the simple 'North West Corner' rule to the more complicated *Vogel's* method. A good compromise is the *least cost method*. This method simply allocates as much as possible to the cheapest routes (excluding the dummy routes). In the BAZ case the cheapest route is A-S at £3 per litre. The requirement at S is for 100 units and this can be met since 175 units are available at A. 100 units are added to this route and a line is drawn in routes B-S and C-S to indicate that nothing can be added to these routes. The next cheapest route is B-Q at £4 per litre. 35 units can be added to this route since the requirement at Q is 35 units and 80 units are available at B. Lines are drawn in routes A-Q and C-Q. There is now a tie for the next cheapest route; routes A-P and A-R both cost £5 per litre. When a choice exists it is often a good idea to choose the route where the most can be added, so on this basis you would choose route A-P since 60 units can be placed here rather than 50 units in route A-R. However, in this particular example you might be better off going for route A-R, since in this case you will avoid having to allocate anything to the two most expensive routes, B-R and C-R. If 50 units are allocated to route A-R, lines can be drawn in routes B-R and C-R. There are now only 3 routes left (excluding the dummy routes); A-P, B-P and C-P. The cheapest of these is A-P but only 25 units can be added to this route since 150 units have already been used up (100 in A-S and 50 in A-R). The requirement at P is for 60 units, so 35 units are placed in route C-P (this is cheaper than route B-P). To make up the availabilities at B and C, 45 units are added to route B-Dummy and 115 units to route C-Dummy. The completed table is shown in Figure 3, opposite.

Circles have been drawn round the quantities to be delivered to avoid confusion with the other numbers that will soon be added to the table. This is your initial feasible solution and the cost of this solution is:

$$(25 \times 5) + (35 \times 7) + (35 \times 4) + (50 \times 5) + (100 \times 3) = £1060$$

That is £106,000.

Is this the best that can be achieved? That is, is the solution optimal?

Step 2: (Test to see if the solution is optimal)

In order to decide if this is the optimal solution, the opportunity (or *shadow*) costs are calculated for the routes that are *not* used. If any of these shadow costs are negative it means that for every unit that can be placed in the relevant route, this amount of money will be saved. (Compare this idea to shadow prices in linear programming).

Depot \ Refinery		V_1 A	V_2 B	V_3 C	Required
U_1	P	(25) 5	— 13	(35) 7	60
U_2	Q	— 6	(35) 4	— 8	35
U_3	R	(50) 5	— 22	— 20	50
U_4	S	(100) 3	— 9	— 4	100
U_5	Dummy	— 0	(45) 0	(115) 0	160
Available		175	80	150	405

Figure 3 – Initial feasible solution

You do not need to know the detailed mathematical reasoning behind the calculation of the shadow costs but some justification will now be attempted.

Each route that is currently being used has a cost. This cost can be thought of as being made up of two costs – a cost at a depot (U) and a cost at a refinery (V). These 'U's and V's' have been added to the diagram in Figure 1, above. (Subscripts have been used to distinguish one depot or refinery from another). For example, if U_1 represents the cost at depot P and V_1 represents the cost at refinery A, then $U_1 + V_1 = 5$. This procedure is repeated for the other 6 routes and the result is as follows:

$$U_1 + V_3 = 7$$
$$U_2 + V_2 = 4$$
$$U_3 + V_1 = 5$$
$$U_4 + V_1 = 3$$
$$U_5 + V_2 = 0$$
$$U_5 + V_3 = 0$$

In order to solve for 8 variables using only 7 equations, it is necessary to allocate an arbitrary value of zero to one of these variables. If $U_1 = 0$ then the value of the other variables (in the order in which they can be calculated) are:

$$V_1 = 5, V_3 = 7, U_3 = 0, U_4 = -2, U_5 = -7, V_2 = 7, \text{ and } U_2 = -3$$

167

These values can be placed alongside the relevant U or V.

The shadow cost for each unused route is defined as:

Actual cost – (cost at the origin + cost at the destination)

For example, the shadow cost of route B-P is $13 - (0 + 7) = 6$. These shadow costs have been calculated for all the 8 unused routes and have been added to the table shown in Figure 4, below.

The only route that has a negative shadow cost is C-S. Therefore this solution is *not* optimal as a saving of £1 per litre will be achieved on any quantity of oil delivered by this route. This brings you to step 3.

Step 3: (*If not optimal, improve the solution and repeat step 2*).

As much oil as possible should be sent via route C-S, but care must be taken to ensure that the solution remains feasible. One method of achieving this is the *stepping stone* method.

The idea behind this method is that the rows and columns must remain balanced if the solution is to remain feasible. A '+' is first added to route C-S to indicate that a quantity of oil should be added to this route. It is now necessary to add a '–' to a route in the *same* row or column that is currently being used. C-P is the only used route in the same column and a '–' has been added to this route.

Refinery / Depot	(5) V_1 A	(7) V_2 B	(7) V_3 C	Required
U_1 (0) P	(25) [5]	6 [13]	(35) [7]	60
U_2 (-3) Q	4 [6]	(35) [4]	4 [8]	35
U_3 (0) R	(50) [5]	15 [22]	13 [20]	50
U_4 (-2) S	(100) [3]	4 [9]	-1 [4]	100
U_5 (-7) Dummy	2 [0]	(45) [0]	(115) [0]	160
Available	175	80	150	405

Figure 4 – Calculation of shadow costs

Another '+' is now added to route A-P to balance this row and a '–' is added to route A-S. This completes the 'loop'. (Note that if a '–' had been added to route A-R instead of A-S rows R and S would have been unbalanced). A dotted line has been drawn around the diagram in Figure 5 to show that the loop is closed. (The loop doesn't need to be rectangular – provided it arrives back at the starting place the rows and columns should remain balanced)

Refinery / Depot	(5) V$_1$ A	(7) V$_2$ B	(7) V$_3$ C	Required
U$_1$ (0) P	(25) **5** +	6 **13**	(35) **7** −	60
U$_2$ (-3) Q	4 **6**	(35) **4**	4 **8**	35
U$_3$ (0) R	(50) **5**	15 **22**	13 **20**	50
U$_4$ (-2) S	(100) **3** −	4 **9**	-1 **4** +	100
U$_5$ (-7) Dummy	2 **0**	(45) **0**	(115) **0**	160
Available	175	80	150	405

Figure 5 – The stepping stone method

The next stage of the procedure is to decide how much to add to route C-S. To avoid making any quantities negative you can only add *the minimum quantity of the routes with a '-' sign*. The two routes with a '-' sign are C-P and A-S, and the smallest quantity is route C-P at 35 units. This quantity is now added or subtracted from each of the 4 'stepping stones' identified. This gives you your new table and you now have to repeat step 2 by recalculating the U's and V's and the shadow costs. This has been done and the result is shown in Figure 6, below.

Since all shadow costs are non-negative this solution is optimal. The final solution is therefore:

   Refinery A should deliver 6000 litres to depot P, 5000 litres to depot R and 6500 litres to depot S.

   Refinery B should deliver 3500 litres to depot Q only.

   Refinery C should deliver 3500 litres to depot S only.

Refinery / Depot	(5) V$_1$ A	(6) V$_2$ B	(6) V$_3$ C	Required
U$_1$ (0) P	(60) **5**	7 **13**	1 **7**	60
U$_2$ (-2) Q	3 **6**	(35) **4**	4 **8**	35
U$_3$ (0) R	(50) **5**	16 **22**	14 **20**	50
U$_4$ (-2) S	(65) **3**	5 **9**	(35) **4**	100
U$_5$ (-6) Dummy	1 **0**	(45) **0**	(115) **0**	160
Available	175	80	150	405

Figure 6 – The optimal solution

169

The cost of this new solution is:

$$(60 \times 5) + (35 \times 4) + (50 \times 5) + (65 \times 3) + (35 \times 4) = 1025$$

That is, £102,500, a saving of £3500. This figure could also have been found by multiplying the quantity delivered by route C-S (3500) by the shadow cost (£1).

This is the basis of the transportation algorithm and can be applied to any size of problem. However there are various refinements that can or need to be applied under certain situations.

Alternative solutions

When there are zero shadow costs in the optimal solution, it is possible to find alternative solutions at the same cost. This is achieved by allocating a '+' to the route with the zero shadow cost and then repeating step 3.

Forbidden routes

There are occasions when certain routes cannot be used. Perhaps there are physical or political reasons why one origin cannot supply a particular destination. This can easily be overcome by giving that route a very high cost.

Degenerate solutions

The transportation method will only work if the number of used routes is equal to:

number of rows + number of columns – 1

For the BAZ example there were 5 rows and 3 columns, so:

$$5 + 3 - 1 = 7$$

This agrees with the number of used routes in all the tables above.

However, sometimes the number of used routes can be *less* than the required figure. If this occurs it is necessary to 'pretend' that an empty route is really used by allocating a *zero* quantity to this route. You then proceed as before.

Maximisation problems

The transportation algorithm assumes that the objective is to minimise costs. However, it is possible to use the method to solve maximisation problems by either

multiplying all the unit contributions by –1

or   by subtracting each unit contribution from the maximum contribution in the table.

You then proceed as before.

Sensitivity analysis

It is often necessary to see the effects of changes to the original problem without having to repeat the whole analysis.

For example, you may only have been able to estimate some of the transportation costs, in which case you could re-calculate the shadow costs for the optimal table using different values. If any of these shadow costs now turn out to be negative, the solution has become sub-optimal and you would need to repeat step 3.

Sometimes the optimal solution is not acceptable. Maybe it is politically desirable to use a particular route. The additional cost of using a sub-optimal route is simply the shadow cost of that route.

The assignment algorithm

This is a special case of the transportation algorithm where the number of origins equals the number of destinations and the allocations are a either a '1' or a '0'. For example, suppose that there are 4 machines and 4 operators and the operators are better (that is, more efficient) on some machines than on others. How do you *assign* each operator to one and only one machine so that some performance measure (such as cost or time) is minimised?

Suppose you timed how long each operator took to complete a certain task on each machine. The results (in minutes) are as follows:

Machine	Operator			
	1	2	3	4
A	168	172	175	183
B	156	160	158	163
C	138	140	135	145
D	147	142	140	145

This could be solved by the transportation algorithm but there is another method that takes advantage of the particular structure of the problem. The procedure is called the *Hungarian algorithm* and is designed to find the optimal solution very quickly.

Step 1:

For each row in the table, subtract the smallest element from each of the remaining elements in that row. For example, in the first row the smallest element is 168 and this is subtracted from every other element in the first row.

Machine	Operator			
	1	2	3	4
A	0	4	7	15
B	0	4	2	7
C	3	5	0	10
D	7	2	0	5

Step 2:

For each column of your new table, subtract the smallest element in a column from all other elements in the column. For example, column 1 doesn't change because the smallest is zero, but in column 2 the smallest is 2 and this value is subtracted from all other values in that column.

Machine	Operator			
	1	2	3	4
A	0	2	7	10
B	0	2	2	2
C	3	3	0	5
D	7	0	0	0

Step 3:

For the solution to be optimal it must be possible to allocate one zero to each operator. In order to see if this can be done, it is necessary to draw the minimum number of vertical and/or horizontal lines through all the zeros. If the number of lines is less than the number of rows (or columns) the solution is not optimal.

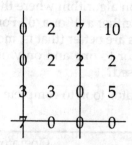

The minimum number of lines is 3 and therefore the solution is not optimal.

Step 4:

The next step is to improve the solution. This involves the following procedure:

For the elements that do not have a line through them, note the smallest.

Subtract this number from every element without a line through it.

Add this number to elements that are crossed by two lines.

Elements that are crossed by only one line are left untouched.

The minimum number is 2 and the new table is as follows:

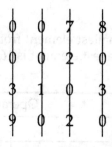

Step 5:

If the table is still not optimal, step 4 is repeated until it is. The table above though, is optimal since it is not possible to cover all the zeros with less than 4 lines

Each zero indicates the cheapest solution and it is now a question of assigning an operator to a machine using the various combinations of zeros. Because there are more than 4 zeros, there is more than one solution. For the table above it is possible to come up with 3 different allocations as shown below:

Option 1				Option 2				Option 3			
[0]	0	7	8	0	[0]	7	8	[0]	0	7	8
0	[0]	2	0	[0]	0	2	0	0	0	2	[0]
3	1	[0]	3	3	1	[0]	3	3	1	[0]	3
9	0	2	[0]	9	0	2	[0]	9	[0]	2	0

The assignments, with the relevant times in brackets are:

Operator	Option 1	Option 2	Option 3
1	A (168)	B (156)	A (168)
2	B (160)	A (172)	D (142)
3	C (135)	C (135)	C (135)
4	D (145)	D (145)	B (163)
Total time	608	608	608

The times of the three options are all equal at 608 minutes.

Like the Transportation algorithm, there are similar refinements that can be applied to the method. *Forbidden* allocations can be handled in the same way as can *maximisation* problems. If there are unequal numbers of rows and columns it is necessary to add dummy rows or columns to enable the method to be used.

Further reading

Introduction to Management Science, Cook and Russell, (PRENTICE-HALL)

Quantitative Approaches in Business Studies, Morris, (PITMAN)

Quantitative Techniques, Lucey, (DP PUBLICATIONS)

Quantitative Analysis, Stansfield, (LONGMAN)

Simulation

Introduction

The quantitative techniques that you have met so far have allowed analytical solutions to problems to be found. For example the inventory control (EOQ) model is a simple formula that will enable you to calculate the order quantity that will minimise inventory costs. (See Unit 17 page 40). These techniques or models are called *deterministic* because it is assumed that the variables (for example demand in the inventory control model) are known precisely and there is a fixed relationship between the input to the model and its output. In practise very few variables are known precisely but this fact is frequently ignored and averages are used to represent the variable.

However there is another model class called *stochastic*. A stochastic model has at least one variable that does not have a single value – it has many possible values defined by some probability distribution. (see Units 2,3 or 4, from page 6).

Where the probability distributions are assumed to follow specific distributions, such as the Poisson distribution a stochastic model can, under certain conditions, be solved analytically. The best example is queueing theory which allows you to calculate such things as average time in the queue, or the probability of a queue of a certain size. Unfortunately queueing theory can only be used for very simple queueing systems because of the number of assumptions that have to be made.

The majority of stochastic models have to be solved by simulation. Simulation is essentially a technique of replicating the behaviour of a real system over time. Although a simulation can be carried out manually it is normal to use a computer for this task. The 'instructions' for the simulation could be programmed using a programming language but these days most people use a simulation package.

The rail ticket office problem

To illustrate the technique, imagine passengers arriving at a suburban rail ticket office during the morning peak commuter period. There is one clerk who issues tickets and provides an information service for passengers. Maybe the manager has received complaints regarding the time passengers spend in the queue waiting to be served and she wishes to investigate possible methods of reducing the queueing time. Possible ideas include employing a second ticket clerk who could either duplicate the existing clerk or perhaps handle enquiries only. Another idea may be to collect fares on the train but without the technique of simulation all these ideas would require experimentation on the real system, which would cost money without any guarantee that the service would improve.

To use simulation to test these ideas you would build a 'model' of the existing system. The 'model' in this case is the arrival of passengers (*entities*) who join a *queue*, and then obtain a *service*. Following this service the passengers depart. This model is best illustrated by the diagram (Figure 1) below.

Arrivals   Queue   Service   Departures

Figure 1 – Ticket office system

Validation of simulation models

Before experiments can be carried out on a simulation model, you would need to validate the model; that is the results from the model of the existing system need to be compared to the real system. If these results agree with the real system then you would have more confidence that the results from the modified model accurately reflect what would happen to the real system. If these results do not agree then reasons for the discrepancy need to be discovered and perhaps changes made to the model. For example in the rail ticket office example the fact that some passengers 'balk' from the queue, that is do not wait to be served, has not been included and may be important.

Before the validation is carried out you would need to collect the data that will 'drive' the model. The data in the above example would be the number of passengers that arrive at the ticket office and the time to be served. The use of averages here would be useless as this would ignore the variations that occur in real life.

Data on arrivals is normally collected by timing the *inter-arrival* time of customers; that is the time between arrivals. This is illustrated below in the form of a frequency distribution.

Inter-arrival time (secs)	Frequency (%)
0 to under 30	55
30 to under 60	30
60 to under 90	10
90 to under 120	5

This table tells you that 55% of passengers arrived within 30 seconds of each other while 30% of passengers arrived within 30 to 60 seconds of each other, and so on. Notice that the frequency is in percentage form which as you will see is important.

Random numbers

During the running of a simulation, the time for the next arrival is obtained by randomly generating an inter-arrival time. Of course over a long period of time the pattern of arrivals must follow that given by the frequency table but in the short term the pattern should not be predictable. This is achieved by the use of random numbers.

True random numbers can only be generated by physical devices such as a roulette wheel which ensures that the distribution is uniform, that is each number has an equal chance of being picked. In addition the sequence of numbers so produced will be non-repeatable. However most simulations are carried out on a computer and the random numbers in this case are generated by a formula within the computer. Although the random numbers produced are not true random numbers they behave like true random numbers and the fact that the sequence can be repeated has certain advantages which you will soon see.

In the table above the frequency was given as a percentage using two digits. Random numbers can also be given as two digits, from 00 to 99, that is 100 numbers. Since 55% of inter-arrival times are in the range 0 to 30 then the random numbers 00 to 54 could be used to represent this time band. If a computer package was used to simulate this system then a routine within the program would generate a random number and then obtain the appropriate inter-arrival time by interpolation. For example if the random number 15 was generated then the inter-arrival time would be 8.2 seconds ($\frac{15}{55}$ of 30). However when manually carrying out a simulation it is much easier to represent each time band by its mid point, so any random number between 00 to 54 would correspond to an inter-arrival time of 15 seconds. This can be repeated for all bands and to do this you may find it easier to write down the cumulative frequencies as in the modified table below.

Inter-arrival time mid point	Frequency (%)	Cumulative frequency	Random numbers
15	55	55	00 – 54
45	30	85	55 – 84
75	10	95	85 – 94
105	5	100	95 – 99

This procedure is now applied to the service time distribution. This table is shown opposite and would have been obtained by timing a large number of services.

Service time (secs) range	mid point	Frequency	Cumulative frequency	Random numbers
20 – <30	25	17	17	00 – 16
30 – <40	35	28	45	17 – 44
40 – <50	45	25	70	45 – 69
50 – <60	55	20	90	70 – 89
60 – <90	75	10	100	90 – 99

Again a particular service time would be represented by a range of random numbers. For example, a service time of 55 seconds would be represented by the random numbers 70 to 89.

Manual simulation

In order to carry out the simulation manually you would need to obtain a stream of random numbers. These can conveniently be obtained from tables or you could pick a numbered disc or card from a container. These numbers would then be used to sample from the arrival and service time distributions. To illustrate the technique the random numbers 08, 72, 87, 46, 15, 96, 04, 00, 52, 27, 46, 73, 95, 76, 10, 25, 02, and 11 will be used to obtain the first few arrivals and services. A table similar to the one below is normally used to record the simulation.

RNo	Inter-arr.	Clock time	No.in queue	RNo	Service time	Starts	Ends	Waiting time
08	15 A	15	0	72	55	15	70	0
87	75 B	90	0	46	45	90	135	0
15	15 C	105	1 C	96	75	135	210	30
04	15 D	120	2 CD	00	25	210	235	90
52	15 E	135	2 DE	27	35	235	270	100
46	15 F	150	3 DEF	73	55	270	325	120
95	105 G	255	2 FG	76	55	325	380	70
10	15 H	270	2 GH	25	35	380	415	110
02	15 I	285	3 GHI	11	25	415	440	130

If the start is at time zero then the first arrival (A) is at time 15 and if you assume that there is no one in the queue at the start of the simulation then this arrival is served immediately. The inter-arrival time of the second arrival (B) is 75 seconds so the clock time is now 15+75=90. Since A departed at time 70 (15+55) B can also be served immediately. However the third arrival C arrives at time 105 and he must wait for 30 seconds since B does not depart until time 135. Arrival D also has to join the queue and cannot be served until C has been served.

As you can see the calculations are not difficult but they are tedious and time consuming. To obtain reliable results the simulation would need to be continued for the duration of the morning rush hour (say 2 hours or 7200 seconds) and more than one run is necessary. The reason for multiple runs is to improve accuracy and this aspect of simulation will now be explained.

Accuracy of simulation results

In the ticket office example it is likely that estimates of various *performance measures* are required. These performance measures may include the average time a passenger spends in the queue or the average queue length or the proportion of the time that the clerk is busy. Unfortunately simulations are subject to errors and care must be taken to ensure that this error has been reduced or at least can be quantified.

Possible errors include:

> **sampling errors**
>
> **lack of independence**
>
> **initial bias**

Sampling errors arise from the use of random numbers. One run of a simulation uses a stream of random numbers and different streams could give quite different results. There is nothing wrong with this – the variations are reflecting the situations that occur in real life. In fact you can think of simulation as a sampling device. Each stream of random numbers generates one estimate of the required performance measures.

The results from one run of a simulation will provide an estimate of the required performance measures. However it will not be possible to provide a confidence interval of the true mean because the individual results are not independent. For example the time in the queue for one passenger depends on how long the preceding passengers have been in the queue.

When a simulation starts it is normally assumed that all queues are empty. In the real system this may not be the case and a bias is therefore introduced into the simulation, the effects of which will diminish with time. This is known as the initial bias and results from the period where bias is significant may not be desirable.

To overcome the errors associated with sampling and with independence, several runs of a simulation are made and average performance measures recorded for each run. If each run uses a different random number stream these averages will be different. If the averages from each run are then grouped together you could use the usual methods for estimating the true mean of a sample. Lack of independence should not now be a problem, particularly if the method of 'independent replications' is used.

The method of replicating the simulation run depends on whether the system is a *terminating* one or *non-terminating*. A terminating one is, as its name suggests, a system that stops after a certain time or after a certain number of entities have passed through the system. The ticket office is an example of a terminating system as the peak period was assumed to continue for just two hours. Another example is a post office or bank which is open for a certain time each day. For terminating systems the length of the simulation is fixed and this can simply be repeated a number of times using a different random number stream each time. This is called the method of *independent replications*.

Non-terminating systems do not have any natural end and could be considered to continue indefinitely. Examples include airports, harbours, 24 hour casualty departments and many production processes. Although some artificial end could be assumed and the independent replications method used, it is usual to use the *batch means* method. This method makes one very long run of the simulation but is halted at regular intervals. At the end of each interval the average performance measure during the interval is noted. Computer packages handle this automatically. The reason that this method is preferred is to do with the third source of error – the initial bias.

Most terminating systems start in the empty state so initial bias is not a problem in this case. However with non-terminating systems it is a problem and it is necessary for the system to reach *steady state* before results are collected. A system is in steady state if its current state is independent of the starting conditions. The length of time necessary for a system to reach steady state can only be found by experimentation. You should find the diagram (Figure 2.) opposite helpful in understanding the procedure.

If the method of independent replications was used, steady state would need to be reached for each run which is wasteful even with fast computers. With the batch means method, steady state only needs to be found once. Results from the period following steady state only are used in the analysis of the system. Figure 3 opposite illustrates the two methods.

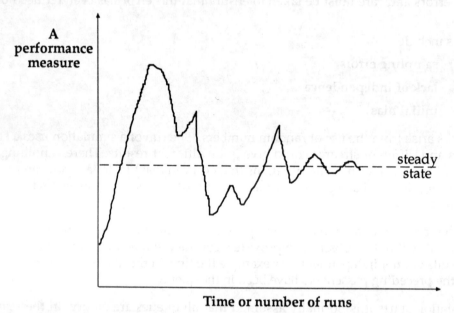

Figure 2 – Steady state analysis

Method of independent replications

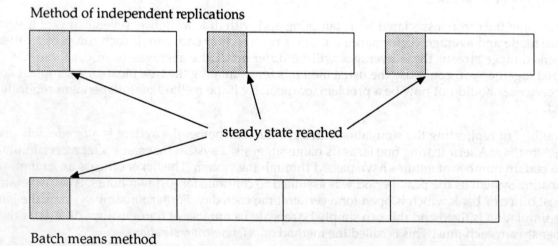

Batch means method

Figure 3 – Methods of replicating runs of a simulation

Analysis of simulation experiments

The ticket office problem was solved using a simulation package. Ten runs of the simulation each of 2 hours duration were made and the average time in the queue for each run was noted. The results are as follows.

Average time in queue (seconds)

387
307
244
227
114
316
125
381
192
221

The mean and standard deviation of this sample of ten values are 251.4 and 95.7 seconds respectively. The 95% confidence interval (see Unit 6, page 13) for the true mean would be:

$$\mu = 251.4 \pm 2.26 \times \frac{95.7}{\sqrt{10}} \text{ (t = 2.26 on 9 degrees of freedom.)}$$

$$= 251.4 \pm 68.4$$

$$= 183 \text{ to } 320 \text{ seconds}$$

You could use this confidence interval for validation purposes by comparing it with the value obtained by observing the real system over a long period of time. Alternatively a hypothesis test could be carried out. (See Unit 8, page 18.)

Provided the validation test was satisfactory the model could be modified to allow the station manager's ideas to be tested. For example the simulation could be re-run with two ticket clerks. The two sets of results could then be compared using confidence intervals or hypothesis testing of two samples (see Unit 9, page 20). If more than two alternatives are to be compared the technique of *analysis of variance* would be used. However before any decision was made some form of cost benefit analysis would probably need to be carried out.

In large simulations there are often many experiments that could be considered and many of the factors affecting the simulation interact. In this case the design of the experiments has to be carefully considered and the *factorial design* method employed.

Variance reduction techniques

If you look at the results from the simulation of the ticket office you will see the results vary considerably; from 114 seconds to 387 seconds. This wide spread is reflected in the confidence interval of ±68.4 seconds. In conventional sampling the only way to reduce this interval is to increase the sample size, which is not always feasible. The sample size in simulation could also be increased by making additional runs but there are alternative methods for reducing the variance of the results. These methods make use of the fact that you are able to control the sources of variability in your experiments and to repeat experiments under identical 'random' conditions.

The most popular method when comparing two or more alternatives is the method of *Common random numbers*. The idea here is that if the sampling variation can be held constant then the observed difference in the results must be due to the differences within the model. To hold the sampling variation constant it is simply a matter of using the same random number stream in all configurations of the model. The results of the experiments can then be analysed using the *paired t-test* (see Unit 10, page 22) for two configurations or the *randomised block design* if more than two configurations are being considered.

Further reading

Introduction to Management Science, Cook and Russell, (PRENTICE-HALL)

Quantitative Approaches in Business Studies, Morris, (PITMAN)

Quantitative Techniques, Lucey, (DP PUBLICATIONS)

Quantitative Analysis, Stansfield, (LONGMAN)

Simulation for Decision Making, Thesen and Travis, (WEST)

Section 3: Developing Knowledge and Skills

Introduction

This section contains further tasks, and professional examination questions. Some of these tasks and questions give you additional practice in the activities found in Section 1, while others extend the knowledge gained in this section.

In some cases the title of a chapter within Section 3 is made up of two chapters from Section 2. This is because of the overlap that exists within many questions. Where overlap does occur, you will not be sent to these questions from Section 1 until all the relevant units have been attempted.

Answers to about half of Section 3 questions are provided in Appendix 1. The answers to the remaining questions are provided in the Lecturers' Supplement (see Preface for details).

Contents

Probability and probability distributions

For help with these tasks and questions see Section 2: Probability, page 55 and Probability Distributions, page 61.

1. a) A computer program is devised for the generation of pseudo-random digits. Calculate the probability that:

    i)   the first two consecutive equal digits which are generated are the fourth and fifth

    ii) the first 6 digits contain exactly three zeros.

2. A security firm delivers wages from a bank to a building site. The driver of the van decides on 1 of 2 routes and on 70% of occaisions he has chosen route 1 (the quickest route) when he is carrying a large amount of cash.

    On other occasions he has chosen both routes equally. Over the past year large amounts of cash were delivered on 25% of occaisions.

    A gang of robbers sees the van take the quick route and decides that a large amount of cash is being delivered. What is the probability that they are correct?

    Answers in Appendix 2, page 245

3. a) In a forthcoming sales promotion each pack of cigarettes is to contain a leaflet with eight 'scratch off' square patches, randomly arranged. The purchaser will scratch off one patch to reveal the value of a small prize. The value of the eight patches on the leaflet is to be as follows:

Value of prize	£0.20	£0.50	£1
Number of patches	5	2	1

    The company has to decide on the number of packs in which to put leaflets, given a budget of £75,000, Find the 'average cost' of a leaflet, and deduce the number of leaflets you would use and why,

    b) In another promotion for cigarettes, a leaflet pictures a roulette wheel with 37 numbers, seven of which are randomly-arranged winning numbers. The purchaser is allowed to scratch off seven of the 37 numbers in the hops of winning a prize. It is therefore possible to select 0, 1 , 2, 3, 4, 5, 6 or 7 winning numbers on each leaflet.

    i)   What is the probability of a purchase not winning a prize?

    ii) If there are one million purchases during the promotion, what are the chances of the 'Super Prize' (the Super Prize is when all seven selections are winners) being won?

    (CIMA May 1991)

4. A mail order firm knows that it will receive a 20% response rate to any literature it circulates. In a new geographic location eight circulars are mailed as a market test. Assuming that the response rate is still applicable to this new location, calculate the probability of the following events:

    i)   two people respond

    ii) more than one person responds and

    iii) less than 25% of people respond.

5. A shopkeeper finds that 20% of the cartons containing 6 eggs he receives are damaged. A carton is picked at random, checked and returned to the consignment. The procedure is repeated a further three times. What is the probability that out of the four cartons inspected

    i)   none were undamaged.

    ii) at least three were undamaged?

6. The World Life Assurance Company Limited uses recent mortality data in the calculation of its premiums. The following table shows, per thousand of population, the number of persons expected to survive to a given age.

Age	0	10	20	30	40	50	60	70	80	90	100
Number surviving to given age	1,000	981	966	944	912	880	748	521	261	45	0

Required:

a) Use the table to determine the probability that
   i) a randomly chosen person born now will die before reaching the age of 60,
   ii) a randomly chosen person who is aged 30 now will die before reaching the age of 60,
   iii) a randomly chosen person who is aged 50 now will die before reaching the age of 60.

   Comment on the order of magnitude of your three answers.

b) The company is planning to introduce a life insurance policy for persons aged 50. This policy requires a single payment paid by the insured at the age of 50 so that if the insured died within the following ten years the dependant will receive a payment of £10,000. However if this person survives, then the company will not make any payment.

   Ignoring interest on premiums and any administrative costs, calculate the single premium that the company should charge to break even in the long run.

c) If twelve persons each take out a policy as described in (b) and the company charges each person a single premium of £2,000, find the probability that the company will make a loss.

d) The above table was based on the ages of all people who died in 1986. Comment on the appropriateness to the company when calculating the premiums it should charge.

e) The above table can be expanded to include survival numbers, per thousand of population, of other ages.

Age	50	52	54	56	58	60
Number surviving to given age	880	866	846	822	788	748

   i) Given that a person aged 50 now dies before the age of 60, use this new information to estimate the expected age of death.

   ii) Calculate a revised value for the single premium as described in part (b), taking into account the following additional information:
      ❐ the expected age of death before 60 as estimated at (i)
      ❐ a constant interest rate of 8% p.a. on premiums
      ❐ an administration cost of £100 per policy
      ❐ a cost of £200 to cover profit and commissions.

(ACCA December 1987)
Answers in Appendix 2, page 245

7. Calls arrive at a switchboard according to the Poisson distribution. If the average number of calls received in a 5 minute period is 6.7, find the probability that:
    a) There are less than 4 calls received in a 5 minute period.
    b) There are more than 7 calls received during a 5 minute period.
    c) There are no calls received in a one minute period.

8. Several lengths of glass tubing are examined for the number of flaws in intervals of given length. State what assumptions would be necessary to apply the theory of a Poisson process.

    If 1500 flaws are found in 1000 intervals each of 1 mm find the probability, assuming a Poisson distribution of
    i) at least 2 flaws in an interval of 1 mm
    ii) an interval between two consecutive flaws being greater than 5 mm.

9. a) Describe the main features of the Normal distribution.

   b) The distribution of marks in a certain examination is believed to be represented by a Normal distribution with a mean of 50 and a standard deviation of 23. There are 1000 marked scripts.

      i) How many scripts would be expected in the 'distinction' category for which the qualifying mark is 75?

      ii) How many scripts would be expected in the 'unclassified' category with less than 20 marks?

      iii) What mark should be required for the 'distinction' category if 10% of the candidates are to be given that achievement level?

(CII April 1990)

10. The specification for the length of an engine part is a minimum of 99 mm and a maximum of 104.4 mm. A batch of parts is produced that is Normally distributed with a mean of 102 mm and a standard deviation of 2 mm. Parts cost £10 to make. Those that are too short have to be scrapped; those too long are shortened at a further cost of £8.

You are required

   a) to find the percentage of parts which are (i) undersize, (ii) oversize;

   b) to find the expected cost of producing 1,000 usable parts;

   c) to calculate and to explain the implications of changing the production method so that the mean is halfway between the upper and lower specification limits. (The standard deviation remains the same.)

(CIMA November 1991)

11. A company manufactures automatic vending machines. One of the simplest machines is operated by a £1 coin. Inside the machine a photo-electric cell is used to assess whether a coin is genuine or counterfeit by measuring the time (t) it takes to roll a fixed distance down a slope. Since coins and machines vary a little in size and wear, there is some small variation in time (t).

From extensive testing it has been found that the time (t) taken by genuine £1 coins follows a Normal distribution with a mean of 300 units of time and a standard deviation of 20.

For commonly-used counterfeit coins the tests revealed a Normally distributed time with a mean of 150 time units and a standard deviation of 50.

The manufacturer sets the limits of acceptability at a minimum of 260 units of time.

You are required to find

   a) the percentage of such counterfeit coins accepted;

   b) the percentage of genuine £1 coins rejected;

   c) the changes which would result from restricting the percentage of accepted counterfeit coins to 0.1%.

(CIMA May 1988)
Answers in Appendix 2, page 245

12. State *two* reasons for the importance of the normal distribution in statistical analysis.

Broadway Plastics Limited is a small firm which specialises in the production of heavy-duty plastic springs. The company has secured an order for 800 springs which were basically the same as a standard spring, the SX-1, except for its resulting force. The production manager had initially assumed that a special batch of these 800 springs would have to be made at a cost of £5.20 per spring. This cost took into account the batch set-up cost and all other costs associated with the manufacture of a small batch of non-standard springs.

The production manager has begun to wonder whether it would be necessary to have the springs specially made. The plastic springs required would exert a force of 2.9 kilos at the usual operating length. The tolerance on this specification is 0.2 kilos, so that any spring with a force between 2.7 and 3.1 kilos at the usual operating length would be acceptable. These requirements are not too different from those of the SX-1 standard spring which the company uses extensively and which would therefore cost much less. It is known that the force of SX-1 springs is approximately normally distributed with a mean force of 2.5 kilos at the usual operating length and a standard deviation of 0.2 kilos. The SX-1 springs have a unit price of £3.50 per spring. The production manager has to decide whether he should order the 800 springs as a batch to be specially manufactured, or whether he could select springs within the required tolerance range from the existing stocks of standard springs. The cost of inspection and measurement is estimated at £0.20 per spring.

Required:

a) Determine the percentage of existing stocks of SX-1 springs which lie within the required tolerance limits.

b) Determine the number of SX-1 springs that could be expected to require inspection if the production manager wanted to obtain the 800 springs from existing stocks. Determine the expected cost of inspection.

c) Find the total cost of procuring the 800 springs within the required limits if they were

   i)   selected from existing SX-1 springs.

   ii) manufactured as a special batch.

   Hence decide whether or not the production manager should have the springs specially made.

d) What percentage change in the original special batch cost, £5.20 per spring, is required to alter the decision in part (c)?

e) Broadway Plastics also produces another lesser-used standard spring, SY-2, which is more highly priced at £4.25 per spring. The forces of these springs at the usual operating length have a normal distribution with a mean of 2.7 kilos but an unknown standard deviation, s.

   Assuming that the cost of inspection and measurement is the same as the SX-1 spring, determine the range of values of s for which it would be more preferable to use the SY-2 spring than the SX-1 for the order.

   (ACCA December 1990)

13. As a result of a recent analysis of labour costs throughout all the branches of the Olympus Assurance Company, it has been decided that the total number of employees should be reduced by 3%. The usual retirement age in the company is 65 and it is estimated that the desired reduction can be achieved by offering early retirement to all employees aged 62 and above. For this purpose, an early retirement scheme has been drawn up, based on negotiations with the unions concerned and the informal reactions of employees. It has been estimated that the probability of employees accepting the scheme depends on their age as follows:

Age	Probability of accepting early retirement
62	0.6
63	0.7
64	0.8

In one particular branch of the company, there are 10 employees aged 62 and above as detailed in the following table.

Age	62	63	64
Number	5	3	2

Required:

a) What is the expected number of employees accepting early retirement at this branch? What is the probability of early retirement being accepted by all 10 employees?

b) What is the probability of exactly 9 employees accepting early retirement? Hint: The one person who does not accept early retirement can be aged 62, 63, or 64. These three cases must be considered individually.

c) Given that the variance of a Binomial distribution is np(1-p), determine the variance of the total number of employees accepting early retirement from this branch. Using a Normal distribution approximation, estimate the probability of at least 8 employees accepting the scheme.

(ACCA December 1985)
Answers in Appendix 2, page 245

14. In each of the following three situations, use the binomial, Poisson or normal distribution according to which is the most appropriate. In each case, explain why you selected the distribution and draw attention to any feature which supports or casts doubt on the choice of distribution.

a) Situation 1: The lifetimes of a certain type of electrical component are distributed with a mean of 800 hours and a standard deviation of 160 hours.

Required:

i) If the manufacturer replaces all components that fail before the guaranteed minimum lifetime of 600 hours, what percentage of the components have to be replaced?

ii) If the manufacturer wishes to replace only the 1% of components that have the shortest life, what value should be used as the guaranteed lifetime?

iii) What is the probability that the mean lifetime of a sample of 25 of these electrical components exceeds 850 hours?

b) Situation 2: A greengrocer buys peaches in large consignments directly from a wholesaler. In view of the perishable nature of the commodity the greengrocer accepts that 15% of the supplied peaches will usually be unsaleable. As he cannot check all of the peaches individually, he selects a single batch of 10 peaches on which to base his decision of whether to purchase a large consignment or not. If no more than two of these peaches are unsatisfactory, the greengrocer purchases the consignment.

Required:

Determine the probability that, under normal supply conditions, the consignment is purchased.

c) Situation 3: Vehicles pass a certain point on a busy single-carriageway road at an average rate of two per ten-second interval.

Required:

Determine the probability that more than three cars pass this point during a twenty-second interval.

(ACCA June 1990)
Answers in Appendix 2, page 245

Decision analysis

15. A biologist develops a new product. Having made the product he has three choices of what to do with it.

> For help with these tasks and questions see Section 2: Decision Analysis, page 78.

Either i)   Manufacture the product himself

   ii)   Allow someone else to make it and be paid on a royalty basis.

or iii)   Sell the rights for a lump sum.

The profit which can be expected depends on the level of sales and is shown below (in thousands of £'s).

	High Sales	Medium Sales	Low Sales
Manufacture himself	80	40	–20
Take royalties	50	30	10
Sell all rights	20	20	20

The probabilities associated with the level of sales are:

   High sales   0.2

   Medium sales   0.5

   Low sales   0.3

a)   Obtain the corresponding loss table and write down the best decision using:

   i)   The minimax rule.

   ii)   The maximax rule.

   iii)   The maximin rule

b)   Draw a decision tree for the problem and decide the best course of action using this method.

c)   A survey might help to determine the likely level of sales. What is the maximum amount that you would be prepared to pay for this survey?

(Answers in Appendix 2, page 245)

16. a)   What do you understand by the term 'expected value' of a probability distribution?

b)   A company which supplies venture capital to industry has been asked by a client to supply £1m in order to set up a new process. The company expects to make a return of 30% on the capital in the first year if the client's process is a success and a loss of 20% if the process is a failure. It costs the company £25,000 to analyse the deal whether it accepts the business or not. If, after analysis, the company rejects what turns out to be a successful process it will lose goodwill estimated at £100,000.

   i)   Show the expected profit and loss on the business in the form of the table below.

Decision	Success	Failure
Accept		
Reject		

   ii)   The person who underwrites the venture assesses its chance of success as $\frac{3}{4}$ and its chance of failure as $\frac{1}{4}$. What should be the decision of the company and what would be the expected profit?

   iii)   What probabilities of success and failure would make the company indifferent as to acceptance or rejection?

   iv)   What are the advantages and the disadvantages of using this approach to decision making?

(CII April 1990)

17.   A golf club has to decide how many programmes to produce for a Charity Pro-Am golf tournament. From previous experience of similar tournaments, it is expected that the probability of sales will be as follows:

Number of programmes demanded	Probability of demand
1,000	0.1
2,000	0.4
3,000	0.2
4,000	0.2
5,000	0.1

The best quotation from a local printer is £2,000 plus 10 pence per copy. Advertising revenue totals £1,500. Programmes are sold for 60 pence each. Unsold programmes are worthless.

You are required

a)   to draw up a profit table with programme production levels as columns and programme demand levels as rows;

b)   to find the most profitable number of programmes to produce;

c)   to explain your analysis, including any assumptions.

(CIMA May 1992)

18.   Each week a small hardware shop purchases for £40 per unit a perishable product which it then tries to sell for £70 per item. Every item that is sold incurs a selling cost of £5. At the end of each week any items that are not sold are returned to the manufacturer who refunds £25 for each item returned. From past experience customer demand each week can be described by the following probability distribution.

Customer demand	1	2	3	4	5
Probability	0.05	0.2	0.4	0.25	0.1

Required

a)   Determine the contribution to profit for each combination of weekly purchase quantity and customer demand.

b)   One decision criterion is based on the method of expectation.

   i)   Determine the number of products the store manager should order each week using the criterion of expected value of weekly contribution.

   ii)   Given this order size and with all other data unchanged, obtain the minimum selling price that the store can set without sustaining an expected loss.

c)   An alternative decision criterion is the maximin decision criterion.

Determine the optimum weekly order size using this criterion.

d)   In the context of this question outline briefly the limitations of the two decision criteria used.

e)   The store manager is considering two proposals for increasing sales of the product:

   i)   Advertising in a local newspaper at a weekly cost of £10. which would change the probabilities of customer demand to 0.0, 0.1, 0.2, 0.5, 0.2 respectively and

   ii)   Cutting the price of the product to £60, which would alter the probabilities to 0.0, 0.0, 0.1, 0.3, 0.6 respectively.

Would either of these two proposals be worth while (based on the criterion of expected contribution)? Make a recommendation to the store manager.

(ACCA December 1991)
(Answers in Appendix 2, page 245)

19.   Gordon Electronics are considering the launch of a new range of lighting equipment which will have a project horizon of five years. If the new range is introduced without further market research it is thought that demand will be either high (with probability 0.7) or low (with probability 0.3). However, it is possible to commission a market research survey which will produce either a good forecast (with probability 0.6) or a bad forecast. It has been decided that if the survey

yields a good forecast there will be increased marketing effort which will yield an increased annual contribution. In this case the probability of a high demand is 0.9. However, if the survey produced a bad forecast it has been decided that the company will not introduce the new range but continue with the old range of products.

The accounts department of Gordon Electronics has produced the following financial information.

Annual contribution if the new range of equipment is introduced and no market survey is commissioned.

Year	1	2	3	4	5
High demand	20,000	40,000	50,000	30,000	10,000
Low demand	10,000	15,000	20,000	10,000	5,000

Increased annual contribution if the survey provides a good forecast.

High demand	£10,000 p.a.
Low demand	£5,000 p.a.

The survey cost is £10,000.

Annual contribution if the new range of equipment is not introduced and the old range of products is continued.

Year	1	2	3	4	5
	20,000	20,000	15,000	10,000	5,000

The company's cost of capital is 15% p.a.

Assume that all income occurs at the year-end.

Year	1	2	3	4	5
Present value factors (at 15% p.a.)	0.8696	0.7561	0.6575	0.5718	0.4972

Required:

a)   Draw a decision-tree to represent the various courses of action open to the company

b)   Calculate the present value of contributions for each possible action/outcome combination.

c)   Calculate the expected present value for each of the following three situations:

   i)   launching the new range without a market research survey

   ii)   not introducing the new range of equipment

   iii)   carrying out a market research survey and taking appropriate action.

d)   Recommend a course of action to the company

e)   If the probability that the market survey produces a good forecast changes from 0.6 to 0.5, would this alter your recommendation?

(ACCA December 1990)

Estimation and hypothesis testing

> For help with these tasks and questions see Section 2: Estimation, page 85 and Hypothesis Testing, page 99.

20.   a)   Boxes of pears were packed in Italy with a nominal net mass of 50 kilograms. On arrival in London this has usually decreased due to bruising, ripening and shrinkage. A large batch of these boxes has just arrived in London and a random sample of 15 boxes is chosen and their net masses are recorded in kilograms as listed below.

46.2	50.4	49.6	56.1	52.4	53.6	46.7	48.1
45.2	47.8	51.1	56.9	44.3	49.2	47.5	

Assuming that this sample came from a normal distribution with a standard deviation of 3.74, find a 95% confidence interval for the mean mass of the population.

21. During an internal audit, an accountant had to sample a very large batch of invoices for value and for errors. A simple random sample of 200 invoices revealed a mean value of £90 with a standard deviation of £40.

    You are required to
    a)   find the standard error of the mean;
    b)   find 99% confidence limits for the mean value of the whole batch;
    c)   explain briefly why it is not possible to find 100% confidence limits for the mean value of the batch from a sample;
    d)   find 95% confidence limits for the error rate of the whole batch if 20 invoices showed errors
    e)   find the size of sample required in (b) and (d) in order to double the accuracy of your answers,

    (CIMA November 1989)
    (Answers in Appendix 2, page 245)

22. During an internal audit, a very large number of invoices has to be sampled. The management accountant remembers that the error rate on invoices at the last internal audit was of the order of 10%, but has no record of the limits of accuracy on that figure.

    You are required
    a)   to find the size of simple random sample that should be taken to be 95% confident that the true error rate shall be estimated to within limits of ±3% if
         i)   the last audit's evidence is used;
         ii)   the last audit's evidence is NOT relevant;
    b)   to explain in broad terms how your answers would be affected if the sample were to be stratified by value.

    (CIMA May 1990)

23. a)   What do you understand by the following terms:
         i)   statistical inference;
         ii)   central limit theorem;
         iii) confidence interval?
    b)   An insurance company recognises that 5% of small claims on household policies will be fraudulent and accepts this on the grounds of controlling administration expenditure. In order to verify this the company organises a detailed check on a random sample of 300 such claims and finds that 25 involved a degree of dishonesty.
         i)   Does this investigation justify the maintenance of the 'accepted' 5%?
         ii)   What is the 95% confidence interval for the proportion of fraudulent claims?
         iii) What size sample should have been taken to estimate the percentage of fraudulent claims to within ±2% at a confidence level of 99%?

    (CII April 1990)

24. 'Real Toys' have just negotiated a repeat order from Toy World who have had problems with goods being faulty and are insisting on a quality control procedure being implemented before the order is signed.
    a)   Write a letter to the Managing Director of Real Toys explaining why statistical process control may be worth implementing throughout the Company.

b) The weight of each garden gnome was one of the features chosen for the pilot scheme. The readings from 20 consecutive samples are shown below:

Sample No.	Weight (100's gms)			
1	28.8	29.2	30.8	29.2
2	30.2	30.0	26.8	30.6
3	29.0	27.8	28.6	30.4
4	30.8	29.2	30.4	29.6
5	31.4	30.6	31.0	31.4
6	31.4	30.0	29.0	29.4
7	29.0	28.0	26.5	29.6
8	27.0	23.2	25.2	24.5
9	28.0	27.0	29.4	27.6
10	26.2	25.3	26.8	25.8
11	28.2	28.1	30.0	30.0
12	27.1	26.1	25.4	23.8
13	22.8	23.5	25.5	24.0
14	27.0	28.5	27.2	25.5
15	25.6	24.5	23.5	22.4
16	25.2	27.4	27.0	28.2
17	28.0	28.0	25.8	30.4
18	26.5	25.2	29.3	27.4
19	22.1	26.2	23.8	24.8
20	20.5	20.4	24.6	24.8

i) Use the results to produce a control chart for the means.

ii) What does the chart tell you about the process?

25. The Marathon Drug Company plc, a leading supplier of pharmaceuticals and industrial chemicals, has recently installed a new filling machine for the accurate measurement of powders. For many products, the accuracy of measurement in the filling process is of considerable importance in view of the high unit cost of the materials involved.

A retailing chemist, Nelson Dispensing Chemists, has placed an order for 800 packets of a substance packed by the Marathon Drug Company. Nelson required packs of 500g. After the machine was set up for dispensing 500g of this substance, the quality control manager selected five packs out of each batch of 100 filled, thus obtaining eight samples of five observations. The results of his measurements were summarised by the sample means and ranges as shown below.

Sample number	1	2	3	4	5	6	7	8
Mean	509.6	506.8	508.2	506.2	508.6	507.2	508.6	508.8
Range	6	5	4	4	7	8	12	10

Required:

a) Use this data to find control limits for the mean and range, commenting on the stability, or otherwise, of the manufacturing process.

b) The unit price of the powder is 20 pence per gramme. The Marathon Drug Company usually applies the company policy that no more than 2.5% of all packs are permitted to weigh less than the stated amount and no more than 2.5% are to exceed the nominal weight by more than 4%.

i) If the company policy applies, and assuming the weights of the packs follow a normal distribution, show that the largest standard deviation, σ, allowed for the target population is approximately 5.1g. Identify the corresponding target mean μ.

ii) Using the values of μ and σ found in (i), obtain control limits for the mean of a sample of five observations from the target population.

What can therefore be concluded about the machine's inherent accuracy in relation to the accuracy required?

iii) Using the sample data estimate the cost of the powder dispensed in excess of 500g per pack for the whole order

(ACCA June 1991)
(Answers in Appendix 2, page 245)

26. a) Explain clearly the following terms used in hypothesis testing:
    i) Null and Alternative hypotheses
    ii) Type I and Type II errors
    iii) Significance level

A motorcycle is claimed to have a fuel consumption which is normally distributed with mean 54 miles per gallon and standard deviation of 5 miles per gallon. 12 motorcycles are tested and the mean value of their fuel consumption was found to be 50.5 miles per gallon.

Taking a 5% level of significance test the hypothesis that the mean fuel consumption is 54 miles per gallon.

(Answers in Appendix 2, page 245)

27. a) Outline the central limit theorem and comment on its application to inferential statistics.

    b) Taurus Components Limited, a manufacturer of electrical parts and accessories, is currently examining the cost of assembling one of its major products. From considerable past experience it has been established that the mean labour time to assemble this component is 90 minutes. However the chief works engineer is convinced that the assembly procedures could be improved. Consequently he has developed a new assembly method, and has randomly assigned operators to carry out a trial run. After allowing these operators to get used to the new procedures, he timed the assembly of a sample of ten components. The results (in minutes) are shown below.

79	74	112	95	83	96	77	84	70	90

Required:

i) Calculate unbiased estimates of the mean and standard deviation of the assembly time of the product using the new assembly method.

ii) Test whether the sample observations support the belief that the new assembly method significantly reduces assembly time. State any assumptions you make.

iii) Encouraged by his results, the chief works study engineer timed the assembly of a further 30 components. The unbiased estimates of the mean and the standard for these 30 observations are 84.0 and 14.65 respectively.

From the combined sample of 40 observations obtain further unbiased estimates of the population mean and standard deviation and hence provide a 95% confidence interval for the new mean assembly time.

iv) Estimate the smallest total sample size required for the sample mean to be within three minutes of the underlying population mean with 95% confidence.

v) At the present time the direct labour costs, including allowances for overhead expenses are £8.70 per hour.

If the fixed cost of implementing the new procedure is estimated to be £20,000 and it is assumed that the mean time for the combined sample could be maintained during the full production, then use the results of the combined sample to determine the expected savings of using this method if the company sell a further 50,000 components of this type.

(ACCA June 1989)

28. a) A random sample of eight discount stores in London showed the following prices of a particular compact disc:

£8.60   £9.40   £10.70   £7.80   £10.30   £7.90   £8.30   £11.40

A random sample of ten Bristol discount stores showed the following prices for the same CD:

£10.20 £7.80 £11.00 £11.50 £9.50 £12.20 £10.30 £8.80 £8.90 £9.80.

Working at the 5% significance level, is there evidence that the average prices in discount stores in the two cities differ significantly?

29. A software house has recently developed an improved version of its self-tuition word-processing package QUICKWRITE which it has decided to call SUPERWRITE. It claims that SUPERWRITE is much faster than QUICKWRITE at teaching untrained individuals with no prior experience of word-processing to process and manipulate scripts.

To test the validity of this claim, 19 individuals with no previous word-processing experience were selected and divided into two groups. Ten spent an hour using QUICKWRITE while the remaining nine spent an hour using SUPERWRITE. Each individual was then asked to process, correct, save and print a suitable test script. The time taken, in minutes, in each case is recorded below.

QUICK	40	34	37	41	35	43	39	42	41	38
SUPER	36	41	28	31	36	41	38	34	35	

a) Using an appropriate t-test, test the claim at a 5% level of significance, showing clearly all workings.

b) What reservations do you have about this result? Can you think of an alternative test design which may give more reliable results.

(Answers in Appendix 2, page 245)

30. a) In auditing it is often sufficient to investigate only a sample of the accounts of a company.
Describe the advantages of taking a random sample as opposed to a judgement sample.

b) An auditor undertakes a preliminary spot check of the weekly wage slips of the 50,000 manual workers of a large chemical firm to estimate the percentage which include overtime payment. He takes a random sample of 100 and finds 25 that do include overtime payment.

Required:

i) Provide 90% confidence limits for the percentage of all wage slips which include overtime payments.

ii) How many wage slips need to be inspected if he wishes his estimate to be within 5% of the true percentage with 95% confidence?

c) The weekly wage amounts, in £, of the 25 employees who do have an overtime payment are given in the following table.

70	166	140	150	126
151	133	200	145	170
200	118	132	149	130
125	165	167	240	120
210	137	140	136	130

(You may use the summations $\Sigma x = 3750$, $\Sigma x^2 = 591900$)

Required:

Determine unbiased point estimates of the mean and standard deviation for this population.

d) The weekly wages of the sample of 75 employees who do not have an overtime payment have a mean of $\bar{x}_2 = 140$ and a standard deviation $\hat{\sigma}_2 = 32$

Required:

Is there statistical evidence of a difference between the two sets of wages? Interpret your answer and state any assumptions you make.

(*ACCA June 1991*)

31. A new wages structure is introduced throughout the large number of factories in the Hoopoint kitchen appliance manufacturing industry. The following values of output per man-hour are obtained from eight randomly selected factories just before and another eight just after its introduction (16 different factories in all).

Output per man-hour	
Old wages structure	New wages structure
54	55
81	56
50	47
40	64
49	26
58	51
63	48
45	53

Required:

a)   Calculate a 95% confidence interval for the overall mean output per man-hour under the new wages structure. What assumption are you making when calculating this interval?

b)   It is suggested that the change in the wages structure has in fact produced no overall change in output per man-hour.

   i)   Explain why a match-paired t-test would be inappropriate to test this suggestion.

   ii)   Perform a more appropriate t-test to test the hypothesis and report your conclusion. State any assumptions you make.

   iii)   Explain why it might be thought to be desirable to use a distribution free test with these data.

(*ACCA December 1990*)
(Answers in Appendix 2, page 245)

32.   a)   A car manufacturer has developed a device that is supposed to improve the fuel consumption of its cars. A motoring magazine has decided to test this claim and has hired eight different (unmodified) models of car from this manufacturer. The cars were filled with petrol and driven at a constant 50 mph for exactly 30 miles round a test track. At the end of the test the petrol consumption was measured and the test repeated after the device had been fitted to each of the cars. The petrol consumption (in litres) before and after the modification was as follows:

Car:	A	B	C	D	E	F	G	H
Before:	3.5	4.2	4.7	5.0	2.6	4.5	4.6	6.2
After:	3.3	4.0	4.7	4.5	2.8	4.2	4.7	5.7

Use an appropriate t-test to decide if the claim by the manufacturer is justified.

b)   The car manufacturer wished to discover if the petrol saving device had improved the company's image with the motoring public. Out of 80 people questioned before the new device was developed, 15 indicated that they would consider buying one of the company's cars. Another survey carried out after the device had been developed and advertised gave 18 out of 60 people for the same question. Does this suggest that the company's image has been improved?

(Answers in Appendix 2, page 245)

33. As part of an investment portfolio analysis, two similar companies which operate in the same market are being compared in terms of their earnings per share. The companies' annual results over the last 6 years have provided the following information:

Earnings per share(p)

Year	Company A	Company B
1980	14.3	13.8
1981	15.6	14.6
1982	17.2	16.4
1983	16.4	16.8
1984	14.9	15.0
1985	17.6	16.4

The person performing the analysis calculated the mean and standard deviation of each company's results and then computed a t statistic as follows:

Company	Mean (p)	Standard Deviation (p)
A	16.0	1.2977
B	15.5	1.2050

$$t = \frac{16.0 - 15.5}{\sqrt{\dfrac{1.2977^2}{6} + \dfrac{1.2050^2}{6}}} = 0.69 (10 \, df)$$

He then concluded that the result was insignificant on both a one and two tailed basis, and consequently decided that the two companies have the same average earnings per share.

Required:

a) Critically evaluate the analysis which has been performed and give 3 reasons why the procedure used and the conclusion reached are inappropriate and invalid.

b) Perform an appropriate analysis of the data and state your conclusions.

(ACCA June 1986)

(Answers in Appendix 2, page 246)

34. Northern Electrics Company Limited is a well established manufacturer of a variety of electrical goods; its leading product being the computer colour monitor. The main manufacturing centre for colour monitors has six independent production lines all running at the same speed so that the same large number of monitors are completed each hour. At the end of the manufacturer process all monitors undergo a quality inspection, at which stage a small proportion are rejected as unsatisfactory. The numbers of faulty products are recorded hourly in a log book for each production line. For an eight-hour day the following results were recorded

Production Line	Number of faulty products							
	Hour 1	Hour 2	Hour 3	Hour 4	Hour 5	Hour 6	Hour 7	Hour 8
Line 1	0	3	0	2	0	1	2	4
Line 2	1	1	3	5	2	3	4	3
Line 3	2	3	4	1	4	2	2	7
Line 4	0	0	2	0	0	2	1	2
Line 5	0	2	1	3	1	1	1	2
Line 6	2	0	0	3	1	2	5	6

Required:

a) Construct an ungrouped frequency distribution table for the 48 entries in this table and hence determine its mean.

b) Explain why a Poisson distribution may be expected to be a suitable model for this data.

c) Assuming an appropriate Poisson distribution determine the probabilities that:

    i)   for a given production line, no faulty monitors are discovered during one hour,

    ii) for a given production line, more than three faulty monitors are found during one hour,

    iii) less than five faulty monitors are recorded in total during one hour.

d) Use a standard statistical test to examine whether or not the entries recorded in the table conform to the Poisson distribution.

e) The production manager suspects that there is a tendency for there to be more faulty produced during the last two hours of production than the first six hours.

Explain why it may not be statistical appropriate to carry out a t-test on the data to test this suspicion. Without performing a test how might this suspicion be tested more appropriately?

(ACCA December 1989)

(Answers in Appendix 2, page 246)

35. a) Explain briefly the meaning of the term 'significantly different' in statistical hypothesis testing.

b) The four production plants of Zeus Company Limited are based at Aybridge, Beedon, Crambourne and Deepool. A random sample of employees at each of these four plants have been asked to give their views on a productivity-based wage deal that the company is proposing. The table below summarises these views.

		Production Plant		
View	Aybridge	Beedon	Crambourne	Deepool
In favour	80	40	50	60
Against	35	30	40	25

Required:

i) A chi-squared analysis of the contingency table gave a X^2 value of 7.34.

Test the hypothesis that there is no significant difference in views between the production plants. Explain what action might have been taken to reach a clearer decision.

ii) The employees at Aybridge, Beedon, Crambourne and Deepool were also asked to indicate whether or not they were under forty years of age. The numbers aged under forty for the four production plants were 75, 48, 54 and 57 respectively, of which 60, 28, 30 and 45 respectively were in favour of the wage proposal.

Analyse the two resulting 2 x 4 contingency tables to test separately for the two age groups the hypothesis that there is no significant difference in views between the production plants.

iii) Estimate the overall percentage of the employees in favour of the wage deal for each age group. Are these percentages 'significantly different'?

(ACCA June 1988)

36. Crownhouse Limited is a market research company specialising in the collection of opinions from the general public. The company is currently undertaking a study into the effects of incentives to increase the returns from its surveys. The objective of the study was to compare the effect of a monetary incentive on response rate for two social types.

A number of questionnaires were posted to potential respondents, some containing a financial incentive for a prompt response and others without such an incentive. Each potential respondent was classified as either Social Type X or Social Type Y according to occupation. A follow-up letter was sent to all respondents who had not returned the questionnaire by a two-week deadline. The data obtained from this study are obtained in the table below.

		Questionnaire Response		
Social Type	Financial Incentive Given?	Returned before Deadline	Returned after Follow-up	Not Returned
X	Yes	37	3	20
	No	25	1	19
Y	Yes	39	2	19
	No	18	2	35

Required:

a) Explain why it is preferable to combine the final two columns of data before carrying out an appropriate statistical test on this data.

Produce a fully-labelled table with these two columns combined.

b) By combining the rows appropriately test the hypotheses that

i) The questionnaire response rate is independent of whether or not a financial incentive is provided.

ii) The questionnaire response rate is independent of social type.

c) Provide a full interpretation of the results of the survey.

(ACCA December 1991)
(Answers in Appendix 2, page 246)

37. a) Describe the conditions under which a normal distribution may provide a good approximation to a binomial distribution, and give a reason why this approximation may be useful in practice.

b) A company which manufactures electrical circuits packs these circuits in boxes of 15. These boxes are then distributed to microcomputer assemblers in cartons of 50 boxes. On their arrival, the quality control manager opens a number of cartons, randomly selects from these a total of 100 boxes of circuits and counts the number of defective circuits in each box. The table below summarises the findings.

Number of defective circuits in a box	0	1	2	3	≥4
Number of boxes	57	29	11	3	0

Required:

i) Explain the circumstances under which a binomial distribution might not be a suitable distribution to model the number of defective circuits in a box.

ii) Use the data above to produce a point estimate, p, for the proportion of electric circuits that are defective.

iii) Carry out a chi-squared goodness-of-fit test to determine whether the frequency distribution of defective electric circuits per box is binomial.

iv) A box of electric circuits is rejected if it contains 2 or more defectives.

Use the estimate of p, found in (ii), to find the approximate probability that a randomly chosen carton contains at most 10 boxes that are rejected.

(ACCA June 1989)

Correlation and regression

For help with these tasks and questions see Section 2: Correlation and Regression, page 116.

38. The data below relates to the weight and height of a group of students.

Height (ins)	Weight (lbs)	Sex
68	148	male
69	126	female
66	145	male
70	158	male
66	140	female
68	126	female
64	120	female
66	119	female
70	182	male
62	127	female
68	165	male
63	133	male
65	124	female
73	203	male

a) Draw a scatter diagram of weight against height for the whole data. Alongside each point write either 'm' or 'f' as appropriate.

b) Describe your scatter diagram. Try drawing an ellipse around
   i)   all the points
   ii) the points relating to the male students
   iii) the points relating to the female students.

Is there any indication that the correlation is stronger for either group?

c) Calculate Pearson's Product Moment Correlation Coefficient for the three sets of points identified in (b) above. Comment on the values obtained.

d) Are the correlation coefficients calculated in (c) significantly different from zero?

(Collect data from a group of friends and repeat the analysis)

(Answers in Appendix 2, page 246)

39. At the end of a financial year the chief accountant of each of ten engineering companies was asked to compute six accounting ratios (A, B, C, D, E, F) to describe his company's performance. The accounting ratios D, E and F for the 10 companies were as follows:

Company	Ratio D	Ratio E	Ratio F
1	1.30	1.30	1.45
2	1.45	1.20	1.20
3	1.30	1.25	1.30
4	0.95	0.80	0.75
5	1.80	1.75	1.90
6	1.50	1.60	1.65
7	1.05	1.35	1.50
8	1.30	1.05	0.90
9	0.90	0.95	0.85
10	0.90	1.10	1.00

Required:

a) Calculate Spearman's rank correlation coefficient between:
   i) ratio D and ratio E,
   ii) ratio E and ratio F,

and hence complete the following Spearman's rank correlation matrix.

	A	B	C	D	E	F
A	1.0	−0.7	0.8	−0.8	−0.9	−0.7
B	−0.7	1.0	−0.8	0.9	0.8	0.7
C	0.8	−0.8	1.0	−0.8	−0.7	−0.6
D	−0.8	0.9	−0.8			
E	−0.9	0.8	−0.7			
F	−0.7	0.7	−0.6			

b) Use the correlation matrix described in (a) to divide the six accounting ratios into two distinct groups. Explain your reasoning.

c) Use the test statistic $T = \dfrac{R\sqrt{n-2}}{\sqrt{1-R^2}}$ which has a $t_{(n-2)}$ distribution under H_0.

   to investigate whether there is a significant rank correlation between ratios D and E.

d) Explain why a set of data can give a value of exactly 1.0 for R, Spearman's rank correlation coefficient, and a value of less than 1.0 for r, the product moment correlation coefficient. Is it possible for a set of data to give r = 1.0 and R < 1.0? Support your arguments with a suitable sketch.

(ACCA December 1988)
(Answers in Appendix 2, page 246)

40. A company has analysed its expenditure in relation to sales with the following results.

Sales ('000 items):	49	61	73	80	89	98
Total Expenses (£'000s):	73	77	83	86	93	97

i)   Draw the scatter diagram.
ii) Use the method of least squares to find the line of best fit and draw it on your diagram.
iii) Estimate the total expenses for sales of 85,000 items.

(CII April 1990)
(Answers in Appendix 2, page 246)

41. Prior to privatisation, the most recent annual sales and profit data (£ million) for distribution companies within the Central Electricity Generating Board (England and Wales) were as follows:

Distribution company	Sales (£m)	Profit (£m)
Norweb	1,129	32.1
Manweb	808	26.6
Midland	1,181	38.4
South Wales	551	10.3
South West	687	30.0
Southern	1,134	65.4
Seeboard	912	27.2
LEB	1,050	39.9
Eastern	1,497	58.9
East Midlands	1,165	52.1
Yorkshire	1,140	49.3
North East	740	31.9

[Source: The Times, Monday 16 April 1990]

Σ(Sales) = 11,994 Σ(Profit) = 462.1 Σ(XY) = 498,912.2

Σ(Sales)^2 = 12,763,470 Σ(Profit)^2 = 20,459.35

You are required

a)   to find the regression equation of profit on sales, to plot it on a scatter diagram and to predict profit for a similar company with sales of £1,000 million ;

b)   to interpret your analysis.

(CIMA November 1991)

42.   The management accountant of Pan Products has been analysing the manufacturing times of all the company's major products. He has obtained the following data for one particular item which is produced in batches to satisfy specific customer orders.

Batch Number	Batch Size	Manufacturing Time (hours)
1	32	21.4
2	24	17.0
3	30	20.4
4	45	29.6
5	15	12.6
6	26	19.1
7	50	34.2
8	18	15.2
9	20	16.3
10	40	29.2

The data show, in chronological order, the manufacturing times of all batches of this item produced in the last year.

Having obtained these times, the accountant developed a regression relationship between manufacturing time (Y) and batch size (X) of the form

$$Y = 3.5 + 0.6X$$

with a correlation coefficient of 0.99. In the light of the high value, he concluded that batch size was a reliable and effective predictor of manufacturing time:

Required:

a)   Explain the meaning of the regression coefficients in the context of this example.

b)   Calculate the deviations of the observed manufacturing times from the regression line and show that these deviations sum to zero. Explain why the deviations will always sum to zero.

c)   Calculate the sum of squared deviations and explain the importance of this value.

d)   Plot the deviations against both the batch size and batch number. What do you deduce from the form of your graphs? Would you agree with the view that batch size is a 'reliable and effective predictor of manufacturing time'?

(ACCA December 1986)
(Answers in Appendix 2, page 246)

43.   It seems reasonable to assume that the second hand price of a particular make of car is dependent on its age. Decide on a particular make and model of car and a suitable source for the data, such as your local newspaper. Collect data on the age and price of around 20 cars and do the following:

i)   Plot a scatter graph of the data. Does the scatter graph indicate that a linear relationship exists for all or part of the range of the data?

ii)   Calculate the regression equation that would enable the price of the car to be obtained given its age.

iii) Using the equation obtained in (ii) above and suitable examples, illustrate how the price of a car could be found if its age was known. Within what age range is your equation valid? Why is this so?

iv) What proportion of the variability in price is explained by the age factor? What other factors could affect the price of a car?

44. The Genesis Driving School Ltd possess a fleet of cars of the same make and model, each having approximately equal usage. The assistant chief accountant is currently reviewing the company's vehicle replacement policy with the aim of deciding the optimum age at which to replace cars. Over the past 12 months the company has kept a full record of the service and maintenance costs for each of its cars. The following table shows, for a random sample of 12 cars, the age (in years) and their annual costs of service and maintenance (in £).

Car	Age (years), X	Cost (£), Y
A	1	300
B	4	660
C	3	500
D	4	600
E	5	750
F	2	420
G	2	450
H	1	340
I	3	520
J	5	700
K	4	640
L	2	480

You can use the following summations:

$\Sigma X = 36$ $\Sigma Y = 6360$ $\Sigma XY = 21250$

$\Sigma X^2 = 130$ $\Sigma Y^2 = 3593000$ $\hat{\sigma} = 28.564$

Required:

a) Draw a scatter plot of the data and comment on the appropriateness of fitting a straight-line relationship.

b) Using the method of least squares, estimate a relationship of the form $Y = a + bX$, where Y is the annual cost and X is the age of the car. Interpret your values of a and b in the context of this question.

c) The cost information concerning one of its cars, aged five years, has been mislaid.

Obtain a 95% interval estimate for the cost of this car over the previous 12 months.

d) What other information would the assistant chief accountant need to establish an optimum replacement policy?

(ACCA June 1991)

45. Fast foods Limited is a major food retailing company which has recently decided to open several new restaurants. In order to assist with the choice of siting these restaurants the management of Fast Foods Limited wished to investigate the effect of income on eating habits. As part of their report a marketing agency produced the following table showing the percentage of annual income spent on food, Y, for a given annual income (£), X.

X	Y
5000	62
7500	48
10,000	37
12,500	31
15,000	27
20,000	22
25,000	18

Required:

a) Plot, on separate scatter diagrams,
   i) Y against X,
   ii) $\log_{10}Y$ against $\log_{10}X$,
   and comment on the relationship between income and percentage of family income spent on food.

b) Use the method of least squares to fit the relationship
   $Y = aX^b$
   to the data. Estimate a and b.

c) Estimate the percentage of annual income spent on food by a family with an annual income of £18,000.

(ACCA December 1987)
(Answers in Appendix 2, page 246)

46. You have been asked by a housing association to provide them with a formula that would allow the cost of a second hand house to be estimated given various factors concerning that house.

   a) Make a list of all the possible factors that you think may influence the cost of a house in a particular locality.

   b) Obtain details on at least 60 houses from estate agents or other sources. From these details decide on about 5 factors (variables) that you think important and use a spreadsheet to obtain the product moment correlation coefficient r between the cost and each of the chosen variables. Start with the variable that gives the largest r^2 and obtain the regression equation. Repeat this with two variables, the one just used and the variable with the next largest r^2. Repeat this process until no further improvement in the multiple r^2 is obtained. Demonstrate how your multiple regression model would be used and comment on the validity of your model.

Time series

47. You have just completed an analysis into the Sales of a computer game over the past 3 years and the result is shown below:

> For help with these tasks and questions see Section 2: Time Series Analysis, page 127.

Year	Period	Sales (000's)
1990	1	30
	2	35
	3	35
	4	40
	5	50
	6	60
1991	1	30
	2	40
	3	38
	4	35
	5	52
	6	60
1992	1	35
	2	33
	3	37
	4	43
	5	50
	6	65

a) From the raw data, calculate the moving average series and plot this on the graph. Comment on both series of data.

b) Use the additive decomposition model to obtain forecasts for 1993.

c) Comment on the accuracy of your forecasts. What error 'statistics' could be obtained from your model?

48. The number of claims on household policies for property damage which were submitted to a district office is as follows:

	1st Q	2nd Q	3rd Q	4th Q
1986	745	432	507	652
1987	762	520	460	685
1988	691	370	398	974
1989	786	481	440	721

a) Show this information on a carefully prepared graph.

b) Superimpose your estimate of a trend line on the graph using the moving average method.

c) Estimate the quarterly seasonal effects.

(CII April 1990)
(Answers in Appendix 2, page 246)

49. The number of daily visitors to a hotel, aggregated by quarter, is shown below for the last three years.

Year	Quarter 1	Quarter 2	Quarter 3	Quarter 4
1986	–	–	–	88
1987	90	120	200	28
1988	22	60	164	16
1989	10	80	192	–

The following additive model is assumed to apply:

Series = Trend + seasonal variation + Residual (Irregular)

You are required to

a) find the centred moving average trend;

b) find the average seasonal variation for each quarter;

c) plot the original data and the trend on the   same time-series graph;

d) predict the number of daily visitors tor the fourth quarter of 1989, showing clearly how this is calculated, and state any assumptions underlying this answer.

(CIMA Nov 1989)
(Answers in Appendix 2, page 247)

50. In June 1990 the managing director of a large furniture store, Cushair Designs, engaged a management consultant to devise a simple and practical method of forecasting the store's quarterly sales levels for a period of six months ahead. On taking up the task the consultant felt that a forecasting method appropriate for the purpose would first require him to deseasonalise the store's gross quarterly sales over the last 30 months. The time series obtained could then be plotted, a line of best fit determined and extrapolated over the next two quarters. By applying an appropriate seasonal index to these figures, sales for the two periods ahead could be estimated.

Gross sales data for Cushair Designs	
Sales period	Value of retail sales (£000)
Jan–Mar 1988	285
Apr–Jun 1988	310
Jul–Sep 1988	315
Oct–Dec 1988	385
Jan–Mar 1989	340
Apr–Jun 1989	370
Jul–Sep 1989	375
Oct–Dec 1989	460
Jan–Mar 1990	395
Apr–Jun 1990	425

The management consultant also gave some thought to how he could avoid getting the store to compute its own seasonal indices, an operation he felt inappropriate considering the small amount of past data he had available. He decided to use a national quarterly seasonal index as published in a national journal. He thought that his client's furniture store had a product mix not too different from the aggregate mix on which the index was based.

National quarterly seasonal index for furniture

Multiplicative	Jan–Mar	Apr–Jun	Jul–Sep	Oct–Dec
Seasonal index	94	98	96	112

Required:

a) Plot the actual quarterly sales figures on graph paper and explain why the multiplicative model may be more appropriate for these data than the additive model.

b) Calculate the values of the deseasonalised data and plot these data on your graph.

c) Use the method of least squares to determine the equation of the straight line through the deseasonalised data.

d) Comment on the likely accuracy of your estimates.

(ACCA June 1990)

51. The personnel department of BBS plc, a large food processing company, is concerned about absenteeism among its shop floor workforce. There is a general feeling that the underlying trend has been rising, but nobody has yet analysed the figures. The total number of shop-floor employees has remained virtually unchanged over the last few years.

The mean number of absentees per day is given below for each quarter of the years 1989 to 1991 and quarter 1 of 1992.

	Q1	Q2	Q3	Q4
1989	25.1	14.4	9.5	23.7
1990	27.9	16.9	12.4	26.1
1991	31.4	19.7	15.9	29.9
1992	34.5			

a) Plot the above data on a graph (leave space for the remaining 1992 figures).

b) Use the method of moving averages to determine the trend in the series and superimpose this on your graph. Interpret your graph.

c) Use an appropriate method to measure the seasonal pattern in the data. *Briefly* give reasons for your choice of method.

d) Use your analysis to produce rough forecasts of the mean number of absentees there will be in the remaining quarters of 1992.

e) Discuss the limitations of the forecasting method which you used in part (d) above. Would exponential smoothing be a better method? Give reasons for your answer.

(UWE, Bristol September 1992)

52. a) Briefly describe the terms:
    i) additive model,
    ii) multiplicative model,

    as applied to time series analysis. Explain how to distinguish between the appropriateness of these models.

    b) The table below gives the production figures (in thousands of tonnes) of ceramic goods for 1988.

Jan	Feb	Mar	Apr	May	Jun	Jul	Aug	Sep	Oct	Nov	Dec
335	325	310	354	360	338	333	270	375	395	415	373

As the data exhibit seasonal fluctuations, multiplicative seasonal indices have been calculated using data from several years and are shown below.

Jan	Feb	Mar	Apr	May	Jun	Jul	Aug	Sep	Oct	Nov	Dec
96	93	90	102	105	96	94	78	110	115	120	108

Required:

i) Calculate the values of the deseasonalised data for each month of 1988.

ii) Plot the monthly production figures and the deseasonalised data on the same graph. Comment on any apparent trend of the data.

iii) Use the exponential smoothing model, applied to the deasonalised data, to produce a forecast of the deseasonalised data for the first month of 1989 using the smoothing constant $\alpha = 0.2$ and starting with a forecast of 350 for August 1988.

iv) Use your answer to part (iii) and the seasonal indices to forecast the production figures of ceramic goods for each of the first three months of 1989, stating any assumptions that you are making.

(ACCA December 1988)
(Answers in Appendix 2, page 247)

Network analysis

53. Yachtsteer manufacture a self-steering device for pleasure yachts and as a result of increased competition from foreign manufacturers, it has decided to design and manufacture a new model in time for the next Boat show. As a first step in planning the project, the following major tasks and durations have been identified:

> For help with these tasks and questions see Section 2: Network analysis, page 138

	Task	Time (Weeks)	Preceding Tasks
A	Design new product	8	–
B	Design electronics	4	–
C	Organise production facilities	4	A
D	Obtain production materials	2	A
E	Manufacture trial gear	3	C,D
F	Obtain electronic circuit boards	2	B
G	Decide on yacht for trials	1	–
H	Assemble trial gear and electronics	2	E,F
I	Test product in workshops	3	H,G
J	Test product at sea	4	I
K	Assess product's performance	3	J
L	Plan national launch	4	K

a) Draw a network to represent the logical sequence of tasks and determine how long it will be before the new product can be launched.

b) The time taken to complete tasks A,B,D,K and L is somewhat uncertain and so the following optimistic and pessimistic estimates have also been made to supplement the most likely figure given above. These additional estimates are:

Task	Optimistic Time (weeks)	Pessimistic Time (weeks)
A	5	13
B	2	6
D	1	4
K	2	6
L	2	8

What now is the expected time until the product can be launched and what is the probability of this time exceeding 35 weeks? (Assume duration times follow a Beta distribution and completion time is normally distributed).

54. The following table gives data for a simple project:

Activity	Preceding activity	Duration (days)
A	–	3
B	–	3
C	–	7
D	A	1
E	D, J	2
F	B	2
G	C	1
H	E,F,G	1
J	B	1

You are required

a) to draw a network diagram for the project;

b) to draw up a table, with a list of activities, durations, earliest start and finish times, latest start and finish times, and total floats;

c) to state and to explain the critical path.

(CIMA November 1991)

55. The Airdale Electronics Company has been awarded a contract to develop radar components for the armed forces of an overseas country. The development manager of the company has analysed the requirements of the contract and has split the overall project into eight separate activities. The following table gives the normal time to complete each activity, the normal cost of each activity and each activity's immediate predecessors.

Activity	Immediate Predecessors	Normal Duration (months)	Normal Cost (£000)
A	–	4	20
B	–	5	20
C	A	2	8
D	A	3	15
E	B,C	3	12
F	B,C	4	24
G	D,E	5	10
H	F	2	12

In addition to the above costs there is a penalty cost of £10,000 per month for each month that the overall project exceeds 12 months.

Required:

a) Using the normal durations and costs construct an activity network for the project. Determine the critical path and associated total cost.

b) Determine the total float of each activity. Explain clearly what this means.

c) The development manager is aware that six of the activities can be shortened by bringing in extra resources. The following table shows the minimum durations and the extra cost required to attain this minimum duration.

Activity	Minimum Duration (Months)	Extra Cost (£000)
B	3	4
D	2	4
E	2	6
F	3	2
G	3	8
H	1	4

Assume that it is possible to reduce the normal time to minimum time in steps of one month and that the extra cost is proportional to the time saved.

i) Find the minimum project time and the minimum cost of attaining this minimum project time.

ii) What is the minimum overall cost of the project? State the associated activity durations.

(ACCA December 1991)

(Answers in Appendix 2, page 247)

56. The production manager at Gemini Machines Limited has been asked to present information about the times and costs for the development of a new machine that the company may choose to manufacture. The managing director requires accurate time and cost estimates since the project will involve a fixed-fee contract offering no provisions for later renegotiation, even in the event of modifications.

	Activity	Preceding Activities	Duration (weeks)	Cost (£000)
A	Obtain engineering quotes	I	1	4
B	Subcontract specifications	A,J	4	8
C	Purchase of raw materials	–	3	24
D	Construct prototype	I	5	15
E	Final drawings	I	2	6
F	Fabrication	H	6	30
G	Special machine study	–	4	12
H	Subcontract work	B,E	8	40
I	Preliminary design	G	2	8
J	Vendor evaluation	C,D	3	3

The production manager has been asked to identify the critical activities, to determine the shortest project duration and to provide a week by week cost schedule.

Required:

a) Draw a network to represent the inter-relationships between the activities indicated, and insert earliest and latest event times throughout.

b) Determine the critical path and the shortest possible duration of the project.

c) Assuming each activity commences at the earliest start date, and that for each activity the cost is incurred evenly over its duration, construct a week by week schedule of cash flows.

The project is to be financed by £50,000 available initially, a further £50,000 available at the start of week 9 and the final £50,000 available from week 20.

Identify any particular problems and suggest solutions.

(ACCA June 1991)

57. Revor plc are urgently planning the production of their new light weight car battery, the 'Epsilon'. They would like to exhibit their battery at a trade fair, which is to take place in 48 weeks time. Various activities had to take place before production could start and these are shown below:-

Activity	Description	Immediate Predecessors	Duration (Weeks)
A	Clear designated area for the installation of equipment	–	20
B	Commission consulting engineers to design equipment	–	2
C	Receive consultant's report	B	10
D	Place equipment out to tender	C	1
E	Obtain equipment	D	6
F	Install equipment	A,E	30
G	Recruit additional staff	C	6
H	Train new staff	G	4
I	Order and obtain materials	–	16
J	Pilot production run	F,H,I	3
K	Advertise new product	–	2

a) Draw the network and show that it is not possible to start production within 48 weeks. What are the critical activities and how much total float do the non-critical activities have?

b) It is possible to 'crash' (i.e. reduce the duration of) certain activities at increased cost. These activities are as follows:

Activity	Crashed Duration (Weeks)	Normal Cost (£000's)	Crashed Cost (£000's)
A	18	4	10
E	5	1	3
F	28	15	27
I	8	0.5	8.5
J	2	16	26

i) Ron Smith the Production Manager suggests that only activity I need be crashed because this is the cheapest option and allows the greatest reduction in time to be made. Explain why this would not help the situation.

ii) It has been estimated that for every week over 48 weeks that this project takes, a loss of £8000 is made as a result of lost profits. Decide on the strategy that will minimise the sum of crashed costs and loss of profits.

c) After further discussions it was revealed that the durations of activities B,C and H are only estimates whereas the duration of the other activities are known with certain. To help achieve more reliable estimates, information was obtained for a pessimistic time, most likely time and an optimist time for each of the activities B,C and H. This is shown below:

Activity	Pessimistic Time (Weeks)	Most Likely Time (Weeks)	Optimistic Time (Weeks)
B	3	2	1
C	13	11	3
H	5	4	3

Using the PERT method and the revised activity times arrived at in (b)(ii), estimate the probability that the project time will in fact be greater than 50 weeks.

d)   Briefly comment on any assumptions that you have made and any reservations that you might have with your answers to the above questions.

(UWE, Bristol June 1992)

58. Shipways boatyard undertakes spring refits on cabin cruisers and yachts and in the past the company has received complaints from customers regarding the time taken to complete the job. As a consequence the M.D, Alan Waters has decided to carry out a critical path analysis on the cabin cruiser refit. Table below gives, for each activity, the duration, immediate preceding activities and the number of yard assistants required.

Activity	Description	Duration (Days)	Immediate preceding activities	Yard assistants required
A	Bring craft up slipway	1	–	2
B	Check and overhaul seacocks etc	3	A	1
C	Scrape and prepare hull for painting	7	A	2
D	Paint hull	4	C	1
E	Remove engine	2	A	3
F	Overhaul engine	16	E	1
G	Clean and paint engine bilges	3	E	1
H	Refit engine	3	F and G	3
I	Apply antifoul paint to hull	2	D and H	2
J	Refloat	1	B and I	2

Note – the reason that I follows from both D and H is that a boat must be refloated no more than 48 hours after the antifouling paint has been applied. Antifouling should not therefore be started until the boat is ready for the water.

a)   Draw the network and determine how long the refit will take. What are the critical activities and how much float do the non-critical activities have?

b)   i)   Draw a Gantt chart and resource histogram for the refit. What is the maximum number of yard workers required and when is this required?

   ii)   Unfortunately there are only 4 yard workers available during the period of the refit. Using your Gantt chart and/or histogram reschedule the activities so that no more than 4 yard workers will be required.

c)   There is some uncertainty with the durations of some of the activities. Briefly explain how uncertainty can be taken into account using the PERT technique.

(UWE, Bristol June 1993)
(Answers in Appendix 2, page 247)

Inventory control

> For help with these tasks and questions see Section 2: Inventory Control, page 148.

59. The production of Revor plc's electronic ignition range requires the purchase of various components. The annual demand for component 'A' is 138,000 and the current policy is to order 23,000 every period (8 weeks).

a)   If it costs £1,000 to place an order, stock holding costs are 17% of the average value of components held and the value of component A is £600 per 1000 calculate the total cost associated with the current policy. (It can be assumed that all components arrive at the beginning of a period and are used up at a uniform rate over the period).

b) Looking back at the past year what would have been the best ordering policy and what costs would this have incurred?

c) Management are concerned that the recommended ordering policy could result in a stock-out which they want to avoid. They have however indicated that they would be prepared to accept a probability of no more than 5% of a stock-out occurring. If it is assumed that component requirements vary according to the normal distribution with a mean of 23,000 units per period and a standard deviation of 1730 units, and that delivery time is 16 weeks, what would you recommend? What increase in costs would your recommendation cause?

d) An alternative supplier has been found for this component which charge £580 per 1000. However, the order quantity must be at least 100,000. What would you recommend?

(UWE, Bristol June 1992)

60. K & L Games Ltd is re-evaluating its stock control policy. Its daily demand for wooden boxes is steady at 40 a day for each of the 250 working days (50 weeks) of the year. The boxes are currently bought weekly in batches of 200 from a local supplier for £2 each. The cost of ordering the boxes from the local supplier is £64, regardless of the size of the order. The stockholding costs, expressed as a percentage of stock value, are 25%.

You are required to

a) determine the economic order quantity and frequency of replenishment, and the annual saving to be made by implementing these;

b) recommend whether or not it is worthwhile to make use of the local supplier's new quantity discount scheme, shown below.

Local Supplier's New Discount Scheme

Quantity	Discount
0 – 999	0%
1,000 – 4,999	5%
5,000 +	10%

Note: The EOQ formula is on page 27 of the CIMA Mathematical Tables for Students.

(CIMA November 1987)
(Answers in Appendix 2, page 247)

61. The Oxygon Office Supplies Company Limited is a well established firm of paper merchants and stationers, which is open for 50 weeks each year and specialises in the retailing of general office supplies. Its many customers include financial institutions, legal establishments and insurance companies. However, steadily increasing operating costs have diminished their financial reserves which has prompted the chief accountant to recommend a reduction in overall stock levels. Whereas in previous times it was common for the company to hold over twelve months' stock for many stock items in order to guarantee availability, pressures on liquidity seemed to demand a reduction in inventory levels.

The company's main selling item was a high quality typing paper which tended to have erratic demand but can be assumed to have a normal distribution with a mean of 800 boxes each week and a standard deviation of 250 boxes per week. This paper is supplied by the Tiara Paper Company at a cost of £2.50 per box. It was found that the lead time of supply of this paper recently had been very consistent at three weeks.

The annual cost of stockholding was estimated at 15% of the stock item value and is based on the cost of storage and the company's cost of capital. In order to estimate the cost of a delivery of paper from Tiara the cost of making and receiving the order together with the associated accounting and stock control tasks requires a total effort of approximately twelve man hours, where the average wage rate is £160 per week for a 40 hour week.

Required:

a) Outline the basic principles of inventory control policy and explain why a good inventory policy is of value to Oxygon.

b) Calculate the economic order quantity for this stock item, together with the average length of time between replenishments.

c) Determine the recommended buffer stock if there is to be no more than a 1% chance that a stockout will occur in any one replenishment period.

d) Determine the total stockholding cost (storage and delivery costs) per annum using the calculated values of the economic order quantity and reorder level.

(ACCA December 1987)
(Answers in Appendix 2, page 247)

62. A manufacturer has a steady demand for one of his products of 200 units per week. The set up cost is £300 per production run and the cost of holding stock is reckoned to be 20p per unit per week. If it is possible to produce this product as a rate of 600 units per week, calculate the economic batch quantity and the cost associated with this policy.

Just as a new batch is to be produced one of the unions calls its members out on strike. This results in a cut of output of 70%. Explain what affect this will have and what action the company could have taken had it been given warning of the strike. (From past experience, this strike could last 5 weeks).

(Answers in Appendix 2, page 247)

Linear programming

63. A company has been set up in Bristol to manufacture rowing dinghies. Currently they have plans to produce a basic and a deluxe version. The two dinghies are similar and both take 1.5 man-days to manufacture. However, the deluxe version is much stronger and the profit is higher as can be seen in the table below:

> For help with these tasks and questions see Section 2: Linear Programming, page 157.

	Basic	Deluxe
Resin	10 kgms	16 kgms
Glass Fibre Mat	30 m	50 m
Profit	£50	£80

Due to safety regulations the company is only allowed to store a limited amount of the raw material, which is 200 kgms of resin and 900 m of mat. The required raw material is delivered on a daily basis.

The basic dinghy is likely to be a good seller but it is assumed that the deluxe dinghy will be limited to a maximum of nine per day. All boats produced by the end of the day are delivered to a distribution depot as there are no storage facilities available at the Plant.

a) If the current labour force is 27, use the graphical method of linear programming to demonstrate that there are multiple solutions to the problem. Hence suggest a sensible mix of dinghies to produce on a daily basis and show that this results in a profit of £1,000 per day.

b) i) What is the Shadow Price of the resin resource?

ii) As a result of improved storage facilities more resin can be held at the plant. What is the maximum amount of resin that would be worth storing and how would this affect the profit calculated in (a)?

c) The company is thinking about making a third type of dinghy. Explain why the problem cannot now be solved by the graphical technique.

64. Revor plc has one production line for the manufacture of the ELEN PLUS and ELEN SUPER ignition systems. Both models use similar components in their manufacture but the SUPER model usually requires more of them and takes longer to produce. Relevant detail is shown below.

	ELEN PLUS	ELEN SUPER
No. of component A	4	8
No. of component B	2	3
No. of component C	0	10
Manufacturing time(hours)	5	7

There are supply problems for components A and B and daily usage is limited to 400 and 250 respectively. For component C, the company has entered into a contract with its supplier to take at least 150 per day.

It is also found that at least twice as many ELEN PLUS models are sold as ELEN SUPER, so production should reflect this fact.

The contribution to profits for the PLUS and SUPER models are £60 and £85 respectively.

You can assume that there are 60 employees engaged in the production of these ignition systems and each employee works an 8 hour day.

a) Formulate this as a linear programming problem, assuming that it is required to maximise profits.

b) Use the graphical technique of linear programming to determine the optimal numbers of ELEN PLUS and ELEN SUPER models to produce each day. What is the daily profit associated with this production?

c) Identify the scarce resources (binding constraints) for this problem. For each determine the *shadow price* (opportunity cost). It is possible to purchase additional quantities of component A from an alternative supplier at a premium of £10 per component. Would it be worthwhile?

d) The unit costs associated with the production of these systems is known to vary. However the selling price is only changed annually. How much can the profit on the ELEN PLUS model be allowed to vary before the optimal solution found in (b) changes?

(UWE, Bristol June 1992)
(Answers in Appendix 2, page 247)

65. As part of a corporate rationalisation programme, the Nemesis Company has decided to merge its two factories at Abbotsfield and Birchwood. The Abbotsfield factory will be closed down, and production capacity will be expanded at Birchwood. At the present time, the numbers of skilled and unskilled men employed at the two factories are

	Abbotsfield	Birchwood
Skilled	200	100
Unskilled	300	200
Total	500	300

whereas after merger, the enlarged factory at Birchwood will employ 240 skilled and 320 unskilled men.

After extensive negotiation with the unions involved, the following financial arrangements have been agreed.

1. All workers made redundant will receive redundancy payments as follows

Skilled men	£2,000
Unskilled men	£1,500

2. Workers from the Abbotsfield factory who are retained will receive a relocation payment of £2,000.

3. To avoid any bias towards the workers from the Birchwood factory, the proportion of the Abbotsfield men retained should be equal to the proportion of the Birchwood men retained.

Required:

a) Construct a linear programming model to determine how the new labour force will be selected from the two factories in order to minimise total redundancy and relocation costs. You should use the following variables:

S1 = Number of skilled men retained from Abbotsfield

S2 = Number of skilled men retained from Birchwood

S3 = Number of unskilled men retained from Abbotsfield

S4 = Number of unskilled men retained from Birchwood

b) Using two of the equality constraints, eliminate two of the four variables and solve the problem graphically. What is the minimum total redundancy and relocation cost?

(ACCA June 1987)
Answers in Appendix 2, page 247)

66. a) In what areas of a firm's activities might linear programming prove to be a useful technique?

b) The Stonehouse Electronics Company manufactures four technical products, which it supplies to the computer industry. Each of the four products must pass through the following four processes: forming, wiring, assembly, and inspection. The time requirements (in hours) for each product together with the production time available (also in hours) for each process each month are summarised in the following table.

Product	Process			
	Forming	Wiring	Assembly	Inspection
XL35	1	2	4	0.5
RK27	2	3	2	0.5
RM93	2	1	3	1
TS15	1	3	2	0.5
Production time	2,500	4,000	4,500	1,200

The profit for each product together with the minimum monthly production requirement to fulfil contracts are as follows:

Product	Unit Profit	Minimum Production Level
XL35	£25	200
RK27	£30	150
RM93	£20	300
TS15	£22	200

The production manager, a person with virtually no quantitative background, has the responsibility of specifying production levels for each product for the coming month.

Help him by formulating the problem.

c) An extract of the output from a computer package for this problem is given below

Solution:

X1 = 425, X2 = 525, X3 = 300, X4 = 425.

Shadow prices:

Constraint 1 8.00,   Constraint 2 2.75   Constraint 3 2.875

where variables X1,...X4 are the production levels for XL35, RK27, RM93, TS15 respectively, and constraints 1-4 describe the limited production time for forming, wiring, assembly and inspection respectively.

Required:

i) Provide a full and clear interpretation of this output for the production manager. Include information concerning the product mix, optimum monthly profit, unused process time, and shadow prices.

ii) There is a proposition that the company manufactures an additional product, YX49, which would yield a unit profit of £35. Each unit would require a time allocation of 2 hours for forming, 3 hours for wiring, 3 hours for assembly and 1 hour for inspection.

Justify whether this is a worthwhile proposition or not.

(ACCA June 1991)
(Answers in Appendix 2, page 247)

Transportation and assignment algorithms

67. REVOR plc, a car component manufacturer, has factories at Aberdeen, Bristol and Colchester. It sells its goods to a national distributor which owns 4 warehouses, located in different parts of the U.K. Due to the recession, the quantity required by the supplier

For help with these tasks and questions see Section 2: transportation and assignment algorithms, page 165.

has fallen but REVOR has not reduced its production capacity. Excess capacity is stored on the factory premises.

Goods purchased by the supplier are transported to its warehouses by container. Due to the competitive nature of the car component industry all transport costs are borne by REVOR and clearly it is in their interest to keep transport costs as low as possible.

A recent analysis has revealed that transport costs vary considerably and the cost (in £00's per container) from each factory to each warehouse is shown below. Also shown is the normal weekly production at each factory and the requirements at each warehouse. Not shown is the cost of production at each factory because there is very little difference between factories.

		Aberdeen	Bristol	Colchester	Quantity Required
	I	5	13	7	60 containers
Warehouse	II	*	4	8	35 containers
	III	5	22	25	50 containers
	IV	3	9	4	100 containers
Quantity Produced		175	80	150	

* For operational reasons it is not possible to deliver to warehouse II from Aberdeen.

a) The current transportation plan is as follows:

Aberdeen	to Warehouse	I	25	containers
"	to "	III	50	"
"	to "	IV	100	"
Bristol	to "	II	35	"
Colchester	to "	I	35	"

Calculate the cost of this plan and show that it is not the cheapest plan that could be achieved.

b) Use the transportation algorithm to find the optimum solution. What is the cost of this solution?

c) To reduce production capacity it has been suggested that the Bristol factory could be shut down. If this was done, the site would fetch about £2m and redundancy and disturbance allowance would cost the Company £1.2m. Investigate this suggestion from a practical as well as from a financial point of view. (Assume the Company works a 48 week year). Write a short memo to the M.D. discussing the implications of the closure of the Bristol factory.

(UWE, Bristol June 1992)
(Answers in Appendix 2, page 248)

68. a) Explain briefly how the transportation algorithm can be modified for profit maximisation rather than minimisation of costs.

b) The Orange Computer Company manufactures one product, a dot-matrix printer, which is currently in short supply. Four of Orange's main outlets, large speciality computer shops at Abbotstown, Beswick, Carlic and Denstone, already have requirements which in total exceed the combined capacity of its three production plants at Rexford, Seadon and Triston. The company needs to know how to allocate its production capacity to maximise profits.

Each printer is packed in a separate box after being carefully wrapped to prevent damage. Distribution costs(£) per unit from each production plant to each speciality shop are given in the following table.

From	To Abbotstown	To Beswich	To Carlic	To Denstone
	£	£	£	£
Rexford	22	24	22	30
Seadon	24	20	18	28
Triston	26	20	26	24

Since the four speciality shops are in different parts of the country, and as there are differing transportation costs between the production plants and the speciality shops, along with slightly different costs at each of the production plants, there is a pricing structure that enables different prices to be charged at the four shops. Currently the price per unit charged is £230 at Abbotstown, £235 at Beswich, £225 at Carlic and £240 at Denstone. The variable unit production costs are £150 at plants Rexford and Triston, and £155 at plant Seadon.

Required:

i) Set up a matrix showing the unit contribution to profit associated with each production plant/speciality shop allocation.

ii) The demands at Abbotstown, Beswich, Carlic, and Denstone are 850, 640, 380, and 230 respectively. The plant capacity at Rexford is 625, at Seadon is 825, and at Triston is 450.

Use the transportation algorithm to determine the optimal allocation.

iii) Determine the contribution to profit for the optimal allocation

(ACCA June 1990)
(Answers in Appendix 2, page 248)

69. a) Explain the terms
    i) degeneracy,
    ii) inequality of supply and demand,
    iii) non-unique optimal solution,

in transportation problems. Explain how the transportation algorithm is adapted to overcome these difficulties.

b) The Royal Wedgetown Pottery Company has orders to be completed next week for three of its products – mugs, cups, bowls – as given in the table below.

Product	Order (units)
Mugs	4,000
Cups	2,400
Bowls	1,000

There are three machines available for the manufacturing operations, and all three can produce each of the products at the same production rate. However, the unit costs of these products vary depending upon the machine used. The unit costs (in £) of each machine are given in the following table.

		Product		
		Mugs	Cups	Bowls
	A	1.20	1.30	1.10
Machine	B	1.40	1.30	1.50
	C	1.10	1.00	1.30

Furthermore, it is known that capacity for next week for machines B and C is 3,000 units and for machine A is 2,000 units.

Required:

i) Use the transportation model to find the minimum cost production schedule for the products and machines. Determine this minimum cost.

ii) If this optimal solution is not unique, describe all other production schedules with the minimum cost. If the production manager would like the minimum cost schedule to have the smallest number of changeovers of production on machines, recommend the optimal solution.

(ACCA June 1989)
(Answers in Appendix 2, page 248)

70. a) The assignment problem can be regarded as a special case of a transportation problem.

    Describe these special features of the assignment problem and explain why the transportation algorithm tends not to be used to solve such problems.

    b) The Midland Research Association has recently been notified that it has received government research grants to undertake four major projects. The managing director has to assign a research officer to each of these projects. Currently there are five research officers – Adams, Brown, Carr, Day, Evans – who are available to carry out these duties. The amount of time required to complete each of the research projects is dependent on the experience and ability of the research officer who is assigned to the project. The managing director has been provided with an estimate of the project completion time (in days) for each officer and each project.

	Project			
Research Officer	1	2	3	4
Adams	80	120	60	104
Brown	72	144	48	110
Carr	96	148	72	120
Day	60	108	52	92
Evans	64	140	60	96

As the four projects have equal priority, the managing director would like to assign research officers in a way that would minimise the total time (in days) necessary to complete all four projects.

Required:

i) Determine an optimal assignment of research officers to projects, and hence determine the total number of days allocated to these four projects.

ii) State any further allocations that would result in the same total number of days. If research officers Brown, Carr and Day express a preference for projects 2 or 3, whilst officers Adams and Evans express their preference for projects 1 or 4, which of the optimal allocations seems to be the most sensible for the managing director to make?

iii) What feature of this particular project duration matrix could be exploited to simplify the problem?

(ACCA December 1989)
(Answers in Appendix 2, page 248)

Simulation

71. Customers arrive at a single cash dispenser with the following inter-arrival time distribution:-

For help with these tasks and questions see Section 2: Simulation, page 174.

Inter-arrival time (secs)			% Frequency
20	to under	50	5
50	"	100	20
100	"	150	30
150	"	200	45

The service time is 45 seconds.

Using the random numbers below, manually simulate the system and find the average time spent waiting for service and the utilisation of the cash dispenser.

08,72,87,46,75,73,00,11,27,07,05,20,30,85,22,21,04,67,19,13

(Answers in Appendix 2, page 248)

72. Customers arrive at a bank, which has only a single cashier, with the inter-arrival time and service time distributions shown below.

Inter-arrival time (minutes)	% of customers	Service time (minutes)	% of customers
0 to under 4	30	0 to under 1	0
4 to under 6	40	1 to under 3	50
6 to under 8	20	3 to under 5	40
8 to under 10	10	5 to under 7	10

Using the random numbers given below, simulate the next 6 arrivals and find the mean time that they spend queueing for the cashier.

04, 10, 59, 07, 38, 98, 01, 75, 48, 91, 04, 12

73. Brightside Chemicals, a firm that manufactures non-hazardous chemicals, distributes its product in barrels from its main depot. The premises, having a congested inner-city location, have only one loading bay. If further vehicles arrive whilst the loading bay is being utilised then they have to form a queue. This queue takes place on the local road system and often causes traffic congestion.

The effective utilisation of the loading bay and the queuing up of vehicles waiting to be loaded has been a consistent problem for some time. In August 1991 the transport manager decides to examine the queuing problem more closely. He knows from past observation that large queues tend to form in the morning period so on two consecutive Mondays in August he records the arrival times and service times of the vehicles to be loaded.

The distribution of interarrival times and service times is shown in the table below .

Time (minutes)	Interarrival times (%)	Service times (%)
0-10	18	12
10-20	25	20
20-30	36	45
30-40	13	23
40-50	5	0
50-60	3	0

Required:

a) Comment briefly on the transport manager's sampling method.

b) Assuming initial conditions at 9.00 a.m. with no customers in the system simulate, using the following random numbers, the arrival and service sequences until 1.00 p.m. State clearly, for each vehicle, the arrival time at the firm's premises, together with the start and finish time at the loading bay.

Interarrival times:	57	23	85	03	48	28	89	44	37	76	15	98	12
Service times:	42	01	67	34	63	21	80	11	83	89	58	16	51

c) Use your simulation results to estimate

i) The level of utilisation of the loading bay between 9.00 a.m. and 1.00 p.m. (that is, the time for which the loading bay is in use as a percentage of the total time).

ii) The average queuing time for each of the vehicles arriving between 9.00 a.m. and 1.00 p.m.

iii) The average queue length between 9.00 a.m. and 1.00 p.m.

Briefly explain why it may have been more sensible to base these three estimates on the simulation results for the time period between 10.00 a.m. and 1.00 p.m. only.

d) Briefly suggest ways in which the queuing time of the vehicles might be reduced.

(ACCA December 1991)

74. Ajax Food Products has its main factory in the centre of Bristol. Lorries arrive at a constant rate from 08.00 to 18.00 five days a week where they are either loaded or unloaded using the single loading/unloading bay and on a first come first served basis. The area around the factory is frequently congested with lorries because the loading/unloading depot is not large enough for all arriving lorries to wait. A suggestion has been made that an improvement in numbers queueing might result if priority was given to lorries that required unloading. This is because unloading is generally a faster operation. However before any decision is made it has been decided to build a simulation model of the current system.

a) Briefly discuss the advantages and disadvantages of simulation as a means of experimenting on this system.

b) Using the random numbers 42, 17, 38 and 61, demonstrate how four unloading times could be generated from the frequency distribution given below.

Unloading times

Time (minutes)	% frequency
0 to under 30	20
30 to under 40	35
40 to under 50	22
50 to under 60	15
60 to under 70	8

c) Ten separate runs of the model were made, each of one days operation (10 hours). Five runs were for the current operation (FIFO) and five runs for the proposed operation (unloading priority). The method of *common random numbers* was used and the results are as follows:

Day	Current operation Av. queue size	Proposed operation Av. queue size
1	4.2	4.0
2	3.3	3.2
3	6.4	5.7
4	4.1	4.1
5	5.2	4.9

i) Briefly explain how the technique of common random numbers is implemented. What is the advantage of using this technique rather than making ten independent runs?

ii) Use an appropriate t test to decide if a significant improvement in queue size would result from a change in priority?

iii) What other statistics might be useful as a means of comparing the performance of the two systems.

(UWE, Bristol June 1993)
(Answers in Appendix 2, page 248)

75. A large garage, open for 50 weeks each year, is examining its inventory policy in relation to one type of tyre it stocks. Weekly demand for the tyre is distributed according to the following table.

Weekly demand	Probability
20	0.1
30	0.6
40	0.3

The garage uses a reorder level of 100 for this tyre and the lead time is fixed at three weeks.

Required:

a) Determine

  i) the expected annual demand

  ii) the probability that demand exceeds 100 during the lead time period of three weeks.

The cost of placing each order for tyres is estimated to be £12. For any tyre in stock it is estimated that the annual storage cost is equal to 15% of its cost. A tyre costs £10.

b) Use the simple EOQ formula to show that the optimum order quantity for this tyre is 160.

c) Use the random digits below to simulate the inventory operation for a period of 10 weeks in order to estimate the total weekly stockholding costs of this garage. Start with an initial stock of 150, use the order quantity found in (b) and assume that the cost of being out of stock is £0.25 per tyre. State any further assumptions made and explain how the demand data is generated.

  Random digits: 6 9 1 4 7 1 8 9 3 0

d) Explain how this simulation method might be used to determine the optimum order quantity and reorder level.

(ACCA December 1990)

Appendix 1
Solutions to tasks and problem-solving activities in Section 1

Unit 1 Probability *(page 3)*

Tasks

(i) $1400 + 200 = 1600$

(ii) (a) $P(\text{A broken down}) = \frac{200}{1600} = \frac{1}{8} (= 0.125)$

(b) $P(\text{A working}) = 1 - \frac{1}{8} = \frac{7}{8} (= 0.875)$

(iii) $P(\text{B broken down}) = \frac{350}{1600} = \frac{7}{32} (= 0.0273)$

$P(\text{A and B broken}) = \frac{1}{8} \times \frac{7}{32} = \frac{7}{256} (= 0.02734)$

(iv) $P(\text{A or B broken}) = \frac{1}{8} + \frac{7}{32} - \frac{7}{256} = \frac{81}{256} (= 0.3164)$

(iv) 0.3164

(v)   (a)

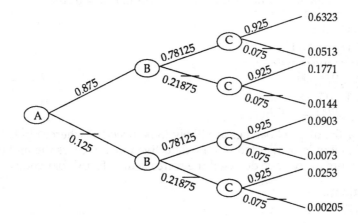

(b)   0.6323

(c) $P(\geq 1) = 1 - P(0)$
$= 1 - 0.6323$
$= 0.3677$

(d) $P(2) = .0253 + .0073 + .0144$
$= 0.0470$

Problem-solving activities

(i)   Machine A works for $\frac{7}{8}$ of the time. Therefore on average machine A works for $\frac{7}{8} \times 80 = 70$ hours a week.

Expected number of pies made each week by machine A is $70 \times 2000 = 140{,}000$.

Similarly for machine B the expected number of pies made per week is: $\frac{25}{32} \times 80 \times 2000 = 125{,}000$

and for machine C $\frac{37}{40} \times 80 \times 2000 = 148{,}000$

The total weekly pie production for all three machines is therefore 413,000

For the new machines each will work for $0.95 \times 80 = 76$ hours per week. Production rate is therefore $3 \times 76 \times 2000 = 456{,}000$.

The difference in production rate is $456{,}000 - 413{,}000 = 43{,}000$ and this represents a profit of $43{,}000 \times £0.1 = £4{,}300$.

The cost of the new machines is 3×1500 per week $= £4500$ and since this is more than the extra profit, replacement on financial grounds cannot be justified.

Unit 2 The binomial distribution (page 6)

Tasks

(i)

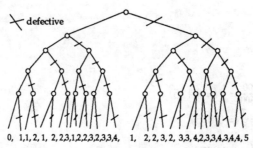

(ii) 1, 5, 10, 10, 5, 1 ways respectively

(iii) P(0)= 0.95 × 0.95 × 0.95 × 0.95 × 0.95 = 0.7738

(iv) Each route has probability 0.95 × 0.95 × 0.95 × 0.95 × 0.05 = 0.0407. Since there are 5 such routes the combined probability (using the addition law) is P(1) = 5 × 0.0407 = 0.2036
Similarly for 2,3,4,5 defective bar codes:

P(2)= 10 × 0.002143= 0.0214,
P(3)= 10 × 0.000113 = 0.00113,
P(4)= 5 × 0.000006 = 0.00003,
P(5)= 1 × 0.00000 = 0.00000

(v) (a) P(≥1)= 1-P(0) = 1 – 0.7738 = 0.2262,
(b) P(≥2)= 1 – [P(0) + P(1)] = 0.0226

(vi) In the first scheme 22.6% of good batches are likely to be rejected, whereas in the second scheme only 2.26% of good batches would be rejected. As the defective rate increases the higher rejection rate of the first scheme would more likely have detected the increase in defective bar codes.

Problem-solving activities

(i) Previous scheme:

P(good batch rejected)= 22.62% (from task (vi))
The probability of accepting a batch with 20% defectives can be found by calculating the probability that no defectives will be found in a batch of 5 items.

That is P(0) = 1 × 0.80⁵ = 0.3277

So P(bad batch accepted)= 32.77%

Current scheme:

In this case P(good batch rejected) = 2.26% (from task(vi))
The probability of accepting a batch with 20% defectives is now P(0) + P(1). That is:

P(1) = 5 × 0.80⁴ × 0.2 = 0.4096 and
P(bad batch accepted) = 0.3277 + 0.4096 = 0.7373 or 73.73%

(ii) In this case the probability of rejecting a batch with 5% defectives is when there is 3 or more defectives in a batch of 20. P(≥3) = 1 – [P(0) + P(1) +P(2)]

$P(0) = 1 \times 0.95^{20} = 0.3585$
$P(1) = {}^{20}C_1 \times 0.05 \times 0.95^{19} = 0.3774$
$P(2) = {}^{20}C_2 \times 0.05^2 \times 0.95^{18} = 0.1887$
Therefore P(good batch rejected) = 1 – [0.3585 + 0.3774 + 0.1887) = 0.0754 or 7.54%

The probability of accepting a batch with 20% defectives is P(0) + P(1) + P(2)
$P(0) = 1 \times 0.8^{20} = 0.01153$
$P(1) = {}^{20}C_1 \times 0.20 \times 0.80^{19} = 0.0576$
$P(2) = {}^{20}C_2 \times 0.20^2 \times 0.80^{18} = 0.1369$
Therefore P(bad batch accepted) = 0.01153 + 0.0576 + 0.1369
$$= 0.2060 \text{ or } 20.6\%$$

So this scheme is better.

Unit 3 The Poisson distribution *(page 8)*

Tasks

(i)   mean $= \dfrac{24}{5} = 4.8$ accidents a year

(ii) $P(0) = \dfrac{e^{-4.8} \times 4.8^0}{0!} = 0.0082$

$P(1) = \dfrac{e^{-4.8} \times 4.8}{1!} = 0.0395$

$P(2) = \dfrac{e^{-4.8} \times 4.8^2}{2!} = 0.0948$

Continuing this process gives
$P(3) = 0.1517$, $P(4) = 0.1820$, $P(5) = 0.1747$, $P(6) = 0.1398$,
$P(7) = 0.0958$

(iii) $P(\geq 8)$ $= 1 - [P(0) + P(1) + ... + P(7)]$
$= (1 - 0.8865)$
$= 0.1135$ or 11.35%

(iv) 2.4 accidents in 6 months

(v) $P(0) = 0.0907$, $P(1) = 0.2177$, $P(2) = 0.2613$, $P(3) = 0.2090$
Therefore $P(\geq 4) = 1 - (0.0907 + 0.2177 + 0.2613 + 0.2090)$
$= 0.2213$ or 22.13%

(vi) The chance of 4 or more accidents in six months, based on an average of 2.4, is quite small which suggests that the mean number of accidents has increased. Also the probability that no accidents will occur in the next 6 months is small (9%) so it is highly likely that the year will end with 5 or more accidents.

Unit 4 The normal distribution *(page 9)*

Tasks

(i)

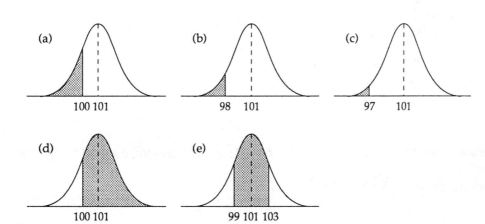

(a) $Z = \dfrac{100 - 101}{1.5} = -0.667$
$(P(Z < -0.667) = P(Z > 0.667) = 0.2514$ or 25.14%

(b) $Z = \dfrac{98 - 101}{1.5} = -2.0$
$P(Z > 2) = 0.0228$ or 2.28%

(c) $Z = \dfrac{97 - 101}{1.5} = -2.67$
$P(Z > 2.67) = 0.0038$ or 0.38%

(d) $P(X > 100) = 1 - P(X < 100) = 1 - P(Z > 0.667)$ from (a) $= 1 - 0.2514 = 0.7486$ or 74.86%

(e) Area from 99 to 101 is the same as the area from 101 to 103.

$$Z = \frac{103 - 101}{1.5} = 1.33$$

$$P(99 < X < 103) = 1 - 2 \times 0.0918$$
$$= 0.8164 \text{ or } 81.64\%$$

(ii) Number less than 98g in weight = 50000×0.0228
$$= 1140 \text{ jars}$$

(iii) Need to find the probability of 1 or more underweight jars in a sample of 10
That is: $P(\geq 1) = 1 - P(0)$
$P(0) = (0.9772)^{10} = 0.7940$
So $P(\geq 1) \ 1 - 0.7940 = 0.206$ or 20.6%

(iv) $P(X < 98) = 0.001$, so $Z = -3.10$

$$-3.10 = \frac{98 - \mu}{1.5}$$

$\mu = 98 + 4.65 = 102.65$
So mean should be set to 102.65g

Problem-solving activities

(i) $Z = \dfrac{98 - 102.5}{1.5} = -3.0$

$P(Z > 3) = 0.0013$ or 0.13%

Many reasons why the actual proportion is different. The distribution of weights may not be normal or the standard deviation may not be 1.5g. Perhaps the sample was biased in some way.

(ii) $P(Z) = 0.005$, therefore $Z = -2.575$

$$-2.575 = \frac{98 - 102.5}{\sigma}$$

$$\sigma = \frac{4.5}{2.575} = 1.75$$

so the standard deviation = 1.75

(iii) $Z = -3$ from (i)

$$-3 = \frac{98 - \mu}{1.75}$$

$\mu = 3 \times 1.75 + 98 = 103.25$
so mean = 103.25g

(iv) The increase in the mean weight is 2.25g. For 50,000 jars the extra coffee would be 50000×2.25
$= 112.5$ kg

This is equivalent to $112.5 \times 2 = £225$ per week

Unit 5 Decision analysis *(page 11)*

Tasks

(i) $1 - (0.3 \times 2.5 + 0.7 \times 0.7) = £0.24$m

(ii) and (iii) See diagram opposite.

(iv) £0.269m. Conduct a survey first and then if the survey indicates a favourable response go into full production, otherwise abandon project.

Problem-solving activity

(i) Let probability of high sales be p.

At the node 'a', EMV = $2.5 \times p + (1-p) \times 0.7 - 1.0$

At the node 'b', EMV = $1.23 \times p + (1-p) \times 0 - 0.1$

You will be indifferent to the decision when these EMV's are equal. That is:
$2.5p - 0.7p + 0.7 - 1 = 1.23p - 0.1$
$0.57p = 0.2$
$\quad p = 0.351$

Also need to consider the decision to abandon.

At node 1, the EMV is $1.23p - 0.1$. Providing this is greater than zero, the survey should be carried out.

That is $1.23p - 0.1 > 0$
So $p > 0.081$

If the probability is greater than 0.35, decision changes from survey first to full production. If the probability is less than 0.08 decision changes from survey first to abandon project.

Diagram for Unit 5 Tasks (ii) and (iii)

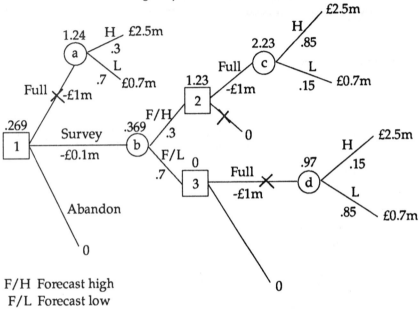

F/H Forecast high
F/L Forecast low

Unit 6 Confidence intervals *(page 13)*

Tasks

(i) $\dfrac{27}{75} \times 100\% = 36\%$

(ii) STEP $= \sqrt{\dfrac{36 \times 64}{75}} = 5.54$

(iii) 95% confidence interval is: $36 \pm 1.96 \times 5.54 = 25.1\%$ to 46.9%

(iv) STEM $= \dfrac{35.97}{\sqrt{52}} = 4.988$ (it is not really necessary to adjust the standard deviation since n is large)

(v) $£37.26 \pm 1.96 \times 4.988$
$= £27.48$ to $£47.04$ (the normal approximation is justified here since n is large)

(vi) No - the interval includes £45.45

Problem-solving activities

(i)

$$1.96 \times \sqrt{\frac{36 \times 64}{n}} = 3$$

So: $$\frac{36 \times 64}{n} = 2.3428$$

$$\therefore \qquad n = 983.4$$

That is a sample of at least 984 is required.

(ii)

$$1.96 \times \frac{35.97}{\sqrt{n}} = 5$$

$$\sqrt{n} = \frac{1.96 \times 35.97}{5}$$

$$n = 198.8$$

A sample of around 200 is required

(iii) Can you be sure that the people who are interviewed are telling the truth? Unless data can be measured you can never be sure how accurate your data really is.

Unit 7 Statistical process control (page 15)

Tasks

(i)   1.96 and 3.10

(ii) STEM $= \dfrac{1.5}{\sqrt{4}} = 0.75$

(iii) 95%: $20 \pm 1.96 \times 0.75 = 18.5, 21.5$
      99.8%: $20 \pm 3.10 \times 0.75 = 17.7, 22.3$

(iv)

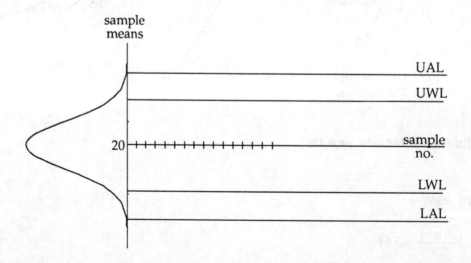

Problem-solving activities

(i)

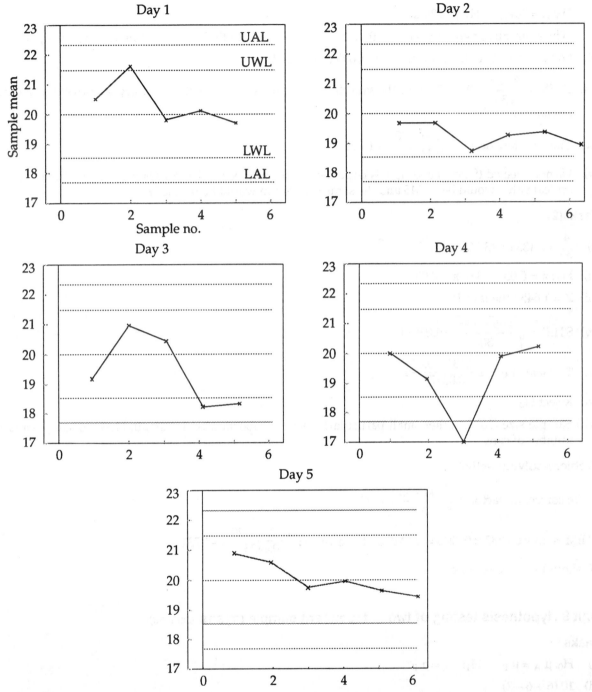

Day 1: Process in control
Day 2: Process in control, but the true mean may be less than 20 microns
Day 3: Not in control. Last two points are both outside the warning limits.
Day 4: Not in control. One point is outside the action limit. (It looks as if process has been re-set.)
Day 5: Not in control. There appears to be a trend downwards.

(ii) There is no mean below 15mm but it is possible that individual values may have been below this figure, particularly in sample number 3 in day 4.

Unit 8 Hypothesis testing of a sample mean and proportion (page 18)

Tasks(1)

(i) $H_0: \mu = 20kg \qquad H_1: \mu < 20kg$

(The alternative hypothesis is less than because you want to find out if the tins are underweight)

(ii) t on 29 degrees of freedom at 5% = –1.699 (one tailed)

(iii) STEM $= \dfrac{2.622}{\sqrt{30}} = 0.4787$ (Since the sample size is large it is not really necessary to correct the standard deviation).

(iv) The test statistic, $t = \dfrac{19.234 - 20}{0.4787} = -1.600$

(v) H_0 not rejected (Since the sample is large the Z test could be used as an approximation. In this case the critical value would be –1.645 and the same conclusion would be reached)

Tasks(2)

(i) $\dfrac{4}{30} = 0.133$ or 13.3%

(ii) $H_0: \pi = 0.05 \qquad H_1: \pi > 0.05$

(iii) Z = 1.645 (one tailed)

(iv) STEP $= \sqrt{\dfrac{0.05 \times 0.95}{30}} = 0.03979$

(v) Test statistic $Z = \dfrac{0.133 - 0.05}{0.03979} = 2.086$

(vi) Reject H_0

(vii) Sample size (30) is rather small particularly as the proportion is also small. Need to sample a larger number of cans.

Problem-solving activity

Finite correction factor is $\sqrt{\dfrac{200 - 30}{199}} = 0.9243$

STEM is now $0.4787 \times 0.9243 = 0.4425$ and t becomes: $\dfrac{19.234 - 20}{0.4425} = -1.731$

H_0 should now be rejected.

Unit 9 Hypothesis testing of two independent sample means (page 20)

Tasks

(i) $H_0: \mu_A = \mu_B \qquad H_1: \mu_A \neq \mu_B$

(ii) 10 (6 + 6 – 2)

(iii) t = 2.228 on 10 degrees of freedom (two tailed so 0.025 in each tail)

(iv) $\overline{X}_A = 5.517; S_A = 1.375; \quad \overline{X}_B = 4.567; S_B = 1.598$

(v) $\hat{\sigma} = \sqrt{\dfrac{6 \times 1.375^2 + 6 \times 1.598^2}{10}} = 1.633$

(vi) Standard error $= 1.633 \times \sqrt{\dfrac{1}{6} + \dfrac{1}{6}} = 0.9428$

(vii) $\quad t = \dfrac{5.517 - 4.567}{0.9428} = 1.008$

(viii) H_0 cannot be rejected so it is not possible use these results to decide on the best filter.

Unit 10 Hypothesis tests on paired data *(page 22)*

Tasks

(i) $H_0: \mu_D = 0$ $H_1: \mu_D > 0$ (one tailed since it is hoped that the campaign would not decrease sales)

(ii)   t = 1.895 at 5% and 2.998 at 1% (1 tailed on 7 degrees of freedom)

(iii) Differences are:

	A	B	C	D	E	F	G	H
	28,	-15,	40,	100,	60,	-20,	0,	50

(iv) $\overline{X}_D = 30.375$; $S_D = 38.288$; $\hat{\sigma}_D = 40.932$

(v)   Standard error = $\dfrac{40.932}{\sqrt{8}} = 14.472$

(vi) $t = \dfrac{30.375}{14.472} = 2.099$

(vii) H_0 can be rejected at 5% but not at 1%. Therefore not conclusive proof that campaign has worked.

Unit 11 The χ^2 hypothesis test *(page 24)*

Tasks

(i) H_0: There is no association between age and level of improvement.

   H_1: There is an association between age and level of improvement.

(ii)   (a) $\dfrac{60}{110}$ (b) $\dfrac{5}{110}$ (c) $\dfrac{60}{110} \times \dfrac{5}{110}$

(iii) $\dfrac{60}{110} \times \dfrac{5}{110} \times 110 = 2.7$

(iv)   Formula is $\dfrac{\text{row total} \times \text{column total}}{\text{Grand total}}$

   Expected values are:
   2.7, 5.5, 30, 21.8
   2.3, 4.5, 25, 18.2

(v)   There are 3 values below 5 so the first two columns should be combined. That is the 'worse' and 'none' categories should be combined. The table now becomes (expected values in brackets):

Age of employee	Level of improvement			Total
	Worse/none	Some	High	
Below 40	6 (8.2)	24 (30)	30 (21.8)	60
40+	9 (6.8)	31 (25)	10 (18.2)	50
Total	15	55	40	110

(vi) to (viii)

O	E	(O – E)	(O – E)^2	$\dfrac{(O-E)^2}{E}$
6	8.2	-2.2	4.84	0.5902
24	30.0	-6.0	36.00	1.2000
30	21.8	8.2	67.24	3.0844
9	6.8	2.2	4.84	0.7118
31	25.0	6.0	36.00	1.4400
10	18.2	-8.2	67.24	3.6945

10.721

(ix) Test statistic = 10.721

(x) 2 degrees of freedom

(xi) Critical value at 1% is 9.210, therefore reject H_0

(xii) It appears that younger employees did better than expected and older employees did worse than expected.

Problem-solving activity

$\pi = 0.3636 \pm 1.96 \times 0.04587$
$= 0.2738, 0.4537$

$P = \dfrac{40}{110} = 0.3636$, $STEP = \sqrt{\dfrac{0.3636 \times (1 - 0.3636)}{110}} = 0.04587$

95% confidence interval is: $0.3636 \pm 1.96 \times 0.04587 = (0.2737, 0.4535)$
That is between 27.4% to 45.4% of all employees are likely to show a high level of improvement at their job.

Unit 12 Correlation *(page 26)*

Tasks
(i)   and (ii)

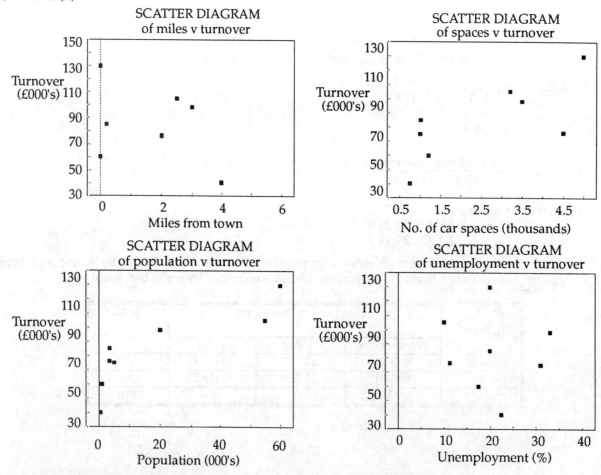

SCATTER DIAGRAM of miles v turnover

SCATTER DIAGRAM of spaces v turnover

SCATTER DIAGRAM of population v turnover

SCATTER DIAGRAM of unemployment v turnover

(iii) The distance factor: **Weak negative** association.
Car spaces: **Strong positive** association.
Population: **Positive** but probably **non-linear**.
Unemployment: **No correlation**.

(iv) All factors except unemployment seem to have some association. Car spaces appears to be the most important.

Problem-solving activities

(i)   (ii)

The distance factor:

Let X be miles and Y be turnover

X	Y	X^2	Y^2	XY
0.2	85	0.04	7225	17
0.0	60	0.0	3600	0.0
2.5	105	6.25	11025	262.5
3.0	98	9.0	9604	294
4.0	40	16.0	1600	160
0.0	130	0.0	16900	0.0
2.0	76	4.0	5776	152
6.5	75	42.25	5625	487.5
18.2	669	77.54	61355	1373

$$r = \frac{8 \times 1373 - 18.2 \times 669}{\sqrt{\left[8 \times 77.54 - 18.2^2\right]\left[8 \times 61355 - 669^2\right]}}$$

$$= \frac{-1191.8}{\sqrt{289.08 \times 43279}}$$

$$= \frac{-1191.8}{3537.1024}$$

$$= -0.3369$$

This suggests that there is a weak negative correlation between miles and turnover.

Car spaces:

X is car spaces (000's)

$\sum X = 20.15$, $\sum X^2 = 77.54$, $\sum XY = 1373$

$$r = \frac{8 \times 1933 - 20.15 \times 669}{\sqrt{\left[8 \times 71.742 - 20.15^2\right]\left[8 \times 61355 - 669^2\right]}}$$

$$= 0.7358$$

A fairly strong positive correlation between number of car spaces and sales.

Population:

X is population (000's)

$\sum X = 148.6$, $\sum X^2 = 7076.46$, $\sum XY = 16562$

$$r = \frac{8 \times 16562 - 148.6 \times 669}{\sqrt{\left[8 \times 7076.46 - 148.6^2\right]\left[8 \times 61355 - 669^2\right]}}$$

$$= 0.8558$$

A strong positive correlation between size of population and sales.

Unemployment:

X is percentage unemployment

$\sum X = 165.25$, $\sum X^2 = 3889.062$, $\sum XY = 13714$

$$r = \frac{8 \times 13714 - 165.25 \times 669}{\sqrt{\left[8 \times 3889.062 - 165.25^2\right]\left[8 \times 61355 - 669^2\right]}}$$

$$= -0.0655$$

No correlation between unemployment and sales.

It is interesting to note that population has the highest correlation even though there is some indication from the scatter diagram that the association is not likely to be linear.

(iii) **H$_0$:** There is no correlation, $r = 0$
   H$_1$: There is some correlation, $r \neq 0$

$$t = \sqrt{\frac{r^2(n-2)}{1-r^2}} \text{ on 6 degrees of freedom}$$

The distance factor: **t = 0.877** (Not significant)
Car spaces: **t = 2.661** (Significant at 5%)
Population: **t = 4.052** (Significant at 1%)
Unemployment: **t = 0.161** (Not significant)

The critical value on 6 degrees of freedom at 5% significance level is 1.943 so only car spaces and population has a significant correlation. However from the scatter diagram it appears that the association for the population factor was non-linear. This is a good example of the importance of always drawing a scatter diagram before doing any calculations.

Unit 13 Linear regression (page 28)

Tasks

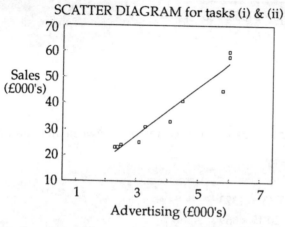

SCATTER DIAGRAM for tasks (i) & (ii)

(i) The scatter graph suggests that their is a strong association between sales and advertising expenditure and that this is a *positive* association.

(ii) Possibly at both low and high values of advertising expenditure.

(iii) The values obtained will depend on the line drawn. For the regression line the values are:

Advert.	Sales	Pred.	Error
6.0	60	55.5	4.5
6.0	60	55.5	4.5
6.0	58	55.5	2.5
5.8	45	53.7	-8.7
4.5	41	41.6	-0.6
4.1	33	37.9	-4.9
3.3	31	30.4	0.6
3.1	25	28.6	-3.6
2.5	24	23.0	1.0
2.4	23	22.1	0.9
2.3	23	21.1	1.9
2.3	23	21.1	1.9

(iv) See the table above. The largest error is when advertising expenditure is £5800.

(v) The positive and negative errors would cancel each other. You could take the absolute value or square the errors to remove the negative sign.

Problem-solving activities

(i)   Y = a + b X; where Y is Sales and X the advertising expenditure.
From the table in Task (iii) the following can be obtained:
$\sum X = 48.3$, $\sum X^2 = 221.79$, $\sum Y = 446$, $\sum XY = 2049.6$
The value of '*a*' and '*b*' can be found from the least squares formula:

$$b = \frac{12 \times 2049.6 - 48.3 \times 446}{12 \times 221.79 - (48.3)^2} = \frac{3053.4}{328.59} = 9.292$$

and

$$a = \frac{446}{12} - 9.292 \times \frac{48.3}{12} = -0.234$$

So the line of best fit is given by: Y = -0.23 + 9.292X

(ii) The correlation coefficient is 0.966 so the coefficient of determination, $R^2 = 0.933$ or 93.3%.

(iii) Y = -0.23 + 9.292 × 5
= 46.2 (000's)
That is £46,200

(iv) From the regression and from the scatter graph it appears that sales should respond to increased advertising. However, it would be unsafe to extrapolate outside the range of data or to generalise to other products. Also and most importantly this is not necessarily a causal relationship. It could be that the sales are being affected by a third variable, e.g the economy, or the promotion of a rival product etc.

(v)   A fixed budget seems preferable but before a figure was recommended further analysis and study would be required. For example what are Riglen's competitors' doing?

Unit 14 Time series analysis *(page 31)*

Tasks

(i)   A great deal of information is lost through this method.

(ii) Moving averages are:

	Mon	Tues	Wed	Thurs	Fri
Week 1			61.4	64.2	62.8
2	61.4	59.4	61.8	58.4	60.0
3	62.0	62.8	58.6	68.6	78.2
4	83.6	90.4	95.4	86.6	75.0
5	67.4	58.4	52.4		

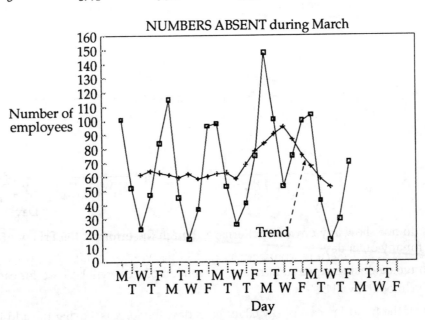

NUMBERS ABSENT during March

(iii) The moving average series represents the trend of the original time series. The seasonal fluctuations have been removed.

(iv) The trend has been affected by the high figures in week four but there are indications that it is returning to normal. A steady forecast around the 60's for each day is probably reasonable but there are other possibilities.

Problem-solving activities

(i) For the additive model, the seasonal differences are:

	Mon	Tues	Wed	Thurs	Fri	
	47.65	−7.25	−39.32	−19.45	19.75	unadjusted
and	47.4	−7.5	−39.6	−19.7	19.5	adjusted

For the multiplicative model, the seasonal factors are:

	Mon	Tues	Wed	Thurs	Fri	
	1.692	0.864	0.384	0.707	1.307	unadjusted
and	1.707	0.872	0.387	0.714	1.320	adjusted

(ii) The predicted values of the numbers absent are T + S for the additive model and T + S for the multiplicative model.

These values areP:

Additive model – 21.8, 44.5, 82.3, 108.8, 51.9, 22.3, 38.7, 79.5, 109.4, 55.3, 19.0, 48.9, 97.7, 131.0, 82.9, 55.8, 66.9, 94.5, 114.8, 50.9, 12.8

Multiplicative model – 23.8, 45.8, 82.9, 104.8, 51.8, 23.9, 41.7, 79.2, 105.9, 54.7, 22.7, 49.0, 103.2, 142.7, 78.8, 37.0, 61.8, 99.0, 115.1, 50.9, 20.3

(iii) The value of MAD and MSE for both models are as follows:

	Additive	Multiplicative
MAD	7.93	8.60
MSE	98.88	124.79

This suggests that the additive model gives smaller errors. The graph of errors over time for both models can be seen below:

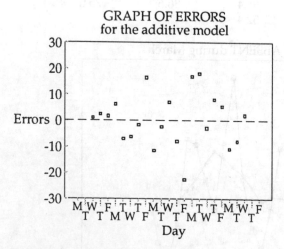

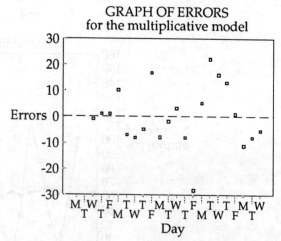

The graphs do not show any obvious patterns, although the error for the Friday of the third week is larger than for any other day.

(iv) For the additive model the expected number of absent employees will be T + S for each day and for the multiplicative model it will be T × S.

For example if the trend forecast is, say 60 for each day, the forecasts using the additive model would be:

Monday	$60 + 47.4 = 107.4$,	that is 107 employees
Tuesday	$60 - 7.5 = 52.5$	(53)
Wednesday	$60 - 39.6 = 20.4$	(20)
Thursday	$60 - 19.7 = 40.3$	(40)
Friday	$60 + 19.5 = 79.5$	(80)

For the multiplicative model the forecasts would be:

Monday	$60 \times 1.707 = 102.4$	(102)
Tuesday	$60 \times 0.872 = 52.3$	(52)
Wednesday	$60 \times 0.387 = 23.2$	(23)
Thursday	$60 \times 0.714 = 42.8$	(43)
Friday	$60 \times 1.320 = 79.2$	(79)

(v) The original series is de-seasonalised by either *subtracting* the seasonal differences from the data (additive model) or *dividing* by the seasonal factors (multiplicative model). For example for Monday, the de-seasonalised value would be $101 - 47.4 = 53.6$ using the additive model and $101/1.707 = 59.2$, using the multiplicative model.

For the additive model the figures are:

Mon	Tues	Wed	Thurs	Fri
53.6	59.5	62.6	66.7	64.5
67.6	52.5	55.6	56.7	76.5
50.6	60.5	65.6	60.7	55.5
100.6	108.5	92.6	94.7	80.5
56.6	50.5	54.6	49.7	50.5

For the multiplicative model the figures are:

Mon	Tues	Wed	Thurs	Fri
59.2	59.6	59.4	65.8	63.3
67.3	51.6	41.3	51.8	72.7
57.4	60.7	67.2	57.4	56.8
86.7	115.8	137.0	105.0	75.8
60.9	49.3	38.8	42.0	53.0

(vi) Using the de-seasonalised figures from the additive model.

Actual	F'cast	Error	.3× err	F'cast	
50.5	56.6	–6.1	–1.83	$56.6 + (-1.83)$	= 54.8
54.6	54.8	–0.2	–0.06	$54.8 + (-0.06)$	= 54.7
49.7	54.7	–5.0	–1.50	$54.7 + (-1.50)$	= 53.2
50.5	53.2	–2.7	–0.81	$53.2 + (-0.81)$	= 52.4

For the multiplicative model.

Actual	F'cast	Error	.3× err	F'cast	
49.3	56.6	–7.3	–2.19	$56.6 + (-2.19)$	= 54.4
38.8	54.4	–15.6	–4.68	$54.4 + (-4.68)$	= 49.7
42.0	49.7	–7.7	–2.31	$49.7 + (-2.31)$	= 47.4
53.0	47.4	5.6	1.68	$47.7 + 1.68$	= 49.4

For the additive model the forecast for Monday of week 6 is $52.4 + 47.4 = 99.82$, i.e about 100 employees.

For the multiplicative model the forecast is $49.4 \times 1.707 = 84.3$, i.e about 84 employees.

Unit 15 Network analysis *(page 34)*

Tasks

(i) to (iii) See diagram overleaf

(iv) 29 weeks

(v) Floats are the difference between the EST and EFT:
A-0, B-12, C-0, D-1, E-0, F-0, G-14, H-0, I-0, J-0
Critical activities are A,C,E,F,H,I,J

Diagram for Unit 15 Tasks (i) to (iii)

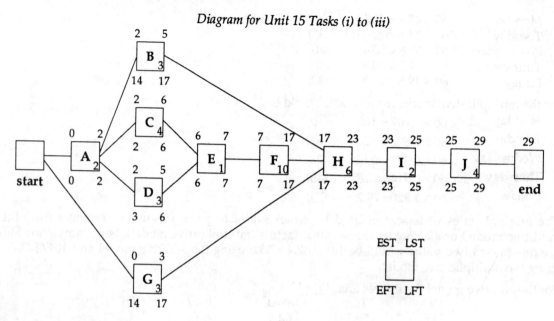

Problem-solving activities

(i) Activity B already has a float of 12 weeks so reducing the duration by 2 weeks will simply increase the float. Activity F is on the critical path so any reduction in time will reduce the project time. The critical path stays the same and the project duration is reduced by 2 weeks. (No other path becomes critical).

(ii)

Activity	t_o	t_p	t_m	$\bar{t}$	σ_t
C	2	7	3	3.5	0.913
D	2	6	3	3.3	0.816
J	3	6	5	4.8	0.707

Project duration now becomes 27.3 weeks

(iii) The mean time is 27.3 weeks and since activities C and J are on the critical path, the standard deviation of the project time is $\sigma = \sqrt{0.913^2 + 0,707^2} = 1.155$

The equation for Z can now be used. That is $Z = \dfrac{29 - 27.3}{1.155} = 1.47$.

From the Z table, this gives a probability of $1 - 0.0708 = 0.9292$

That is there is a probability of about 93% that the project duration will be less than 29 weeks.

Unit 16 Resource and cost scheduling *(page 36)*

Tasks(1)

(i)

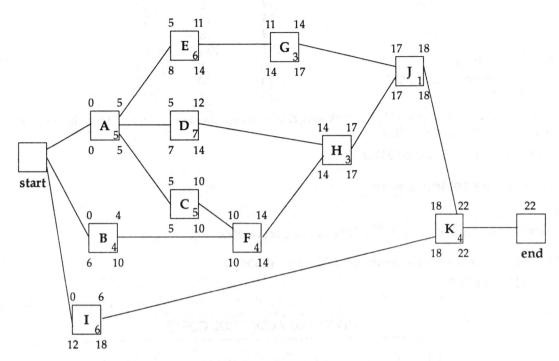

Project will take 22 weeks. Critical activities are A,C,F,H,J,K

(ii) to (iv)

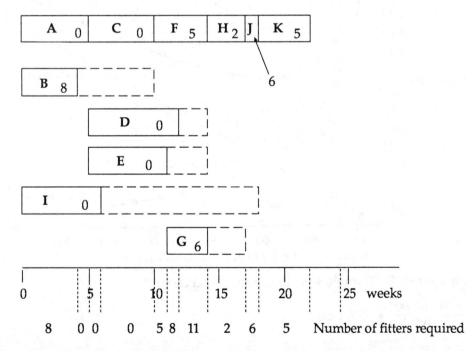

11 fitters are required during weeks 11 to 14

8 fitters only will be required if the start of activity G is delayed for 3 weeks.

Tasks(2)

(i)   £343,000 (£123,000 + 22 × £10,000)

(ii)   B$-\frac{6000}{2}$= £3000, D$-\frac{6000}{1}$= £6000, F$-\frac{15000}{3}$= £5000, G$-\frac{7000}{1}$= £7000, and K$-\frac{8000}{1}$= £8000 per week.

(iii) and (iv)

ACFHJK-	22	20	19	18
ADHJK-	20	20	19	18
AEGJK-	19	19	18	18
BFHJK-	16	14	13	12
IK-	19	19	18	18
Activities crashed		F(2)	K(1)	F(1),D(1)
Extra cost (£000's)		10	8	11
Reduction in overheads (£000's)		20	10	10
Project cost		333	331	332

If F is reduced by 3 weeks, D by 1 week and K by 1 week, the total time will be reduced to 18 weeks. Total cost of project is £332,000.

(v) At 19 weeks the total cost is £331,000.

Unit 17 Inventory control *(page 40)*

Tasks

(i) Average quantity in stock $= \frac{10,000}{2} = 5000$, holding cost $= 5000 \times 0.015 = £75$ p.a

(ii) Number of orders = 50, and order cost $= 50 \times 50 = £2500$ p.a

(iii) £75 + £2500 = £2575

(iv)

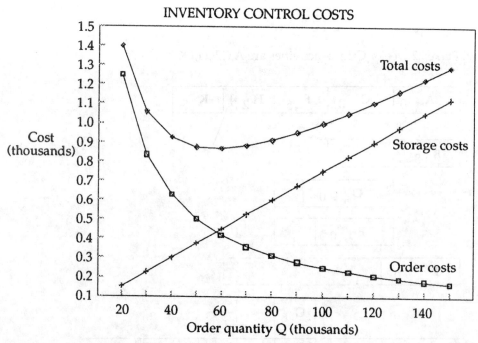

INVENTORY CONTROL COSTS

Cost (thousands) vs Order quantity Q (thousands)

An order quantity around 60,000 would seem to minimise total costs.

(v) $\text{EOQ} = \sqrt{\dfrac{2 \times 50 \times 500000}{0.015}} = 57,735$ cans.

Holding cost $= 0.015 \times \dfrac{57735}{2} = £433$

Order cost $= 50 \times \dfrac{500000}{57735} = £433$

So total cost = £866, which is a saving of £2575 − £866 = £1709 p.a. There will be $\frac{500,000}{57735} = 8.66$ orders a year on average, which is one every 5.8 weeks.

Problem-solving activities

(i)   If the order size is 60,000

Holding cost $= 0.015 \times \frac{60000}{2} = £450$

Order cost $= 50 \times \frac{500000}{60000} = £417$

Total cost $= £867$

Since this is only £1 more than before order 60,000 (12 boxes)

(ii) Order when down to 40,000 cans (average demand in 4 weeks)

(iii) Product cost when ordering 60,000 cans is $100 \times 100 = £10,000$

So total cost $= 10,000 + 867 = £10,867$ p.a

If order 100,000 then product cost $= 100 \times 99 = £9,900$ p.a

Holding cost $= 0.015 \times \frac{100000}{2} = £750$

Order cost $= 50 \times \frac{500000}{100000} = £250$

Total cost $= £10,900$

This is more than ordering 60,000 cans.

(iv) The mean demand over the 4 week delivery time is 40,000 cans. The standard deviation of the demand is $\sqrt{4 \times 5000} = 10,000$ and the Z value from the normal table for a probability of 1% is 2.33

Therefore $2.33 = \frac{X - 40000}{10000}$ where X is the re-order level

The value of X is 63,300, which implies a buffer stock of 23,300 cans.

Unit 18 Linear programming *(page 42)*

Tasks

(i)   to (v)

        Max $0.12F + 0.15P$

subject to:

        $F + P \leq 12000$

        $3F + 5P \leq 43200$

        $5F + 10P \leq 120000$

        $F \geq 2500$

        $P \geq 2500$

(vi) See diagram overleaf

Diagram for Unit 18 Task (vi)

(vii) Possible solutions are at A, B, C or D

	F	P	Profit
A	2500	2500	£675
B	2500	7140	£1371
C	8400	3600	£1548
D	9500	2500	£1515

Optimal solution is therefore at point C, that is when F = 3600 packets and F = 8400 packets per day. This gives a daily profit of £1548. (Note- the quickest method to find the optimum is to draw the isoprofit line. To do this draw the line $0.12F + 0.15P = Y$, where Y is any reasonable profit figure and can be found by substituting any convenient combination of F and P into this equation).

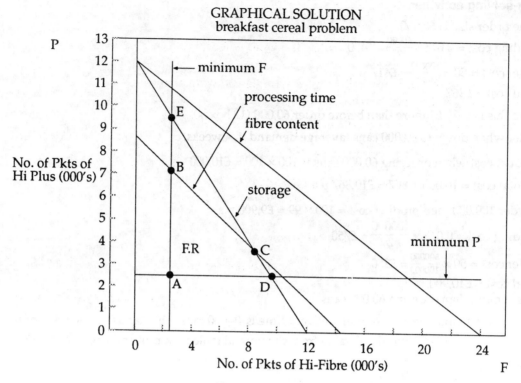

GRAPHICAL SOLUTION
breakfast cereal problem

Problem-solving activities

(i) Storage: 0; Processing time 0; Fibre 4.2kg. So storage and processing time are scarce resources (tight constraints).

(ii) It is only necessary to consider the storage and processing time since fibre is not a scarce resource. To find the shadow price of the storage resource the right hand side of this constraint is increased by 1 to 12,001 and this constraint and the processing one are solved simultaneously.

$$
\begin{aligned}
F + P &= 12001 \quad (1) \quad \text{multiply this equation by 3}\\
3F + 5P &= 43200 \quad (2)\\
3F + 3P &= 36003 \quad (1) \quad \times 3 \text{ subtract the two equations}\\
2P &= 7197\\
P &= 3598.5
\end{aligned}
$$

and $\quad F + 3598.5 = 12001$
giving $\quad\quad F = 8402.5$

The profit = $0.12 \times 8402.5 + 0.15 \times 3598.5 = 1548.075$

This is £0.075 or 7.5p more than before so the shadow price is 7.5p. As this is less than 20p it is not economical to increase the storage space.

The same procedure is repeated for the processing time, except that the storage space is brought back to 12,000 and the processing time is increased to 43,201. The new values for F and P are 8399.5 and 3600.5 respectively. The shadow price is 1.5p per second or £54 per hour. Therefore for every hour of overtime worked, additional profit of £24 (54 – 30) should be realised. The right hand side of the processing time constraint can increase until the line 3F + 5P = Y touches the point E in the graph for Task (vi). At E the value of F and P are 2500 and 9500 respectively. The value of Y is therefore

$3 \times 2500 + 5 \times 9500 = 55000$

This means that the upper limit of the processing time is $\frac{55000}{3600} = 15.27$ hours, an increase of 3.27 hours.

(iii) This question can only be answered accurately if the idea of the isoprofit line is used. To do this let the profit on F be x then the profit equation is

$x\,F + 0.15P$

The gradient of this line is $\frac{x}{0.15}$. When $x = 0.12$ the optimum is at C but this can change to either B or D depending on the value of x.

The gradient of the line F + P = 12000 is 1 and when $\frac{x}{0.15} = 1$, that is $x = 0.15$, the optimum moves to

D. The gradient of the line 3F + 5P = 43200 is $\frac{3}{5}$ and when $\frac{x}{0.15} = \frac{3}{5}$, that is $x = 0.09$, the optimum moves to B. So providing the profit on F stayed within the range 9p to 15p the optimal solution would remain the same. (In fact if the profit was at either extreme you would have multiple optimal solutions). The range for the profit on P is found in a similar fashion and is 12p to 20p.

(iv) A new constraint of F − P ≥ 0 needs to be added to the graph. (See below). The new optimum is at point C and the solution is now F = 5400, P = 5400 giving a profit of £1458. The £90 'loss' could be made up by increasing the profit contribution of Hi-Fibre Plus by 1.7p per packet.

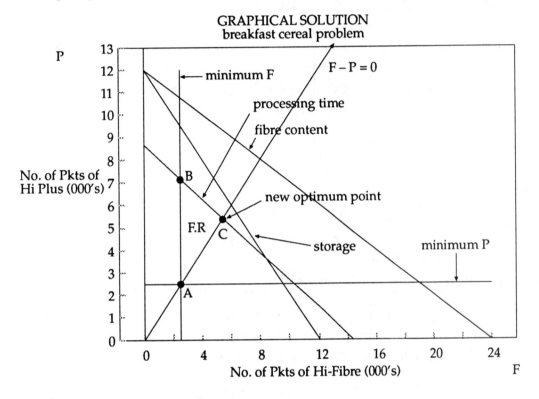

GRAPHICAL SOLUTION
breakfast cereal problem

Unit 19 Transportation algorithm *(page 45)*

Tasks

(i) Watford to London 500 boxes (£900)
Bristol to Wales 100 boxes (£220)
Bristol to the South West 400 boxes (£840)
Birmingham to the North West 450 boxes (£1530)
Birmingham to the North East 450 boxes (£4500)
Total cost = £7990

(ii) and (iii)

	Quantities	1.8	1.4	0.7	7.3	1.3	V's
U's	Destination Warehouse	London	Wales	NW	NE	SW	Available
0	Watford	500	3.6	4.3	-0.2	1.6	500
2.7	Birmingham	30	250	450	170	0.7	900
0.8	Bristol	0.7	100	3.2	-0.2	400	500
-7.3	Dummy	5.5	5.9	6.6	330	6.0	330
	Required	530	350	450	500	400	

Shadow costs

Cost of solution = £6350

(iv) Transfer 170 boxes to Watford-NE route as follows:

		1.8	1.4	0.7	7.1	1.3	V's
U's	Destination Warehouse	London	Wales	NW	NE	SW	Available
0	Watford	330	3.6	4.3	170	1.6	500
2.7	Birmingham	200	250	450	0.2	0.7	900
0.8	Bristol	0.7	100	3.2	0	400	500
-7.5	Dummy	7	6.1	6.8	330	6.2	330
	Required	530	350	450	500	400	

This solution is optimal. Minimum cost is £6316, a saving of £1674 on the current policy.

(v) A saving of 21% is made over the current policy. This would result in an overall saving of approximately £1.7m p.a.

Problem-solving activities

(i) There is an alternative solution because the shadow price for the Bristol-NE route is zero. Transfer 100 boxes to this route. New solution is:

> Watford to London 430 boxes
> NE 70 boxes
> Birmingham to London 100 boxes
> Wales 350 boxes
> NW 450 boxes
> Bristol to NE 100 boxes
> SW 400 boxes

(ii) The shadow price of this route is £0.70 and this will be the additional cost of using this route.

(iii) The shadow cost of this route is 0.2; therefore if the cost could be reduced by this much (that is to £9.80 or less), it would become economic.

Unit 20 Simulation *(page 48)*

Tasks

(i)   and (ii)

| Loading | | | | | Unloading | | |
Time (minutes)	Mid Pt.	%	Cum %	R.Nos	%	Cum %	R.Nos
0 to under 30	15	20	20	00-19	30	30	00-29
30 to under 40	35	35	55	20-54	40	70	30-69
40 to under 50	45	22	77	55-76	25	95	70-94
50 to under 60	55	15	92	77-91	4	99	95-98
60 to under 70	65	8	100	92-99	1	100	99

Inter-arrival time

Time (minutes)	Mid Pt.	%	Cum %	R.Nos
0 to under 10	5	15	15	00-14
10 to under 20	15	40	55	15-54
20 to under 30	25	30	85	55-84
30 to under 40	35	5	90	85-89
40 to under 50	45	5	95	90-94
50 to under 60	55	3	98	95-97
60 to under 70	65	2	100	98-99

Type of lorry

		R.Nos
Loading (L)	70%	00-69
Unloading (U)	30%	70-99

(iii)

Random No.	Loading time
42	35
17	15
38	35
61	45

(iv)

| ARRIVALS | | | | | | | | SERVICE | | |
RNo	Inter arrival time	Clock	Queue Size	RNo	Type	RNo	Time	Starts	Ends	Waiting Time
20	15	15	0	17	L	42	35	15	50	0
96	55	70	0	23	L	17	15	70	85	0
28	15	85	0	66	L	38	35	85	120	0
59	25	110	1	38	L	61	45	120	165	10
73	25	135	1	76	U	80	45	165	210	30
00	5	140	2	20	L	56	45	210	255	70
10	5	145	3	5	L	87	55	255	310	110
88	35	180	2	78	U	15	15	310	325	130

Average waiting time is 43.75 minutes. Maximum queue size is 3

Problem-solving activities

(i)   This would be equivalent to a sample size of 1.

(ii) Steady state only required for non-terminating systems

(iii) Yes- just. t= -2.69 (critical t at 5% is -2.776)

(iv) This will allow you to do a paired t-test on the differences- variation within the samples eliminated.

(v) Yes- obvious without a t-test (t = 20.9)

(vi) Number of lorries in 10 hours $= \dfrac{60}{21.4} \times 10 = 28$

Each lorry queues for 131.3 minutes so total queueing time is $28 \times \dfrac{131.3}{60} = 61.27$ *hours*

Cost at £20 per hour is £1225.40 per day.

For two bays total queueing time is $28\dfrac{49.9}{60} = 23.29$ *hours* and the cost is £465.73 per day. The extra cost of operating this bay is £150 so the saving in cost is $1225.4 - 465.73 - 150 = £609.67$ per day. Assuming a 48 week year the annual saving would be £146,321, and the cost could therefore be recovered in less than a year.

Appendix 2

Answers to selected questions and tasks in Section 3

2. 0.3182

6. (a) (i)   0.252;   (ii) 0.208;   (iii)   0.150
   (b) £1500
   (c) 0.264
   (e) (i)   56; (ii) £1,245 approx.

11. (a) 1.4%
    (b) 2.3%
    (c) Limit of acceptability now 305 units of time. 59.9% of genuine coins would be rejected under this scheme.

13. (a) 0.017
    (b) 0.0875
    (c) 0.2912

14. (a) (i) 10.6%; (ii) 427 hours; (iii) 0.0594
    (b) 0.820
    (c) 0.567

15. (a) (i) Take royalties; (ii) Manufacture;   (iii) Sell
    (b) Manufacture
    (c) £12,000

18. (a)

		Demand				
		1	2	3	4	5
	1	25	25	25	25	25
	2	10	50	50	50	50
Purchase	3	–5	35	75	75	75
	4	–20	20	60	100	100
	5	–35	5	45	85	125

   (b) (i) maximum expected contribution is 63 if 3 ordered
       (ii) £46.67
   (c) 1
   (e) (i) Now order 4 per week giving a profit of £74
       (ii) Maximum expected profit reduced to £60 for a weekly order of 5.

21. (a) £2.83
    (b) £82.71 to £97.29
    (d) 5.84% to 14.16%
    (e) 800

25. (a) mean of sample means = 508.00, mean of sample ranges = 7.00;
       Mean chart: UCL = 512.06; LCL = 503.94
       Range chart: UCL = 14.77
    (b) (i) $\mu = 510$g;   (ii) UCL = 516.84, LCL = 503.15;   (iii) £1,280

26. (b) $Z = -2.425$; H_0 rejected. Fuel consumption not 54mpg

29. (a) $t = 2.088$ so H_0 rejected at 5% (one tailed). Superwrite appears to be faster than quickwrite.

31. (a) 40.8 to 59.2
    (b) (ii) Two sample (2 tailed) t-test. $t = 0.839$ so H_0 accepted. No evidence that output per man has changed.

32. (a) $t = 1.900$; so reject H_0 at 5% (one tailed) on 7 degrees of freedom. The claim does appear to be justified.
    (b) $Z = 1.552$ so H_0 accepted. No evidence that company's image has been improved.

33. (a) Null and alternative hypotheses not stated, samples not independent, formula incorrect, should be two sided (not both), conclusion misleading.

    (b) Use paired t-test. $t = 1.94$ and this is not significant. (Critical value at 5% on 5 degrees of freedom and two tailed is 2.015).

34. (a) mean = 2

    (c) (i) 0.135; (ii) 0.143; (iii) 0.0076

    (d) Use the χ^2 goodness-of-fit test. $\chi^2 = 3.05$ and the critical value on 3 degrees of freedom is 7.81. Therefore accept H_0, that is there is no evidence to suggest that the data do not conform to the Poisson distribution.

    (e) Data not likely to come from a normal distribution. Apply transformation or use non-parametric test.

36. (a) Some expected values are less than 5.

		Questionnaire Response	
		Returned before deadline	Not returned before deadline
	Yes	37	23
X	No	25	20
	Yes	39	21
Y	No	18	37

    (b) (i) $\chi^2 = 8.30$ (don't forget to apply correction since it is a 2 x 2 table). The critical value on 1 degree of freedom at 5% is 3.84 so H_0 rejected. Financial incentive did affect response rate.

    (ii) $\chi^2 = 1.62$. H_0 cannot be rejected.

    (c) Financial incentive appears to have an effect on social type X but not on social type Y.

38. (c) All data: $r = 0.760$; Males: $r = 0.906$; Females: $r = 0.102$

    (d) All data: $t = 4.05$ (significant at 0.1%)

    Males: $t = 4.79$ (significant at 0.5%)

    Females: $t = 0.229$ (not significant)

39. (a) (i) $R = 0.724$;   (ii) $R = 1.00$

	A	B	C	D	E	F
A	1.0	−0.7	0.8	−0.8	−0.9	−0.7
B	−0.7	1.0	−0.8	0.9	0.8	0.7
C	0.8	−0.8	1.0	−0.8	−0.7	−0.6
D	−0.8	0.9	−0.8	1.0	0.7	0.7
E	−0.9	0.8	−0.7	0.7	1.0	1.0
F	−0.7	0.7	−0.6	0.7	0.7	1.0

    (b) B,D,E,F;   A,C;

    (c) $t = 2.97$. Critical value at 5% on 8 degrees of freedom = 2.3. So there is a significant correlation between ratios D and E.

    (d) Pairs of observations can be have the same rank but not be linear whereas if the data lie on a straight line then $r = 1$ and the ranks must be the same.

40. (ii) $E = 47.0 + 0.5049 S$, where E = expenses and S = sales

    (iii) £89,917

42. (a) The 3.5 indicates that a fixed 3.5 hours is required regardless of the size of the batch. The 0.6 is the time required for a batch of size 1.

    (b) −1.3,−0.9,−1.1,−0.9,0.1,0,0.7,0.9,0.8,1.7

    (c) 9.36

45. (b) $Y = 46,452 X^{-0.774}$

    (c) 23.5%

48. (b) Moving average values are (starting from the 3rd quarter 1986):

    586.125, 599.250, 604.375, 602.625, 597.875, 570.250, 543.750, 572.125, 620.125, 645.875, 665.000, 638.625, 508.750, 410.500

    (c) The quarterly seasonal factors are:

Qtr	1	2	3	4
	1.189	0.724	0.754	1.333

49. (a) The centred moving average trend values are (starting from the 2nd quarter 1987):

117, 101, 85, 73, 67, 64, 65, 71,

(b) The average seasonal variations are:

Qtr	1	2	3	4
	–53	1	102	–50

52. (b) (i)

Jan	Feb	Mar	Apr	May	Jun	Jul	Aug	Sep	Oct	Nov	Dec
349	349	344	347	343	352	354	346	341	343	346	345

(iii)

Aug	Sep	Oct	Nov	Dec
350	349.2	347.6	346.7	346.6

The forecast for January 1989 is 346.3

(iv)

Jan	Feb	Mar
332	322	312

55. (a) Project takes 14 months and costs £141,000. The critical path is A C E and G

(b) Floats are A–0, B–1, C–0, D–2, E–0, F–2, G–0, H–2

(c) (i) Minimum project time is 11 months by reducing E by 1 month, G by 2 months and 1 month from either F or H. The minimum overall cost for the project is £137,000 and is achieved when E takes 2 months, G takes 3 months and F takes 3 months.

58. (a) Refit takes 25 days. Critical activities are A, E,F,H,I and J. Floats are B–20, C–10, D–10, G–13 days.

(b) (i) 6 during weeks 2 and 3

(ii) Several possibilities, e.g C starts day 4 and D starts day 12.

60. (a) EOQ = 8 batches (1600 boxes), replenish every 40 days, cost at EOQ is £800 which is a saving of £2,450 p.a

(b) It is worthwhile to take advantage of the discount scheme as a saving of £1000 p.a will be achieved.

61. (b) EOQ = 3,200 boxes, order every 4 weeks.

(c) 1009 boxes

(d) £1,578.37 p.a

62. EBQ = 949 and cost = £126.50 per week. New rate of production would be 180 units per week, which is less than the weekly demand. A buffer stock of 100 units would have allowed demand to be met during the 5 weeks.

64. (a) Max $60P + 85S$

$4P + 8S \leq 400$

$2P + 3S \leq 250$

$10S \geq 150$

$5P + 7S \leq 480$

$P - 2S \geq 0$

(b) $P = 70, S = 15$ giving a profit of £5475 per day.

(c) Components A and C are tight constraints. Shadow prices of A and C are £15 and £3.50 respectively. (Note increasing C would *reduce* profit). It would be worthwhile increasing A since shadow price greater than cost.

(d) No upper limit but lower limit of £42.50.

65. (a) Min $1,350,000 + 500U1 - 2,000S2 - 1,500U2$

$S1 + S2 = 240$

$U1 + U2 = 320$

$S1 \leq 200, U1 \leq 300, S2 \leq 100, U2 \leq 200$

$3S1 + 3U1 - 5S2 - 5U2 = 0$

$S1, S2, U1, U2 \geq 0$

(b) Minimum $S1 + U1 = 350$ (multiple optimal solutions). Total cost = £1,090,000

66. (b) Max $P = 25X1 + 30X2 + 20X3 + 22X4$

$X1 + 2X2 + 2X3 \leq 2500$

$2X1 + 3X2 + X3 + 3X4 \leq 4000$

$4X1 + 2X2 + 3X3 + 2X4 \leq 4500$

$0.5X1 + 0.5X2 + X3 + 0.5X4 \leq 1200$

$X1 \geq 200, X2 \geq 150, X3 \geq 300, X4 \geq 200$

(c)   (i)   Optimum monthly production level is: XL35 = 425, RK27 = 525, RM93 = 300, TS15 = 425. Profit = £41,725. Scarce resources are forming, wiring and assembly. There is 212.5 hours left of inspection time. Shadow prices for forming, wiring and assembly are £8, £2.75 and £2.875 respectively.

      (ii)   Each unit of YX49 would use up scarce resources amounting to some £32.875 of lost profit. However since each unit would realise £35 of profit it may be worthwhile.

67. (a)   Cost = £106,000. It is not optimal because negative shadow cost (-1) in route Colchester to warehouse IV.

    (b)   Optimal solution is when the following plan is adopted:-

Aberdeen to: I- 60;   III- 50;   IV- 65
Bristol to: II- 35
Colchester to: IV- 35
Cost is £102,500

    (c)   New solution is:-

Aberdeen to: I- 60;   II- 35;   III- 50;   IV- 30
Colchester to: IV- 70

Cost is £113,000 per week, an increase of £10,500 per week or £504,000 p.a. A net gain in the first year of £300,000.

68. (b) (i)

To /From	A	B	C	D
R	58	61	53	60
S	51	60	52	57
T	54	65	49	66

      (ii)   The optimal allocation is:

Abbotstown: 625 from Rexford, 25 from Seadon

Beswich: 420 from Seadon, 220 from, Triston

Carlic: 380 from Seadon

      (iii) The optimal contribution to profit is £111,965

69. (b) (i)   Optimal production schedule is:

                Machine   A 1,000 mugs   1,000 bowls
                            B 2,400 mugs
                            C 600 mugs   2,400 cups

        Cost is £8,720

      (ii)   Preferred optimal solution is:

                Machine: A 1,000 mugs   1,000 bowls
                            B 2,400 cups
                            C 3,000 mugs

70. (b) (i)   There are 3 alternative solutions; one is:

Project 1: Day
Project 2: Adams
Project 3: Brown
Project 4: Evans

The total time = 324 days

      (ii)   Project 1:Evans; 2 Day; 3 Brown; 4 Adams

      (iii) Carr takes longer for each project. He can then be disregarded

71. Random numbers are allocated as follows:

I.A.T	Mid point	R.Nos
20 – < 50	35	00 – 04
50 – < 100	75	05 – 24
100 – < 150	125	24 – 54
150 – < 200	175	55 – 99

Random number 08 is equivalent to an inter-arrival time of 75 secs. The first service starts at a clock time of 75 and ends at 120.

74. (b)

Unloading time	Mid Point	R.Nos
0 – < 30	15	00 – 19
30 – < 40	35	20 – 54
40 – < 50	45	55 – 76
50 – < 60	55	77 – 91
60 – < 70	65	92 – 99

(c) (ii) Mean difference = 0.26, and $\hat{\sigma}$ = 0.270 and t = 2.15. This is significant at 5% so some evidence to suggest that an improvement in queue size would result.

(iii) Average queueing time, maximum and minimum queue time/size, utilisation, etc.

Appendix 3

Areas in the right hand tail of the standard normal distribution

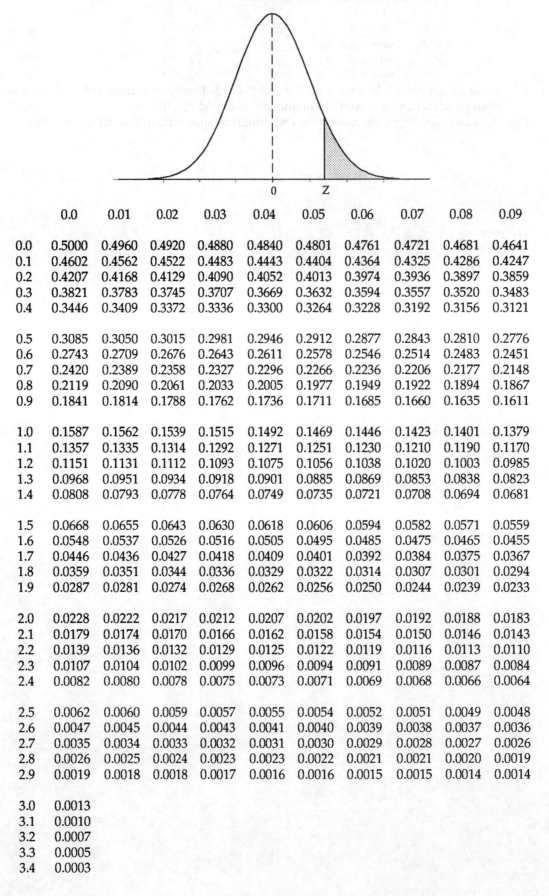

	0.0	0.01	0.02	0.03	0.04	0.05	0.06	0.07	0.08	0.09
0.0	0.5000	0.4960	0.4920	0.4880	0.4840	0.4801	0.4761	0.4721	0.4681	0.4641
0.1	0.4602	0.4562	0.4522	0.4483	0.4443	0.4404	0.4364	0.4325	0.4286	0.4247
0.2	0.4207	0.4168	0.4129	0.4090	0.4052	0.4013	0.3974	0.3936	0.3897	0.3859
0.3	0.3821	0.3783	0.3745	0.3707	0.3669	0.3632	0.3594	0.3557	0.3520	0.3483
0.4	0.3446	0.3409	0.3372	0.3336	0.3300	0.3264	0.3228	0.3192	0.3156	0.3121
0.5	0.3085	0.3050	0.3015	0.2981	0.2946	0.2912	0.2877	0.2843	0.2810	0.2776
0.6	0.2743	0.2709	0.2676	0.2643	0.2611	0.2578	0.2546	0.2514	0.2483	0.2451
0.7	0.2420	0.2389	0.2358	0.2327	0.2296	0.2266	0.2236	0.2206	0.2177	0.2148
0.8	0.2119	0.2090	0.2061	0.2033	0.2005	0.1977	0.1949	0.1922	0.1894	0.1867
0.9	0.1841	0.1814	0.1788	0.1762	0.1736	0.1711	0.1685	0.1660	0.1635	0.1611
1.0	0.1587	0.1562	0.1539	0.1515	0.1492	0.1469	0.1446	0.1423	0.1401	0.1379
1.1	0.1357	0.1335	0.1314	0.1292	0.1271	0.1251	0.1230	0.1210	0.1190	0.1170
1.2	0.1151	0.1131	0.1112	0.1093	0.1075	0.1056	0.1038	0.1020	0.1003	0.0985
1.3	0.0968	0.0951	0.0934	0.0918	0.0901	0.0885	0.0869	0.0853	0.0838	0.0823
1.4	0.0808	0.0793	0.0778	0.0764	0.0749	0.0735	0.0721	0.0708	0.0694	0.0681
1.5	0.0668	0.0655	0.0643	0.0630	0.0618	0.0606	0.0594	0.0582	0.0571	0.0559
1.6	0.0548	0.0537	0.0526	0.0516	0.0505	0.0495	0.0485	0.0475	0.0465	0.0455
1.7	0.0446	0.0436	0.0427	0.0418	0.0409	0.0401	0.0392	0.0384	0.0375	0.0367
1.8	0.0359	0.0351	0.0344	0.0336	0.0329	0.0322	0.0314	0.0307	0.0301	0.0294
1.9	0.0287	0.0281	0.0274	0.0268	0.0262	0.0256	0.0250	0.0244	0.0239	0.0233
2.0	0.0228	0.0222	0.0217	0.0212	0.0207	0.0202	0.0197	0.0192	0.0188	0.0183
2.1	0.0179	0.0174	0.0170	0.0166	0.0162	0.0158	0.0154	0.0150	0.0146	0.0143
2.2	0.0139	0.0136	0.0132	0.0129	0.0125	0.0122	0.0119	0.0116	0.0113	0.0110
2.3	0.0107	0.0104	0.0102	0.0099	0.0096	0.0094	0.0091	0.0089	0.0087	0.0084
2.4	0.0082	0.0080	0.0078	0.0075	0.0073	0.0071	0.0069	0.0068	0.0066	0.0064
2.5	0.0062	0.0060	0.0059	0.0057	0.0055	0.0054	0.0052	0.0051	0.0049	0.0048
2.6	0.0047	0.0045	0.0044	0.0043	0.0041	0.0040	0.0039	0.0038	0.0037	0.0036
2.7	0.0035	0.0034	0.0033	0.0032	0.0031	0.0030	0.0029	0.0028	0.0027	0.0026
2.8	0.0026	0.0025	0.0024	0.0023	0.0023	0.0022	0.0021	0.0021	0.0020	0.0019
2.9	0.0019	0.0018	0.0018	0.0017	0.0016	0.0016	0.0015	0.0015	0.0014	0.0014
3.0	0.0013									
3.1	0.0010									
3.2	0.0007									
3.3	0.0005									
3.4	0.0003									

Table of the t-distribution

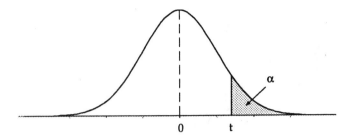

Probability (α)

df	0.2	0.1	0.05	0.025	0.01	0.005	0.001	0.0001
1	1.376	3.078	6.314	12.706	31.821	63.657	318.309	3183.1
2	1.061	1.886	2.920	4.303	6.965	9.925	22.327	70.700
3	0.978	1.638	2.353	3.182	4.541	5.841	10.215	22.204
4	0.941	1.533	2.132	2.776	3.747	4.604	7.173	13.034
5	0.920	1.476	2.015	2.571	3.365	4.032	5.893	9.678
6	0.906	1.440	1.943	2.447	3.143	3.707	5.208	8.025
7	0.896	1.415	1.895	2.365	2.998	3.499	4.785	7.063
8	0.889	1.397	1.860	2.306	2.896	3.355	4.501	6.442
9	0.883	1.383	1.833	2.262	2.821	3.250	4.297	6.010
10	0.879	1.372	1.812	2.228	2.764	3.169	4.144	5.694
11	0.876	1.363	1.796	2.201	2.718	3.106	4.025	5.453
12	0.873	1.356	1.782	2.179	2.681	3.055	3.930	5.263
13	0.870	1.350	1.771	2.160	2.650	3.012	3.852	5.111
14	0.868	1.345	1.761	2.145	2.624	2.977	3.787	4.985
15	0.866	1.341	1.753	2.131	2.602	2.947	3.733	4.880
16	0.865	1.337	1.746	2.120	2.583	2.921	3.686	4.791
17	0.863	1.333	1.740	2.110	2.567	2.898	3.646	4.714
18	0.862	1.330	1.734	2.101	2.552	2.878	3.610	4.648
19	0.861	1.328	1.729	2.093	2.539	2.861	3.579	4.590
20	0.860	1.325	1.725	2.086	2.528	2.845	3.552	4.539
21	0.859	1.323	1.721	2.080	2.518	2.831	3.527	4.493
22	0.858	1.321	1.717	2.074	2.508	2.819	3.505	4.452
23	0.858	1.319	1.714	2.069	2.500	2.807	3.485	4.415
24	0.857	1.318	1.711	2.064	2.492	2.797	3.467	4.382
25	0.856	1.316	1.708	2.060	2.485	2.787	3.450	4.352
26	0.856	1.315	1.706	2.056	2.479	2.779	3.435	4.324
27	0.855	1.314	1.703	2.052	2.473	2.771	3.421	4.299
28	0.855	1.313	1.701	2.048	2.467	2.763	3.408	4.275
29	0.854	1.311	1.699	2.045	2.462	2.756	3.396	4.254
30	0.854	1.310	1.697	2.042	2.457	2.750	3.385	4.234
35	0.852	1.306	1.690	2.030	2.438	2.724	3.340	4.153
40	0.851	1.303	1.684	2.021	2.423	2.704	3.307	4.094
45	0.850	1.301	1.679	2.014	2.412	2.690	3.281	4.049
50	0.849	1.299	1.676	2.009	2.403	2.678	3.261	4.014
60	0.848	1.296	1.671	2.000	2.390	2.660	3.232	3.962
80	0.846	1.292	1.664	1.990	2.374	2.639	3.195	3.899
100	0.845	1.290	1.660	1.984	2.364	2.626	3.174	3.862
∞	0.842	1.282	1.645	1.960	2.327	2.576	3.091	3.720

Table of the χ^2 distibution

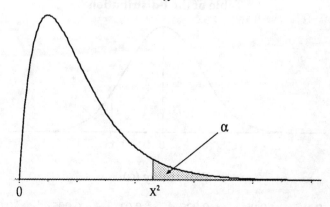

Probability (α)

df	0.995	0.99	0.9	0.1	0.05	0.025	0.01	0.005	0.001
1	0.000	0.000	0.016	2.706	3.841	5.024	6.635	7.879	10.828
2	0.010	0.020	0.211	4.605	5.991	7.378	9.210	10.597	13.816
3	0.072	0.115	0.584	6.251	7.815	9.348	11.345	12.838	16.266
4	0.207	0.297	1.064	7.779	9.488	11.143	13.277	14.860	18.467
5	0.412	0.554	1.610	9.236	11.070	12.833	15.086	16.750	20.515
6	0.676	0.872	2.204	10.645	12.592	14.449	16.812	18.548	22.458
7	0.989	1.239	2.833	12.017	14.067	16.013	18.475	20.278	24.322
8	1.344	1.646	3.490	13.362	15.507	17.535	20.090	21.955	26.124
9	1.735	2.088	4.168	14.684	16.919	19.023	21.666	23.589	27.877
10	2.156	2.558	4.865	15.987	18.307	20.483	23.209	25.188	29.588
11	2.603	3.053	5.578	17.275	19.675	21.920	24.725	26.757	31.264
12	3.074	3.571	6.304	18.549	21.026	23.337	26.217	28.300	32.909
13	3.565	4.107	7.042	19.812	22.362	24.736	27.688	29.819	34.528
14	4.075	4.660	7.790	21.064	23.685	26.119	29.141	31.319	36.123
15	4.601	5.229	8.547	22.307	24.996	27.488	30.578	32.801	37.697
16	5.142	5.812	9.312	23.542	26.296	28.845	32.000	34.267	39.252
17	5.697	6.408	10.085	24.769	27.587	30.191	33.409	35.718	40.790
18	6.265	7.015	10.865	25.989	28.869	31.526	34.805	37.156	42.312
19	6.844	7.633	11.651	27.204	30.144	32.852	36.191	38.582	43.820
20	7.434	8.260	12.443	28.412	31.410	34.170	37.566	39.997	45.315
21	8.034	8.897	13.240	29.615	32.671	35.479	38.932	41.401	46.797
22	8.643	9.542	14.041	30.813	33.924	36.781	40.289	42.796	48.268
23	9.260	10.196	14.848	32.007	35.172	38.076	41.638	44.181	49.728
24	9.886	10.856	15.659	33.196	36.415	39.364	42.980	45.559	51.179
25	0.520	11.524	16.473	34.382	37.652	40.646	44.314	46.928	52.620
26	1.160	12.198	17.292	35.563	38.885	41.923	45.642	48.290	54.052
27	1.808	12.879	18.114	36.741	40.113	43.195	46.963	49.645	55.476
28	2.461	13.565	18.939	37.916	41.337	44.461	48.278	50.993	56.892
29	3.121	14.256	19.768	39.087	42.557	45.722	49.588	52.336	58.301
30	3.787	14.953	20.599	40.256	43.773	46.979	50.892	53.672	59.703
35	7.192	18.509	24.797	46.059	49.802	53.203	57.342	60.275	66.619
40	0.707	22.164	29.051	51.805	55.758	59.342	63.691	66.766	73.402

Appendix 4

Mathematical Formulae used in this book

Probability *(page 55)*

Addition law:

$$P(A \text{ or } B) = P(A) + P(B) - (P(A) \text{ and } P(B))$$
$$= P(A) + P(B) \text{ for mutually exclusive events}$$

Multiplication rule:

$$P(A \text{ and } B) = P(A) \times P(B \mid A)$$
$$= P(A) \times P(B) \text{ for independent events}$$

Bayes' theorem

$$P(A \mid B) = \frac{P(A \text{ and } B)}{P(B)}$$

Expected value $= \Sigma px$

Probability distributions *(page 61)*

$$^nC_r = \frac{n!}{r!(n-r)!}$$

Binomial:

$$P(r) = {}^nC_r . p^r . (1-p)^{n-r}$$
$$\text{Mean} = np$$
$$\text{Standard deviation, } \sigma = \sqrt{np(1-p)}$$

Poisson:

$$P(r) = \frac{e^{-m}m^r}{r!}$$
$$\text{Mean} = m$$
$$\text{Standard deviation, } \sigma = \sqrt{m}$$

Normal Z transformation:

$$Z = \frac{X - \mu}{\sigma}$$

Estimation *(page 85)*

$$\hat{\mu} = \overline{X}$$
$$\hat{\pi} = P$$
$$\hat{\sigma} = s\sqrt{\frac{n}{n-1}} \quad \text{(Bessel's correction factor)}$$
$$= \sqrt{\frac{\sum(X - \overline{X})^2}{n-1}}$$
$$\text{STEM} = \frac{\sigma}{\sqrt{n}}$$
$$\text{STEP} = \sqrt{\frac{P(1-P)}{n}}$$

Confidence interval for a mean based on the normal distribution:

$$\hat{\mu} = \overline{X} \pm Z \times \text{STEM}$$

Confidence interval for a mean based on the t-distribution:

$$\hat{\mu} = \overline{X} \pm t \times \text{STEM}$$

Confidence interval for a proportion:

$$\hat{\pi} = P \pm Z \times \text{STEP}$$

Finite population correction factor:

$$\sqrt{\frac{N-n}{N-1}}$$

Statistical process control:

for the mean chart $\hat{\mu} \pm A \times \overline{R}$

for the range chart $D \times \overline{R}$

Hypothesis testing *(page 99)*

The Z-test for a single sample mean:

$$Z = \frac{\overline{X} - \mu}{\text{STEM}}$$

The t-test for a single sample mean:

$$t = \frac{\overline{X} - \mu}{\text{STEM}}$$

Hypothesis test of two independent sample means: The test statistic is:

$$z \text{ or } t = \frac{(\overline{X}_1 - \overline{X}_2) - (\mu_1 - \mu_2)}{\text{SE}(\overline{X}_1 - \overline{X}_2)}$$

(Note if the t-test is used, t is based on the t-distribution on $(n_1 + n_2 - 2)$ degrees of freedom.)

Standard error of the difference between the two means is:

for the z-test: $\text{SE}(\overline{X}_1 - \overline{X}_2) = \sqrt{\dfrac{\sigma_1^2}{n_1} + \dfrac{\sigma_2^2}{n_2}}$

for the t-test: $\text{SE}(\overline{X}_1 - \overline{X}_2) = \sigma\sqrt{\dfrac{1}{n_1} + \dfrac{1}{n_2}}$

where σ is found from: $\hat{\sigma} = \sqrt{\dfrac{n_1 S_1^2 + n_2 S_2^2}{n_1 + n_2 - 2}}$

Hypothisis test for samples that are not independent

$$t = \frac{\overline{X}_D}{\text{SE}_D}$$

where: $\text{SE}_D = \dfrac{\hat{\sigma}_D}{\sqrt{n}}$

Hypothesis test of a proportion:

$$Z = \frac{P - \pi}{\text{STEP}}$$

where STEP must be found from the following:

$$\text{STEP} = \sqrt{\frac{\pi(1-\pi)}{n}}$$

Hypothesis test on two proportions:

$$Z = \frac{(P_1 - P_2) - (\pi_1 - \pi_2)}{\text{SE}(\pi_1 - \pi_2)}$$

where the standard error of the difference between the two proportions is:

$$SE(\pi_1 - \pi_2) = \sqrt{\frac{\hat{\pi}(1-\hat{\pi})}{n_1} + \frac{\hat{\pi}(1-\hat{\pi})}{n_2}}$$

and the estimate of the population proportion can be found from:

$$\hat{\pi} = \frac{n_1 P_1 + n_2 P_2}{n_1 + n_2}$$

The χ^2 hypothesis test statistic is:

$$X^2 = \sum \frac{(O-E)^2}{E}$$

The degrees of freedom for a goodness-of-fit test is:

$$v = n - 1 - k$$

The expected value for a contingency table is given by:

$$\text{Expected value} = \frac{\text{Row Total} \times \text{Column Total}}{\text{Grand Total}}$$

The degrees of freedom for a contingency table is found from:

$$(\text{number of columns} - 1) \times (\text{number of rows} - 1)$$

Correlation and regression *(page 116)*

Pearson's product moment correlation coefficient:

$$r = \frac{n\sum XY - \sum X \sum Y}{\sqrt{\left[n\sum X^2 - \left(\sum X\right)^2\right]\left[n\sum Y^2 - \left(\sum Y\right)^2\right]}}$$

For a test of significance on the value of r:

$$t = \sqrt{\frac{r^2(n-2)}{1-r^2}} \quad \text{on (n-2) degrees of freedom}$$

Spearman's rank correlation coefficient (R):

$$R = 1 - \frac{6\sum d^2}{n(n^2 - 1)}$$

Line of best fit (method of least squares): $Y = a + bX$

The values of '**a**' and '**b**' that minimise the squared errors are given by the equations:-

$$b = \frac{n\sum XY - \sum X \sum Y}{n\sum X^2 - \left(\sum X\right)^2}$$

$$a = \frac{\sum Y}{n} - b\frac{\sum X}{n}$$

The coefficient of determination: $\quad r^2$

The confidence interval for an estimated value of Y:

$$\hat{Y} \pm t \times \hat{\sigma}_e \sqrt{\frac{1}{n} + \frac{X_0 - \overline{X}}{\sum\left(X - \overline{X}\right)^2}}$$

where: $\qquad \hat{\sigma}_e = \dfrac{\sum\left(Y - \hat{Y}\right)^2}{n-2}$

Time series analysis *(page 127)*

The additive model:

$$Y = T + S + C + R$$

The multiplicative model:

$$Y = T \times S \times C \times R$$

Error statistics:

$$\text{MAD} = \frac{\sum |\text{errors}|}{n}$$

$$\text{MSE} = \frac{\sum (\text{errors})^2}{n}$$

Exponential smoothing:

$$\text{Next forecast} = \text{Last forecast} + \alpha \times \text{error in last forecast}$$

Network analysis *(page 138)*

PERT analysis:

$$\bar{t} = \frac{t_o + 4t_m + t_p}{6}$$

$$\sigma_t = \sqrt{\frac{t_p - t_o}{6}}$$

Inventory control *(page 148)*

EOQ:

$$Q = \sqrt{\frac{2cD}{h}}$$

EBQ:

$$Q = \sqrt{\frac{2cD}{h\left(1 - \dfrac{D}{r}\right)}}$$

Index

All entries refer to topics covered in Section 2: The information bank

Quantitative Techniques

T Lucey

ISBN: **1 873981 26 0** • Date: **1992** • Edition: **4th**
Extent: **544 pp** • Size: **275 x 215 mm**

Courses on which this book is known to be used

BTEC HNC/D, ACCA, CIMA, CIPFA, ICSA, IComA, DMS, IDPM, BA Business Studies; AAT; Graduate Conversion Course (Accounting); BSc Food Manufacture; Dip. in Accounting; BA (Hons) BSc; Management Services Dip.

On reading lists of CIMA, IDPM, IComA and ACP

Contents:

Probability and Decision Making • Decision Trees • Statistics: Statistical Inference, Hypotheses Testing • Correlation and Regression • Multiple and Non-linear Regression • Forecasting and Time Series Analysis • Calculus • Inventory Control • Queueing • Simulation • Linear Programming • Transportation • Assignment • Network Analysis • Financial Mathematics • Investment Appraisal • Matrix Algebra • Replacement Analysis • Statistical and Financial Tables • Examination Techniques • Solutions to Exercises and Examination Questions.

This book provides a sound understanding of quantitative techniques. It includes many exercises and examination questions both with and without answers.

Notes on the Fourth Edition

This new edition is extensively revised and updated. Extensions of coverage include: statistical process control, multiplicative and additive time series models, decision models. It gives full coverage of the latest professional syllabuses including the new ACCA Decision Making Techniques paper. In addition questions have been included from the most recent professional examinations. The lecturers' supplement now includes OHP masters of key diagrams from the text.

Review Comments:

'Unbeatable for the price!' 'The best book for P1 decision making [CIPFA].' 'Extensive syllabus coverage [AAT] and many examples and questions – very good value for money.' – **Lecturers**

'This book is written in the form of a self-study course with plenty of examples and test exercises. Solutions to the exercises are given at the end of the book. One of the best characteristics of the approach is the use of flowcharts to illustrate the procedural steps for each method, and the whole book has a clarity and a sequential development that are highly desirable in a technical workbook.'

"British Book News"

▲ Free Lecturers' Supplement   **Free Lecturers' Supplement ▲**

Quantitative Methods for Computing Students

B Catlow

ISBN: **1 873981 17 1** • Date: **July 1993** • Edition: **1st**
Extent: **400 pp (approx)** • Size: **275 x 215 mm**

Courses on which this book is expected to be used
BTEC Higher National Computing, Computing degree courses and other Computing courses with a quantitative methods component.

Contents:

Section 1 – Scenarios and Related Tasks An ongoing scenario centred around an educational establishment which is the source of a variety of problems that lend themselves to solution using a combination of quantitative methods and computer technology.

Section 2 – Student Information Bank Mathematical Models: Concept of a Model • The Modelling Process • Approximate Nature of Models. Functions and Graphs: Functions as a Means of Expressing Relationships • Interpreting Graphs • Standard Functions and Graphs • Use of Spreadsheets • Curve Sketching. Numerical Analysis: Numbers – Computer Representation, Accuracy and Errors • Iterative Methods. Statistical Analysis: Data Collection, Display and Analysis • Correlation and Regression • Elementary Probability • Probability Distributions • Statistical Tests • Specialised Problem-Solving Techniques: Simulation Techniques • Linear Programming • Transportation and Assignment • Network Analysis – Shortest Route, Travelling Salesman • Network Analysis – Planning, Critical Path.

Section 3 – Further Tasks and Investigation

This book provides all the necessary teaching material for a quantitative methods course for computing students. It enables students to acquire a sound grasp of both the underlying mathematics of constructing an accurate and workable application and the skills of mathematical model formulation and validation, interpretation of results and model evaluation. The three-part, activity based structure of the book is ideally suited to students who have come to expect an investigative and problem-solving approach in their mathematical studies. Students first identify problems in realistic contexts (Section 1) and then are directed to the appropriate information on principles and practices to solve them (Section 2). Further tasks and assignments (with and without answers) develop knowledge and skills (Section 3).

By the end of the book, all necessary mathematical concepts have been covered in such a way as to give the student confidence to choose and implement appropriate problem-solving techniques, aided by computer technology, in any given situation.

⬥ **Free Lecturers' Supplement**   **Free Lecturers' Supplement**⬥

If you liked this book, we may have another that you will find helpful:

Title	Author	Price
☐ Accounting & Finance for Business Students	Bendrey et al	£10.95
☐ Advanced Level Accounting	Randall	£11.95
☐ Advanced Level Biology Practical	Hawkes/Eldridge	£8.95
☐ Advanced Level Business Studies	Danks	£9.95
☐ Advanced Level Maths	Solomon	£9.95
☐ Advanced Level Maths Revision Course	Solomon	£4.95
☐ Auditing	Millichamp	£9.95
☐ BASIC Programming	Holmes	£7.95
☐ Business Accounting I Active Learning	Randall	£12.95
☐ Business Maths & Statistics	Francis	£9.95
☐ Business Law	Abbott/Pendlebury	£10.95
☐ Company Law	Abbott	£9.95
☐ Computer Science	French	£11.95
☐ Computer Studies	French	£7.95
☐ Computing Active Learning	Heathcote	£9.95
☐ Convert to C & C++	Holmes	£9.95
☐ Cost & Management Accounting Active Learning	Lucey	£9.95
☐ Costing	Lucey	£10.95
☐ Data Processing	French	£8.95
☐ dBase for Business Students	Muir	£5.95
☐ Discovering Marketing Active Learning	Stokes	£9.95
☐ Discovering the World of Business	Hillas	£8.95
☐ Easy Guide to Casio Scientific Calculator	Payne	£2.00
☐ Economics for Professional & Business Students	Powell	£9.95
☐ Elements of Marketing	Morden	£11.95
☐ English for Business	Chilver	£6.95
☐ Excel for Bus Students	Muir	£5.95
☐ Finance for Non-Financial Managers	Millichamp	£9.95
☐ Financial Accounting Study Text	Jennings	£11.95
☐ Financial Accounting Solutions Manual	Jennings	£8.95
☐ Financial Management	Brockington	£9.95
☐ Financial Record Keeping	Lee/Jarvis	£8.95
☐ First Course in Business Maths & Statistics	Rowe	£4.95
☐ First Course in Business Studies	Danks	£6.95
☐ First Course in Cost & Management Accounting	Lucey	£6.95
☐ First Course in Marketing	Jefkins	£6.95
☐ First Course in Statistics	Booth	£5.95
☐ First Level Management Active Learning	Lang	£8.95
☐ Foundation Accounting	Millichamp	£9.95
☐ GCSE English	Tarbitt	£6.50
☐ GCSE French	Kambuts/Wilson	£7.50
☐ GCSE Mathematics	Solomon	£7.95
☐ GCSE Maths Higher Level	Solomon	£7.95
☐ GCSE Maths Practice Papers Higher	McCarthy	£3.95
☐ GCSE Maths Practice Papers Intermediate	McCarthy	£3.95
☐ GCSE Maths Revision Course Higher	McCarthy	£3.95
☐ GCSE Maths Revision Course Intermediate	McCarthy	£3.95
☐ GCSE Modern World History	Snellgrove	£6.50
☐ GCSE Science Quizbook	Freemantle	£2.95
☐ Information Technology Skills & Knowledge	Harris/Hogan	£7.95
☐ Intermediate Accounting	Dyson	£7.95
☐ Introductory Pascal	Holmes	£5.95
☐ Introductory Microprocessors & Microcomputer Technology	Hanley	£7.95

Title	Author	Price
☐ Local Area Networks	Hodson	£6.95
☐ Management Accounting	Lucey	£10.95
☐ Management Information Systems	Lucey	£7.95
☐ Management, Theory & Practice	Cole	£10.95
☐ Maths Attainment Tests Key Stage 1	Burndred	£3.75
☐ Maths Attainment Tests Key Stage 2	Burndred	£3.95
☐ Maths Attainment Tests Key Stage 3	Burndred	£3.95
☐ Maths for Engineering	Clarke	£7.95
☐ Maths Key Stage 4 Vol. 1	Solomon	£6.50
☐ Vol. 2	Solomon	£6.50
☐ Vol. 3	Solomon	£6.50
☐ Modula-2 Programming	Holmes	£11.95
☐ Off to University?	Alger	£4.95
☐ Operating Systems	Ritchie	£9.95
☐ MS Works	Weale	£5.95
☐ Paradox 4.0 for Students Active Learning	Heathcote	£5.95
☐ PASCAL CORE Active Learning	Boyle/Margetts	£9.95
☐ PASCAL Programming	Holmes	£11.95
☐ Personnel Management	Cole	£10.95
☐ Quantitative Methods for Computing Students	Catlow	£9.95
☐ Quantitative Techniques	Lucey	£9.95
☐ Refresher in Basic Maths	Rowe	£4.95
☐ Refresher in French	Francey	£7.95
☐ Science Attainments Tests Key Stage 3	Burndred/Turnbull	£3.95
☐ Small Business Management Active Learning	Stokes	£9.95
☐ Spreadsheets for Accounting Students	West	£8.95
☐ Spreadsheets for Business Students	West	£5.95
☐ Structured Programming In COBOL	Holmes	£11.95
☐ Students Guide to Accounting & Financial Reporting Standards	Black	£6.95
☐ Systems Analysis & Design	Hughes	£9.95
☐ Tackling Computer Projects	Heathcote	£6.95
☐ Taxation	Rowes	£11.95
☐ Taxation Questions & Answers	Deane	£7.95
☐ Understanding Business & Finance	Hussey	£9.95
☐ Understanding Business Statistics	Saunders/Cooper	£9.95
☐ Understanding Computer Systems Architecture	Lacy	£10.95

DP Publications' books are available in most academic bookshops or, if you have difficulty finding what you want, UK customers can order direct from us at the following address:

DP Publications Ltd,
Aldine House, Aldine Place, London W12 8AW

Reference: B551

Add £2 postage and packing for one book, or £3 p&p for two or more books.

Please send me the titles indicated. I enclose a cheque for £_____.

Name _____

Address _____

_____

_____